The Myth of Return

Pakistanis in Britain

To my father
and in memory of my mother

The Myth of Return

Pakistanis in Britain

Muhammad Anwar

HEINEMANN · LONDON

Heinemann Educational Books Ltd
22 Bedford Square, London WC1B 3HH
LONDON EDINBURGH MELBOURNE AUCKLAND
HONG KONG SINGAPORE KUALA LUMPUR NEW DELHI
IBADAN NAIROBI JOHANNESBURG EXETER (NH)
KINGSTON PORT OF SPAIN

ISBN 0 435 82022 2

First published 1979

British Library Cataloguing in Publication Data

Anwar, Muhammad
The myth of return.
1. Pakistanis in Rochdale, Eng.
2. Pakistanis in Great Britain — Case studies
I. Title
301.45'19'14120427392 DA690.R55

ISBN 0-435-82022-2

Printed in Great Britain by
Whitstable Litho Ltd, Whitstable, Kent

Contents

List of Figures

List of Tables

Preface

Britain is now a multi-racial and multi-cultural society. It has, over the centuries, received and absorbed large numbers of people from other lands. But it is only in the last three decades that Britain has received, in significant numbers, people whose colour differs from that of the indigenous population. The main sources of this immigration are the West Indies and the Indian sub-continent. The estimated present day number of 'coloured' people is about 3·4 per cent of the total population and of these over 45 per cent are British born.

These newcomers face many difficulties in terms of disadvantage and discrimination which many people see as new but which, in reality, is largely a repetition of the events that followed earlier migrations to this country by large numbers of Jews, Irish, Poles and others. However, what makes the problems of the recent arrivals different and more visible is their colour. Among the new wave of immigrants are the Pakistanis and it is their efforts to adapt to their new environment that have concerned me in this study.

The role of sponsorship and patronage in the process of migration and the way it affected the nature of Pakistani settlement is analysed in this work to show the creation of multi-stranded relationships and extended kinship networks. Resistance to change and non-participation on an individual level in British institutions, in particular where they have a choice, is a feature of the majority of Pakistanis covered in this work. Their participation is limited due to both the external constraints such as prejudice and discrimination and the internal cultural norms and values. There is a further factor which contributes to this—the mythology that they are in Britain to save, invest, and eventually return to their villages back home. In reality, most of them are here to stay because of economic reasons and their children's future.

In approaching this work, I was fortunate in being well placed within the Pakistani community in Rochdale where, for part of the time, I worked with the Community Relations Council.

I hope that this study will throw some much-needed light on a typical Pakistani immigrant community and the social networks that exist within it. Such communities are often discussed—in the Press and elsewhere—in a controversial manner but with little or no real understanding of the people who are under discussion. This is unfortunate and, for this reason, I trust that this work will be of value in helping to close this knowledge gap—not only for academics, but also for social and community workers, the Press and the public at large.

My thanks are due, in the first instance, to Professor Sheila Allen, of Bradford University, and Professor J. C. Mitchell, of Nuffield College, Oxford, for their guidance and help during my formative years in sociology. I am also grateful to Professor Alan Little, Dr. Crispin Cross, Dr. Michael J. Le Lohe, Dr. Verity Saifullah Khan, Dr. Roger Ballard and Dr. Bharti Kansara for their comments and help. But this study would not have been possible without the unselfish co-operation I have had from many others, including the staffs of the Community Relations Commission and the Commission for Racial Equality, Rochdale Community Relations Council, many of my friends outside the community relations field and, last but not least, the Pakistani community in Rochdale.

Finally, it would not be out of place to thank: Dr. A Rauf, J.P., Stanley Hope, M.B.E., Adrian Lord, Qamar Kashmiri, Nasir Malik, S.M. Hayat, M.A. Pasha, Dr. S.H. Syed, Ghulam Yasin, Ghulam Rasul, Muhammad Asghar, Muhammad Ramzan, Amdnat Ali, Noor Muhammad, Mr. and Mrs. Hayee, officers of the local employment office, officers of the local authority, area health authority, employers (including Pakistani businessmen), unions and many others who helped me during my field-work.

Coded names are used throughout the book for reasons of confidentiality.

MUHAMMAD ANWAR
March 1979

Introduction

Most societies in the world today are plural societies, in the sense that they consist of different ethnic and racial groups. One phenomenon which has contributed to the formation of such 'plural' societies was the economic development arising from the growth of capitalism and the Industrial Revolution which led to great international migrations of labour in the seventeenth, eighteenth and nineteenth centuries. This process is a continuing one. A significant coloured population of West Indians, Indians, Bangladeshis and Pakistanis accrued to Britain in the 1950s and 1960s. One third of the labour force of Switzerland, one eighth of the labour force of West Germany and a significant proportion of the labour forces of France, Belgium, Holland and Sweden are made up of foreign workers from various countries such as Italy, Turkey, Yugoslavia, Spain, Surinam, North Africa, and so on.[1] Several special laws have been passed to deal with the new situation created by this presence. Some migrants were relatively permanent settlers and had all the rights of citizenship, such as the New Commonwealth immigrants of Britain up until 1971.[2] Some moved within the European Economic Community, and those from member states were entitled to full social benefits in any state of the Community. Some, such as the Algerians in France, Surinamese in Holland and East African Asians in Britain, came from former colonies under special arrangements. But many (e.g. Turks and Yugoslavs in Germany) came under permits that, theoretically at least, gave them no rights of permanent settlement. In some countries, such as Sweden, government treated all newcomers, whether Italians, Turks, Finns or Yugoslavs, generously, as far as social benefits were concerned. The patterns are extremely varied. Similarly, the distribution of the immigrants in European countries varies. They are mainly to be found in the most industrialized countries, like France, West Germany, Britain, Sweden, Switzerland, and so on, rather than in Italy. Some of these immigrants began arriving from 1945, but the bulk arrived in the late 1950s and early 1960s.

The reasons for the migrations have been primarily economic. Britain's coloured immigrants are mainly from the West Indies, India, Bangladesh and Pakistan. But though they constitute a small proportion of the population, their presence has evoked political issues which far outweigh their representation in the country. The immigration of certain categories had been drastically restricted by successive immigration laws and ultimately stopped by the Immigration Act of 1971. At the same time the existence of official machinery connected with race relations—the Commission for Racial Equality (up to 13th June, 1977 there were two organizations: the Community Relations Commission and the Race Relations Board), the local community relations councils and the House of Commons Select Committee on Immigration and Race Relations—shows the importance of the issues relating to immigrants in public affairs and a trend towards studying the problems involved.[3]

I shall now consider what distinguishes coloured migration from the New Commonwealth from other labour migrations to Britain. Coloured migration has to be seen in this wider context. Indeed a study of previous labour migrations, the need for them and the reactions to them, facilitates an understanding of the presence of ethnic minorities from the New Commonwealth.

Labour Migrations to Britain and Public Reactions

As mentioned above, migration to Britain is not a new phenomenon. Britain was one of the first countries to have large-scale labour immigration in the nineteenth century. The Industrial Revolution rapidly absorbed the surplus of unemployed workers from the countryside and British employers turned their eyes to Ireland.[4]

In 1851 there were 727,326 Irish immigrants in Britain, making up 2·9 per cent of the population of England and Wales, and 7·2 per cent of the population of Scotland.[5] They were concentrated in cities like Liverpool, Manchester and Glasgow, and soon came to form a high proportion of the labour force in unskilled textile occupations and in the building trades. Engels has described at great length the appalling conditions in which the Irish lived and has shown how they competed with the English workers for jobs and houses.[6] Employers often kept Irish and English workers separate to avoid conflict at work. There was frequent discrimination with regard to housing and jobs. 'No Irish' signs were common for over a century in England.

Between 1875 and 1914, 120,000 Jews came to Britain as refugees from Eastern Europe, particularly Russia, to escape persecution. The reaction to these migrants who were poor and largely unskilled was similar to that experienced by the Irish. The majority of them settled in the East End of London. Here they were at the mercy of exploiting landlords and employers. Fear of competition for jobs and housing led to hostility from the local population. Mass demonstrations against immigration were organized, and the newcomers were accused of being the cause of most of the society's ills. This campaign resulted in Britain's first restrictive legislation on immigration, the *Aliens Act* of 1905 and the *Aliens Restriction Act* of 1914.

Immigration to Britain was on a considerably smaller scale during the inter-war period than it had been before the First World War. The reason was the difficulty of finding employment for returning servicemen in the immediate post-war years and later the depressed state of the economy. Britain repatriated nearly all the workers recruited in the colonies during the war. During the Second World War, British labour needs led to direct recruitment in Ireland and elsewhere by the Ministry of Labour. After the war migration continued and estimates indicate a net Irish inflow of around 350,000—or 30,000 per year—between 1946 and 1959.[7] The process slowed down in the 1960s.

It is estimated that about 460,000 foreigners entered Britain between 1946 and 1951. The largest group were the 115,000 Poles who came in under the Polish Resettlement Scheme. They had been members of the Polish armed forces which fought under British command. Due to shopfloor opposition to their employment it was very difficult for them to find jobs, but by 1950 most had found some sort of job. A certain number of former prisoners of war—Germans, Italians and Ukrainians—were also allowed to settle in Britain.[8]

To overcome the labour shortage, the British Government carried out recruitment of European voluntary workers (EVWs). Ninety thousand EVWs were recruited mostly from refugee camps. They were engaged for three years for a specific job chosen by the Ministry of Labour and could be expelled at any time for misconduct.[9] Accidents or ill health were also likely to lead to deportation.[10] Recruitment was confined mainly to single men or women, and only about 4,000 distressed relatives were admitted. Most of the male EVWs were directed to agriculture, textiles, heavy industry or mining. The EVWs, like the earlier immigrant groups to Britain, met with considerable hostility from British labour. The opposition of British workers to the employment of foreigners was strong enough to bring about their complete exclusion from some work places.

Commonwealth citizens had free entry into Britain under the Commonwealth rules. During the 1950s the number of immigrants from the West Indies increased and reached an annual rate of 30,000 in 1955 and 1956. As the pressure for immigration control in Britain grew, more and more West Indians came in to beat the impending ban. Between the beginning of 1961 and the middle of 1962, when the Commonwealth Immigrants Act came into force, 98,000 persons emigrated to Britain from the West Indies. Immigration from India and Pakistan got under way later than that from the West Indies, but also reached a very high level from 1960 onwards, as people tried to enter Britain while there was still time.[11]

The number of New Commonwealth immigrants doubled in the inter-censual period of 1951–61 from 256,000 to 541,000. Those who entered Britain before the Commonwealth Immigrants Act of 1962 were predominantly economically active persons. They included a high proportion of women in the case of West Indians, but the overwhelming majority of the Indians and Pakistanis were men. The voucher system under the Act gave an opportunity for those who were already here to arrange jobs and vouchers for their relatives and friends. This increased the element of sponsorship and patronage. On the other hand, dependants of those already in Britain were allowed to come without vouchers. Between July 1962 and December 1968, only 77,966 voucher holders were admitted, compared with 257,220 dependants.[12] I would argue that the 1962 Act seems to have had a decisive effect on the pattern of migration. It turned a movement of workers, many of whom were probably only interested in staying temporarily, into a relatively permanent immigration of families. Also the voucher system initially reinforced the kinship and friendship bonds and therefore reinforced the pattern of settlement. The net immigration from India, Pakistan and the West Indies between 1955 and 1968 is shown in Table 1.

The British public reaction to the immigration from the Commonwealth during these years was the same as it had been to the previous waves of migrations. Signs such as 'All blacks go home' and 'Send them back' were quite common. 'Paki bashing' and other anti-immigrant demonstrations and movements are still taking place. The British Campaign to Stop Immigration and the activities of the National Front are prime examples. However, looking at the occupations which most of the immigrants have taken up, we can see that the labour migration from other countries to Britain was an important factor in running expanding industries and services. In 1978 the estimated number of ethnic minorities was about 3·4 per cent of the total population but the reactions to their presence are out of all proportion to their numbers. (About 40 per cent of the

Table 1
Net immigration from India, Pakistan and the West Indies between 1955 and 1968*

Indians	200,130
Pakistanis (inc. Bangladeshis)	145,960
Jamaicans	191,330
Rest of Caribbean	132,220
Total	669,640

Source: Nicholas Deakin, op. cit., p. 50

* The number of people arriving for settlement from all the New Commonwealth countries in 1969–77 was 318,521 (out of these 259,646 came as dependants and only 58,875 were male workers.) This means a drastic decline in the number of immigrants coming as workers from the New Commonwealth countries.

1,846,000 of people belonging to ethnic minorities were born in Britain and therefore are not immigrants.)

The National Front has continued to struggle against better race relations in recent years. It has attempted to publicize its offensive doctrines by demonstrating in areas with substantial ethnic minority populations and by putting up candidates at many local and parliamentary elections.

The heat generated by the current debate on immigration which started during 1977 is wasted energy and only strengthens the hands of those who see and treat ethnic minorities as second-class citizens. Immigration has already been brought down to a trickle and should not be a central concern for the society. The important task is to work for a harmonious plural society. It is a paradox that the enactment of the stronger antidiscrimination measures outlined in the Race Relations Act of 1976 is accompanied by a worsening of race relations in the country generally in 1978, with occasional eruption of racial violence in inner city areas of, among others, Wolverhampton, Lewisham and the East End of London. As a response to this growing racial tension many voluntary moves to counter the National Front propaganda and the racialism generally have been made. For instance, among others those worth noting are: the Federation of Conservative Students' Campaign Against Racialism in 1977, Anti-Nazi League and the Joint Committee Against Racialism, which was supported by a wide variety of organizations including the three main political parties and some ethnic minority organizations.

At governmental level efforts have been made to find appropriate ways of responding to the reality of racial/ethnic differences and in particular to the disadvantages and discrimination due to these differences, which some groups face.[13] Recently, the question of the numbers and attitudes of these groups and discrimination against them have been the subject of several research studies. Ethnic differences persist; but there is little information as to the characteristics of these groups which contribute towards or inhibit their assimilation/integration into the wider society. This has, as yet, been inadequately researched. What processes strengthen ethnic group identity? What in effect is happening in ethnic communities? Which minority groups maintain their original ethnic characteristics and which draw away from their origins? The lack of answers to these questions indicates, on the one hand, the need for further research in this field. On the other hand, the ethnic organization and identity of recent immigrants in Britain are such new and complex areas that more knowledge is required to understand the situation. One way of finding out what is happening in these ethnic communities is to examine one particular community.

In this work an effort has been made to demonstrate how far Pakistanis as an ethnic group are transplanting their culture to this country; in particular, to illustrate how sponsorship and patronage result in kinship and friendship networks being re-established in Britain—and how these networks determine a dominant pattern of activity in almost all fields of social interaction among Pakistanis. Further, we consider the extent to which these social networks helped and facilitated the immigration and settlement of Pakistanis in this country and resulted in their 'incapsulation' from the wider society.[14] The field-work for this work was done in Rochdale.[15]

Chapter 1 deals with the theoretical issues related to the study of ethnic minority groups in general and suggests a framework for this study in particular. Chapter 2 describes the migration processes and how they relate to Pakistanis, and Chapter 3 outlines the context in which Pakistanis in Rochdale were living. Chapter 4 and 5 examine the kinship networks with reference to the family and *Biraderi*, extended family relationships, and the role of *Vartan Bhanji*, exchange of gifts and services. Chapters 6 and 7 analyse the situation of Pakistanis in the field of employment. Chapter 8 looks at the participation of Pakistanis in British elections, while Chapter 9 analyses the religious activities of the Pakistanis and Chapter 10 describes their ethnic organizations and leadership. Finally, Chapter 11 provides some case material to illustrate points raised throughout the book and Chapter 12 draws some conclusions related to the migration process and ethnic relations. There are also appendices which help to clarify some points further.

1. Theoretical Issues

The movement of people from one country to another creates new areas of relationships within a new environment. The migrants may have some knowledge about the environment to which they are going, through their relatives and friends, or they may be totally unfamiliar with it. The classic study of Thomas and Znaniecki, *The Polish Peasant in Europe and America*,[1] was one of the first to demonstrate the two distinct worlds of the migrants. The letters writen by the Polish immigrants in America to their relatives at home document the whole set of emotional problems involved in the transition. Since it was written much work using a framework of adaptation/assimilation has been carried out.

American sociologists R. E. Park, E. W. Burgess and Louis Wirth, who laid the theoretical and empirical foundations for the sociology of race relations, studied the impact on Chicago of the mass immigration from Europe and the growing influx of Negroes from the Deep South.[2] The concepts and hypotheses formulated by Park and his contemporaries have become part of the sociology of race relations. But modern post-war industrial societies differ in a number of respects from the cities in the United States in the inter-war years and, therefore, the theories that were developed in the USA during this period are no longer valid for Britain and the USA today. Concepts such as 'assimilation', which seemed to be appropriate in the analysis of these earlier migrations, now prove to be over-simplified in the United States as well as in Europe.[3]

A considerable amount of research has been carried out regarding the process of migration and the ensuing social changes in the migrant. There are diverse definitions of the major processes involved. Assimilation, acculturation, integration and adaptation are often used interchangeably but can have a variety of subtle meanings. For example, Johnston sees assimilation as two-fold:

external, where the migrants' exterior qualities become less distinguishable from the indigenous population, and subjective, where the migrant is willing to identify with the host culture and considers it proper.[4] Similarly, Parsons distinguished social from cultural assimilation. Social assimilation emphasizes the process of adaptation to the receiving society's system of interaction between individuals and collectivities. Cultural assimilation involves adopting the content and patterns of values, ideas and other symbolic systems that are essential in the 'shaping of human behaviour and the artifacts produced through behaviour'.[5]

Two contrasting elements can be noted here which are relevant to the analysis of the migrant situation. Some sociologists maintain that the migrant's previous primary groups and the social and cultural norms governing them are threatened if he does not re-establish these groups within the new social system. Cultural assimilation to the new system is impeded if the migrant has not first anchored himself within such groupings before venturing into the wider society. In such a model kinship—friendship networks and ethnic community relations play an important role in the adjustment period of the immigrant. These assumptions are frequently challenged by other sociologists. For instance, O'Flannery tested these two aspects of the assimilation model with Puerto Ricans in New York and found that the social and cultural assimilation processes were independent to a degree.[6]

Park and Burgess view assimilation as a process of interpenetration and fusion in which persons and groups acquire the memories, sentiments and attitudes of other persons or groups and by sharing their experiences and history are incorporated in a common cultural life.[7] Young has a similar conception of assimilation.[8] On the other hand, Eisenstadt sees 'absorption' as a gradual process consisting of three stages:

(a) redefinition of old established roles . . . so as to make them compatible with the alternative roles of the new society.
(b) acquisition of new roles which have been, as it were, relinquished during the process of migration and which are necessary prerequisites for participation in the new society.
(c) . . . evolution of identification with the new society and its common, shared values and goals.[9]

Duncan and Lieberson define absorption as the entry into the productive activity of the host society.[10] They use socio-economic status as an index to assess immigrant adjustment. Acculturation is another term they apply to 'the adoption of local customs and the relinquishing . . .' of such cultural characteristics as would identify the immigrants as a distinct group.[11] This definition, 'besides its misleading biological connotation too often implies a one-way street in group relations'.[12] More important, these definitions imply the virtual subordination of one culture to another. They suggest that the new migrant is remoulded, reshaped and stripped of all his natural gifts and former ideas, and becomes 'Americanized' or 'Anglicized'.

In a minority–dominant group approach the ideology behind these concepts is seen as the ideology of the dominant group and therefore, any group unabsorbed, or not assimilated is considered to upset the equalization of social relations in the society.

The other problem with these concepts is that they are not precise enough to cover any particular migrant group. This is true of the early 'race relations cycle' of Park and Burgess which used processes of accommodation, competition, conflict and assimilation in the American situation and the modified new terms used in the British situation by Sheila Patterson and Zubrazycki, in particular.[13]

The main criticism of some of these concepts is, as Price says, 'the term accommodation or assimilation is too wide, concealing the fact that there may be complete assimilation in some things (dress, religion and language say), accommodation in other things (economic life and family customs) and conflict in other things (housing or education)'.[14] Similarly there are different types and levels of accommodation and assimilation. Even if a migrant is objectively assimilated, what about his subjective identity, and so on?

The other criticism of these concepts is in relation to the host society. What do we mean by the host society? Rex and Moore argue, 'we have no unitary concept of the host society but see it compounded of groups in a state of conflict with one another about property and about power, as well as of groups with different styles of life arranged in a status hierarchy.'[15] So to discover the rate of adjustment or adaptation of a migrant group it is more realistic to look at particular aspects of the society rather than at society as a whole.

To overcome some of these difficulties Halsey suggests, 'there will be a continuing need for anthropological study of these changing patterns of life, so that the developing heterogeneity of the coloured population can be fully accounted for, not in the theory of assimilation but in a new theory of integration where the process is seen as a highly differentiated one of absorption, incorporation and accommodation to the multiple relationships of locality, occupation, politics and indeed the whole network of society.'[16] Integration is therefore described as a situation in which a group continues to be an integer or unit on its own, but one which as part of a greater whole is accepted by the majority.[17]

This means that a group integrated in this sense would keep its own distinguishing features, such as religion and language, but children would go to state schools and migrants do a job alongside the majority. This situation is the first stage of a newly arrived first-generation migrant which would not involve the social system of the host society but only a contractual tie in the employment and education fields.

The second stage is reached when a migrant still keeps a contractual tie with the host society, but has built up a primary community based on kinship—friendship networks among his other fellow-migrants. Here he tries to reproduce at least some of the social institutions of his country of origin which also provide him with familiar norms and values governing situations.

When this primary community develops to encompass more ethnic institutions and facilities, the members of the community usually prefer to live in the area where these facilities are available and this results usually in a segregated area. This situation keeps migrants within their community and 'incapsulates' them within the host community. The behaviour of Pakistanis (and other ethnic groups) in this situation needs to be understood in the framework of external constraints and their ethnic preferences.

Therefore, we have to find out what kind of community migrants have formed (or are forming) in order to obtain some sort of social and cultural bearings in the new situation, and what relationships exist between their community structure as a whole and the economic, political and social institutions of the host society. How far do the external constraints, such as racial discrimination, faced by the migrant in these institutions, force him to turn back to his own community for security? Ideally one should start with their social structure in the country of origin to understand the situation in the country of settlement. There are three sets of relationships of migrants which can be investigated: one, their relationships with the country of origin, second, their social networks amongst themselves in the country of settlement and, third, the new areas of relations between them and the host society.

The most useful approach to the study of migrants seems to me to be an analysis of the structure of the society in which they live and their relationships with specific groups within that society. These will include both indigenous groups and groups of people sharing their ethnic background. For the latter, one of the main foci of interest is in the processes by which friendship and kinship networks provide support which allows the migrant to cope with the inevitable stresses of the new situation. The continuing ties with people at home are important to consider when describing migrants' relationships. This is the broader framework upon which this work is based. Therefore, a social network analysis both as a theoretical approach and a methodological one has been used.

I argue that there are three inter-related social spheres which help the immigrants to cope with the effects of migration. They are:

(a) residential segregation;
(b) ethnic community; and
(c) ethnic institutions.

(a) Residential Segregation

Extensive research shows that individuals with similar cultural origins tend to cluster together and thus become residentially segregated from the rest of the society.[18] During the first stages of settling in a new society residential proximity enhances interaction and helps to ease culture shock.[19] It allows people with similar values to maintain their group norms to preserve a sense of ethnic identity and to feel secure in a familiar social network.[20] This pattern applies to Pakistanis in Britain.

According to the theory known as the 'race relations cycle', increased segregation of an ethnic group should signify the stoppage, if not the reversal, of the cultural, social and psychological processes of assimilation. But there are studies about other communities such as the Jews in the United States which show that residential segregation facilitates acculturation.[21] We will re-examine the question as to whether, and to what extent, the residential segregation of Pakistanis is affecting the processes of adaptation/acculturation.

(b) Ethnic Community

An ethnic group based on a set of cultural values shares a social organization whose critical characteristics are self-ascription and ascription by others.[22] Its members use their ethnic identity as determined by origin and background, to maintain a distinction between themselves and outsiders,[23] and in order to control the boundaries of their interaction with other groups, especially the indigenous community. Moreover, there are differences in behaviour which become apparent in social contact with persons defined as of different cultures.

It seems that language, religion, national identity and foreignness of Pakistanis are the major sources of structural differentiation. These characteristics are the most important factors to create the feeling of 'insiders' and 'outsiders'.

Religion was the basis used for the creation of a separate Muslim state of Pakistan and it played an important role in creating the feelings of minority status amongst Muslims in British India. It is also crucial for Pakistanis who have settled in Britain and, once again, it is the distinguishing characteristic that identifies them as a minority group.

However, it should be noted that the possession of a common religion and ethnic culture does not automatically produce ethnic action within the community or in relation to the other communities without mobilization. It is also noted that Asians and particularly Pakistanis are community-orientated. This brings us to the idea of an ethnic community.

A community can be said to exist when interaction between individuals has the purpose of meeting individual needs and securing group goals in a geographical area. However, an 'ethnic community' may have social rather than strictly territorial boundaries. Crissman refers to it as 'an order of common life based on common interests which can determine activity and which has ethnicity as well as locality as its basis'.[24] Pakistanis in this work are seen as an ethnic community because they share a common background, have common interests, some form of social structure, hold a common religious belief and a value system and also have a territorial nucleus in parts of Rochdale and in other areas of Britain.

(c) Ethnic Institutions

According to Breton the notion of 'institutional completeness' is more important in attracting the immigrant than merely the idea of community.[25] Institutional completeness and self-sufficiency are measured by the number of available ethnic services, within the boundaries of the ethnic group (see Chapter 3). These include religious and educational facilities, vernacular newspapers, voluntary associations and other services such as shops, cinemas, and so on, catering to ethnic tastes and needs. These services keep the social relations of the immigrants within the ethnic community. Institutional completeness of an ethnic community can be seen as a constructive reaction to the disintegrating processes of migration.[26] Ethnic voluntary associations act as a buffer for culture shock by emphasizing and simulating the traditions and customs of the home country. Pakistani ethnic institutions are seen in this context as providing a familiar frame of reference while at the same time exercising a considerable influence on the Pakistanis' participation in the wider society.

It is often stated that a distinguishing feature of ethnic groups is the fact that individuals are born into them and therefore have no choice in the matter. One does not choose to be a Pakistani, Jew or Chinaman; it is claimed rather that this is determined by fate.[27] There are always individual exceptions such as that a very wealthy Jew may escape the consequences of his 'ethnicity' under some circumstances but for a group generally there are no choices. Pakistanis have a distinguished culture to which they seem to be deeply attached.

Barth has argued that, viewed in terms of what is socially effective, ethnicity becomes a principle of organization. The socially effective turns on a self-ascribed and other-ascribed membership of an ethnic category which 'classifies a person in terms of his basic, most general identity, presumptively determined by his origin and background'.[28] Also that actors use ethnic identity to categorize themselves and others for purposes of interaction. This leads to ethnicity. It is in this simple sense that the term 'ethnicity' has been used in this work.

The more objectively distinguished characteristics, such as race, nationality, language and religion, a minority ethnic group has the more distinctive and visible it is.[29] Taking Pakistanis as an example, the majority are migrants, they are of Indo–Aryan origin, have Pakistani nationality.[30] Their mother tongue in the main is Punjabi or Urdu and they follow the Islamic faith. All these characteristics and other cultural values make Pakistanis in Britain an ethnic minority.

I argue that the significance of ethnicity is better understood looking at the structural form of the ethnic community. The life which Pakistanis live in Britain, in terms of ethnic relations, obligations, values, traditions, and so on, is a reflection of the home culture, and the functions of these norms and values are important for the ethnic group. They are used to maintain group cohesiveness, and to sustain and enhance identity. They establish social networks and communicative patterns which the group then uses in the new situation. The characteristics of an ethnic situation which lead to ethnicity, therefore, are where a group possesses a distinctive culture, interacts in such a way as to be socially distinct, and identifies itself with a common set of beliefs which creates mutual support.[31] Foreignness, minority group status and discrimination by the indigenous population are additional factors which contribute to the strengthening of the ethnic traits and also lead to ethnic mobilization in certain situations. One of the aims of the study was to trace in detail the relationships between the Pakistani community and the various institutions of society at large in Rochdale, economic, political and social. To achieve these aims a particular conceptual model to analyse these data was used.

The Conceptual Model

No race relations theory helps to explain the total structural differentiation of migrants in the new situation. To understand the social relationships of Pakistanis, therefore, I have drawn from a wide field of theoretical concepts to analyse my data. Such concepts as 'social network', 'chain migration', 'incapsulation', 'situational analysis' and 'social conflict' have all been used. These concepts have been used by sociologists for the study of social situations where the structural-functional model is inadequate. In this subsection these concepts have been defined.

The kinship—friendship relationships among Pakistanis and their residential clustering cannot be adequately understood without the concept of 'chain migration'. Chain migration can be defined as the movement in which prospective migrants learn of opportunities, are provided with transportation and have initial accommodation and employment arranged by means of primary social relationships with previous migrants.[32] It is exemplified in the various forms of sponsorship and patronage of relatives and friends by those who are already here. Extended family relationships and relations between friends are certainly crucial to an explanation of social networks, and even types and distribution of occupations among migrants are related to them.

Situational analysis is also adopted because it helps to analyse the unstructured situations and variations which may exist amongst Pakistanis. Van Velsen used a situational frame of reference rather than the structural one to bring order to his analysis of the unstructured Tonga social organization. He argued that the structural analysis aims at presenting an outline of the social morphology; consequently there is a marked emphasis on consistency so that variations are ignored.[33]

He also argued that by presenting a situational analysis the researcher will not only present the reader with abstractions and inferences from his field material, but he will also provide some of the material itself. 'This should put the reader in a better position to evaluate the ethnographer's analysis not only on the basis of the internal consistency of the argument, but also by comparing the ethnographic data and the inferences drawn from them. Particularly when most of the actors appear again and again in different situations, the inclusion of such data should reduce the chance that cases become merely apt illustrations.'[34] This was what I hoped to achieve in my analysis.

The notion of 'social network' used in this work is defined as those interlinkages persons build for themselves with other persons and the social relationships these people have amongst themselves. In providing details about relationships and the individuals involved in them, the sociological account is given more depth and the significance of the social relationships is highlighted.

The use of social network analysis became popular when researchers working in complex societies could not present their findings adequately within the framework of a typical compact institutional analysis characteristic of the structural approach.[35] Consequently they sought concepts within a framework which could reflect what they saw as the relatively unstructured quality of social relationships in large-scale societies. In other words, what Firth referred to as the optative element in social relationships could be analysed.[36] This seems true for the study of immigrants in the new situation.

Philip Mayer's study of African migrants in a South African town shows how ethnic forces 'incapsulate' them from the wider society and slow down the process of integration. He described two patterns of social networks; one, close-knit social networks of 'Red' Xhosa migrants which ensured their strict adherence to rural home-oriented loyalties even while in the city; and two, loose-knit networks of 'School' people who participated in a wider diversity of urban-based institutions and tended to lose their rural-oriented loyalties. The first category Mayer labels as 'conservative' and the second as 'progressive'.[37]

The 'Red' syndrome which has been termed 'incapsulation' features multiplex relations and a close-knit type of network. This makes for consistent moral pressure on individuals and conservatism. The term 'incapsulation' is used in the present work in the same way.[38]

A further aspect, that of 'intensity of relationship', is taken here to be the extent to which individuals linked by some network relationship are prepared to honour obligations stemming from it, or conversely feel free to exercise the rights implied by that relationship. The rationale for this in commonsense terms is that if people are tied to one another by a variety of different links, then they will find it difficult to sever social relationships and therefore are obliged to carry out the expectations and obligations entailed in those relationships.[39] It is important to ascertain the strength of these links as sponsorship and patronage play a role in the formation of social networks. Therefore, the proposition that multi-stranded relationships are more likely to be intense than single-stranded relationships, is relevant to the data presented in this work.

The normative content of network linkages refers to the actor's construction of the meaning of that relationship to him in terms of his understanding of the other person's expectations of his behaviour. The basis of these networks could be kinship—friendship, ethnicity, neighbourhood, religion or political group membership links. An approach to networks analysis from this point of view provides an extension to, and development of, the classical structural–functional approaches in sociology and anthropology.[40]

I use 'social conflict' following Coser in the sense that it is of central importance to an understanding of major areas of social relationships.[41] In accepting Georg Simmel's thesis that to understand conflict situations the causes of the conflict and the mediating processes of conflict, together with the immediate factors and effects which come into play need to be analysed.[42] An attempt has been made in this work to apply this kind of analysis to social networks. For instance, I pose the question: What are the bases of support in a conflict situation and how does conflict divide and unite different sections of the community at various times? The way these concepts have been used in the analysis of the data has led to some modifications as well as testing their applicability in such studies. This has resulted in the redefinition of some concepts, and in the inclusion of ethnographic material in the study.

2 Migration of Pakistanis

Introduction

Looking at the sociological and anthropological literature about ethnic group formation, we find that ethnicity has frequently resulted either from migration, the movement of rural people of varying origins and characteristics to towns and of settlers to new regions and countries, or from the incorporation of previously independent social units into one new unit of larger scale.[1] In this chapter the main factors involved in migration are outlined, and Pakistani migration is discussed in this context. It is also shown how this migration has given support to ethnic group formation and ethnicity.

Migration and Factors Involved

Migration is defined broadly as a permanent or semi-permanent change of residence. It can be from one country to another or simply from one part of a country to another which may involve a move from rural to urban areas. Therefore, no restriction is placed upon the distance of the move or upon the voluntary or involuntary nature of the act, and no distinction is made between external and internal migration.

No matter how short or how long, how easy or how difficult, every act of migration involves an origin, a destination and an intervening set of obstacles. According to Everett S. Lee, the factors which enter into the decision to migrate may be summarized under the following four headings:

1. Factors associated with the area of origin.
2. Factors associated with the area of destination.
3. Intervening obstacles.
4. Personal factors.[2]

Lee presents the first three of these in diagram form to show the movement.

In every area there are countless factors which act to hold people within the area or attract people to it, and there are others which tend to repel them. These are shown in Figure 1 as + and − signs. Some of these factors affect most people in much the same way, while others affect different people in different ways. The set of pluses and minuses at both origin and destination is differently defined for every migrant or prospective migrant depending on the personal factors. The factors that hold and attract people are not fully understood either by the social scientist or the persons directly affected.

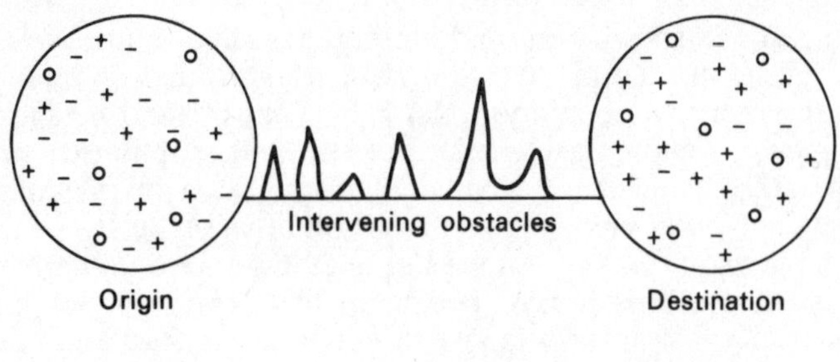

FIGURE 1 *Origin and destination factors and intervening obstacles in migration*

There are, however, important differences between the factors associated with the area of origin and those associated with the area of destination. The knowledge of the area is seldom exact, and indeed some of the advantages and disadvantages of an area can only be weighed up by living there. For instance, the case studies of migrant Pakistanis show that, on the one hand, there is an element of ignorance or even mystery about the area of destination, and, on the other hand, not all persons who migrate make the decision themselves. Children go with their parents and wives accompany or join their husbands at a later stage.

Similarly, the intervening obstacles such as financial outlay, official restrictions and difficulties, particularly the role of immigration laws and their application, the process of chain migration and many personal factors affect individual motivations and facilitate or retard migration. Such obstacles encountered by Pakistanis will be mentioned later. However, there are some general points about migration which are raised here.

The question arises, why do people move? One common attempt to cover all migration under a general heading is the 'push—pull' hypothesis.[3] It suggests that migration is due to socio-economic imbalances between regions, certain factors 'pushing' persons away from the area of origin and others 'pulling' them to the area of destination. It, however, does not take into consideration the intervening obstacles and personal factors involved in the process. Nor does it explain rates of migration since there are many examples where few migrate through 'push' factors.

Petersen argues that the opposite to the 'push—pull' hypothesis could be true, that 'man migrates because of wanderlust'.[4] Neither of these assumptions explains the different behaviour of individuals in similar situations. Nor do they cover the social constraints on individual decision-making. Each individual has reasons for migrating or staying at home, but to interpret migration processes on a personal basis is to treat the individual as an entity independent of social forces and thus fail to take account of the structure and process of migration.[5]

Petersen suggests that people migrate either as a means of achieving new conditions or in response to a change in conditions in order to retain what they had. He further emphasizes that if this distinction between the two types of migration (the innovating and the conservative) and the distinction between the socio-economic causes of migrant's motives are accepted, then a typology of broad classes of migrations can be developed. This typology is presented in Table 2.

Petersen's typology presents different ideal types of migration. It is simple and outlines clear distinctions and relevant features in the migration process. He suggests that this typology is a 'step toward a general theory of migration'. What we need to explain further is the selectivity and localization of emigration which is only from certain parts of Pakistan and the town-by-town pattern of Pakistani settlement in Britain. Sponsorship and patronage are crucial to an understanding of this process. This process clusters Pakistanis on kinship—friendship lines whereby the role of chain migration becomes clear.

Chain migration is distinct from impersonally organized migration, which is movement based on impersonal recruitment and assistance. Chain migration is exemplified in the various forms of sponsorship and patronage of relatives and friends. (See p. 14.) John and Leatrice MacDonald have used 'chain migration' to describe the major process instrumental to ethnic neighbourhood formation.[6] They have used the notion of chain migration to

Table 2

Petersen's Typology*

Relations	Migratory force	Class of migration	Type of migration: Conservative	Type of migration: Innovating
Nature and man	Ecological push	Primitive	Wandering Gatherers and nomads	Flight from the land
State (or equivalent) and man	Migration policy	Impelled Forced	Displacement Flight	Slave trade Collie trade
Man and his norms	Higher aspirations	Free	Group	Pioneer
Collective behaviour	Social momentum	Mass	Settlement	Urbanization

*modified

account for the presence of highly origin-localized Italian neighbourhoods in many American cities.[7]

Larger cities like New York often displayed several districts of Italian neighbourhoods grouped on the basis of common village origin. Thus the clustered residences of Italians from the same regions in American cities were not chance phenomena, but the result of a social process distinguished by the obligations of migrants to provide a stepping-stone for their kind.[8] Louis Wirth's account of the development of the Jewish community in Chicago presents a similar case. [9] The earliest Jewish migrants who came from Europe provided considerable assistance to newcomers. The residential segregation of Jews from Germany and Eastern European origins was based partly on economic differences but also on synagogue affiliation. The clustering of Jews from a single village in the neighbourhood around a small synagogue catering only to those people is noted by Wirth. The notion of chain migration is also to be found well expressed in the work of C. A. Price, particularly in his study of *Southern Europeans in Australia*. [10]

According to this notion, a chain of migration may begin with the arrival of a lone immigrant in a foreign land, where he then 'makes good'. News of his success reaches home, and he recruits other members of his family and friends (often like himself, young, often single) to come and join him if his circumstances permit. The second stage starts when the early arrivals feel sufficiently well established to call their wives, children, or brides to join them. With the reuniting and establishment of families the group starts recreating some of its basic home culture. Traditional ceremonies and social occasions become more numerous and the customs and values of the old country become more strongly entrenched and greater attention is given to education and religion.[11] With community life well established and news of this reaching the area of origin, the older, the younger and the less enterprising begin to follow also. This completes the chain and results in the establishment of a full community life.[12]

The Pakistani Case

The migration of Pakistanis to Britain can be explained in terms of colonial links, political freedom[13] of movement and an economic 'push' and 'pull' which slowly developed into a 'chain migration'. The immigrants left Pakistan in order to return home with money to buy land and build better houses and to raise their social status. One respondent explained, 'I came here to work for a few years to earn money, to buy some land in Pakistan and then go back and settle there.' They did not intend to enter into British society and become acculturated. In my survey of Pakistani workers, economic reasons for migration were given by the majority of the respondents. This was also true of the case studies, the only exception being some of the professionals, for example doctors, who first came to Britain to improve their qualifications but later settled here.

During the First and Second World Wars many people from the areas now constituting Pakistan joined the Allied armies and navies. Mirpur, Jhelum and some parts of the Punjab are particularly well known for the high percentage of their men in the British army. This is still true of present-day numbers in the Pakistani army.

The British maintained that only certain 'races' in India had military capacity. The Sikhs and Muslims were included among these, with the result that in both peace and war over half of the Indian army came from the Punjab. No other province approached it in terms of recruits. During World War I, for example, the Punjab with a population of 20,000,000, provided 350,000 combatants, while Bengal with a population of 45,000,000 supplied only 7,000.[14] Army service gave the men widening experience and often offered them opportunities to go overseas. Another reason for migration from Mirpur has long been the need to look for work. As well as joining the army, many Mirpuris joined the British steamship companies, who recruited many of their Lascar seamen from the district.[15] The 'push' factors were mainly the poor quality of land in these areas and a tradition of this type of service. Unemployment was quite high due to a predominantly agricultural economy and limited industrialization. Thus, it is reasonable to suggest that a traditionally close link existed between these areas and Britain which had its influence on the migration in the 1950s and 1960s.

Early Settlers

After the Second World War some of the Pakistanis who were in the army decided to try their luck in Britain. Former seamen began settling in Britain after 1941 leaving the ports and moving inland.[16] Some Pakistanis tell stories about being stationed in Britain while in the army during the Second World War and afterwards deciding to try their luck in this country. 'I was stationed in Scotland during the war and I decided to come to Britain when ex–army soldiers got special vouchers in 1962.' Another Pakistani who claimed to have been in this country since 1930 told me that he came as a seaman and then decided to stay here. He did 'door' business first. He was called back to the Navy during the Second World War. After the war he came to stay with another Pakistani in Birmingham and then after a few years when his other relatives came to join him he moved to Manchester. In 1962 he decided to settle in Rochdale 'as houses were cheap there and there was no difficulty in finding jobs for the newcomers'. Shortly afterwards, other relatives followed him. In 1975 there were at least 20 families related to each other in the town. The earlier arrivals who settled in the 1940s and 1950s sponsored their kinsmen by arranging for their recruitment as seamen hoping that they would eventually arrive in Britain. One respondent explained, 'My uncle arranged for me to join a ship in 1955 and after four years I left the service and came to live with him in Bradford, then my brother-in-law came to join us at the end of 1961, and we decided to move here from Bradford.' The pioneer Pakistani migrants became a source of the voluntary chain migration process.

Mass Migration

The mass migration of Pakistanis started in the late 1950s and early 1960s when migrants followed the routes established by the pioneer

Pakistanis. Aurora writes that once a tradition of migration is established it acts as a 'social force' and many people who may not have an economic reason to migrate are drawn into it.[17] The flow of knowledge back from the migrants' destinations to areas of origin is important. The sponsorship and patronage by the pioneers help to overcome the intervening obstacles. This leads to a chain of migrants on the kinship—friendship basis, which in the case of the Pakistani migrants continued even after the Commonwealth Immigrants Act 1962.[18]

A typical case is that of A. G., a spinner, who came to Britain in 1961 to improve his financial position. One of his relatives, A. A., a pioneer settler (arrived in early 1950s), sent for him. His sponsor arranged his air ticket through an agent in Pakistan who also helped him with other paperwork. On A. G.'s arrival his sponsor also arranged his accommodation and supported him during the first thirteen weeks when he was looking for a job. Another example is that of M. A., also a textile worker, who came to Britain in 1964. His work voucher and air ticket were arranged through a distant relative and friend of his father's who came to Britain in 1960. M. A. lived with his sponsor and received all kinds of help, particularly for the first few months, to familiarize himself with the new situation. This pattern was common among my respondents.

Two other reasons for migration of Pakistanis to Britain were:

(1) Partition of India in 1947 when Pakistan was created, and
(2) the construction of the Mangla Dam.

In both these cases large numbers of people were displaced. At the time of the Partition in 1947, large-scale movements of population took place between India and Pakistan. Practically the whole of the Muslim, Hindu and Sikh population of East and West Punjab was exchanged and there was also a large exchange of population between East (now Bangladesh) and West Bengal. Many Muslims from all over India, especially from its northern parts, took refuge in Pakistan. These refugees (*Muhajirs*), according to the Census of 1951, constituted 9·81 per cent of the total population of Pakistan. In East Pakistan (now Bangladesh) the percentage was only 1·7.[19]

The largest number of refugees settled in the Punjab. The eastern districts near the border or India were very heavily settled. Most of the Pakistanis (from Punjab) in this country come from these districts. These refugees formed 55 per cent of the population of Karachi, more than 28 per cent of the old Punjab, and 20 per cent of former state of Bahawalpur. This migration at the time of the Partition fits into Petersen's category of the impelled—flight type.

Out of a sample of 211 heads of households, 201 came from Punjab and most of them were *Muhajirs* (i.e. 70 per cent).

The second group of displaced people was the Mirpuris. About 100,000 people were moved from the area in the early 1960s when the Mangla Dam was constructed. The purpose of the dam was to increase the volume of irrigation water for the Punjab and to generate electricity for a large area of the Punjab. At the end of the 1950s, and the beginning of the 1960s, the villagers of the proposed dam area were given compensation. Some bought land in the Punjab, others received cash and settled in other areas of Pakistan. Some who had relatives in Britain used the compensation money to come to Britain to find work. It has been suggested that the large numbers of Mirpuris in Britain are a direct result of displacement by the dam, and an arrangement at Government level to admit them into Britain.[20] It is not the only factor, but seems to have been a contributory one to the large-scale migration of Mirpuris.[21]

The people involved in this forced move from their villages were in a position to consider a number of alternatives. It is difficult to say, as no records are available, how many people displaced as a result of the building of the dam chose to use their compensation money to join relatives and fellow villagers in Britain. These events happened to take place at the same time as news of the possible introduction of immigration laws in Britain was reaching Pakistan. This resulted in Mirpuris and other Pakistanis joining the 'beat-the-ban-rush' to come to Britain. Thus the main period of mass migration from Pakistan to Britain was in the early 1960s. Few families had settled here before 1965.[22] Out of a sample of 570 Pakistani workers from Rochdale, both Punjabis and Mirpuris, only 29 came to Britain before 1960, while 273 came in 1960–63 (see below, pp. 36–8).

Petersen outlines the importance of the individual migrants' motives and decisions but this is of less consequence in a mass migration, such as the Pakistani migration to Britain. The feed-back of information and other help given by pioneer Pakistanis was an important factor in stimulating others to join the movement. Examples of the successful pioneers were an incentive in themselves. The mass migration also resulted in the establishment of agents and other institutions at both the Pakistani and British ends to facilitate the migration process and to make money out of it.

The point to be stressed here is not so much the incentive to migration but the fact that the majority of Pakistanis who have emigrated to Britain had some experience before coming here. As Everett S. Lee rightly says, 'a person who has once migrated and who has broken the bonds which tie him to the place in which he has spent his childhood is more likely to migrate again than is the person who has never previously migrated.[23] This certainly applied to Pakistani *Muhajirs* who first migrated from India to Pakistan and then to Britain later.

Without carrying out any systematic study of conditions in Pakistan, it is clear from the evidence available that lack of work and opportunities, along with other factors mentioned above, produced most of the 'push' towards migration to Britain. The availability of jobs in Britain 'pulled' the migrants to come and work here. C. Peach at a much earlier stage of the migration suggested that employment was a major factor attracting people to Britain. If the level of Commonwealth immigration was plotted against the level of job vacancies in this country a strong relationship was found. When job vacancies went up, immigration also went up, and when vacancies went down, immigration went down.[24] Many Pakistanis came to work, save enough to improve their economic position at home, support their dependants and eventually bring them over to Britain. This behaviour affected the settlement process of Pakistanis in this country which is discussed elsewhere in the book.

The main reason for migration given by a sample of 103 is outlined in Table 3. The economic incentive to migration was clearly the main reason. Over three-quarters said they came to Britain 'to get work or to earn money' or 'to have a better future for the children and the family'. Some mentioned reasons such as 'due to the Partition, lost everything and decided to try luck in Britain where some relatives were living before the Partition'. The category of education includes some of those young people, who came to join their parents; one of their parents' main reasons for calling them

Table 3

Main reasons for coming to Britain

N–103

Reasons	*No.*
Economic	81
Education	10
To join parents	5
Visit	5
Political	1
Other (air force deserter)	1
Total	103

was education. Those who had come for a visit and then decided to stay usually had a relative or friend in Britain. As one respondent put it, 'due to misleading stories about opportunities first many came for a visit and then decided to stay for a few years.'

Information about better wages and better opportunities was transmitted through friends or relatives. One respondent came 'due to other relatives who arranged everything; I decided to try my luck and help my family to improve their economic situation'. Another explained, 'followed other relatives' example who were improving their economic situation'. This supports my earlier assumption that Pakistanis came using their kinship—friendship networks before the immigration restrictions and even after the Commonwealth Act, 1962.

Whatever the other evidence, the fact remains that there were necessary and sufficient conditions to start the chain migration process. Pioneer migrants decisively influenced those who followed, by their letters, visits and remittances home demonstrating the economic opportunities. One of the characteristics of the Pakistani mass migration was that these following migrants were given financial assistance by way of sponsorship to help to pay the fare when necessary. They were also given hospitality on arrival in terms of accommodation, meals and help for looking for a job by the established migrants.[25]

The settlement patterns of Pakistanis in different towns or on a smaller scale within towns on the basis of their home origins, I suggest, came about as a result of the kin—friend chain migration. The importance of the kinship—friendship networks becomes clear in analysing the persistence of ethnic values and norms among the Pakistanis in Britain. It appears that Pakistani settlement has reached a stage where their communities are structurally, socially and culturally distinctive. As Eisenstadt points out from a sociological point of view, immigrants do not simply recreate their society of origin but produce a new direction as the immigrant community adapts itself to different aspects of the host society. The Pakistani chain migration process has contributed to the building up of interconnected communities. Such a development lends itself to a study based on the social network approach. The role of these networks of sponsorship and patronage in the formation of Pakistani communities and the processes involved form an important part of the study of Pakistani ethnicity.

3. Context of the Study

The Environmental and Social Context

Rochdale is an industrial town in the Manchester conurbation. Like many other Lancashire towns, Rochdale's population rose from approximately 11,000 in 1801 to 83,112 in 1901.[1] When Lancashire changed from woollen to cotton, Rochdale concentrated on her flourishing wool trade and became the most prosperous woollen town in the North West. At the end of the eighteenth century, the town was balanced between the old and the new industry. Although Rochdale moved late into cotton it soon caught up with its neighbours.[2] James Butterworth, the Rochdale historian, wrote in 1928, 'The Rochdale workhouse, or House of Industry, is situated above Entwistle Place; it is a neat stone building with a small garden in front.' Adjoining the workhouse was the town prison, both of which were in a new part of town which he describes as 'pleasant, neat and clean'.[3] It was named 'Mount Pleasant'. In fact, it was an amorphous cluster of cheap jerry-built dwellings, lacking space, and recreation area. It was here that John Bright (industrialist father of the town) brought the starving Irish labourers who would work for a bare pittance at his Cronkeyshaw Mills.[4]

In good times, wages in Rochdale averaged 3*s*. to 5*s* a week. In bad times, whole families faced starvation. In 1829, only one-third of the woollen weavers were working. In 1842, Sharman Crawford, the Rochdale MP, told the House of Commons that 3,000 heads of families were earning less than 1*s*.10*d*. per week. Yet Rochdale continued cording, twisting, spinning, winding, beaming, weaving, dying and tenting. Within fifty years its population trebled to 80,000.

Self-help, independence and co-operation were the watchwords of nineteenth-century Rochdale. It was on 21 December 1844, at

No. 31 Toad Lane that the Rochdale experiment in co-operative retailing began, which was to lead to the world-wide movement of production and wholesale and retail distribution.[5]

Describing the towns of Lancashire in the nineteenth century, Engels writes:

> These towns are almost wholly industrial and conduct their business through Manchester upon which they are in every aspect dependent. They are totally working people's districts, interspread only with factories, a few thoroughfares lined with shops and a few lanes along which gardens and houses of the manufacturers were scattered like villas. The towns themselves are badly and irregularly built with foul courts, lanes and back alleys, reeking of coal smoke, and especially dingy from the originally bright red brick, turned black with lime which is here the universal building material. Cellar dwellings are general here. Wherever it is in any way possible, these subterranean dens are constructed and a very considerable portion of the population dwells in them.[6]

Rochdale was such a town, and one can see even today some traces of what it looked like in the nineteenth century.

Its progress as an industrial town took place amid the conditions outlined; production changed from wool manufacturing to cotton, and later from cotton to fibres. Large national companies like Dunlop and Courtaulds came to Rochdale; and others like Turner Brothers started to spread to the neighbouring towns. Migrant workers from Ireland, the Ukraine, Hungary and Poland and the more recent group, mainly Asians, settled in to meet the labour needs of the town.

Housing

As people moved to Rochdale in the nineteenth century more houses were built; for example, from 1870 to 1885 many houses were built by private speculative builders to fulfil the demand for housing in the area.[7]

Structurally, many properties in Rochdale still do not have facilities such as baths and indoor lavatories. A recent survey of the Wardleworth area showed that only 40 per cent (292 properties) had indoor baths and only 36 per cent (268 out of 717 houses) had indoor lavatories.[8] Another study in the Deeplish area recommended extensive environmental improvement.[9] Besides the areas of poor-quality housing, new housing of higher quality has become available. From 1963 to 1970 the number of private houses completed in Rochdale was 2,396 (estimated population in 1968: 89,000)—see Table 4.

Table 4

Private houses completed in Rochdale, 1963–70

Year	*Number of private houses completed*
1963	330
1964	416
1965	324
1966	157
1967	164
1968	200
1969	341
1970	464
Total	2,396

Note: From 1971 to the end of the 1977–8 financial year, 5221 houses were completed in the private sector in the Metropolitan Borough of Rochdale.

Source: Planning and Estates Department, Metropolitan Borough of Rochdale.

Although the prices of these houses varied every year, in 1968 a new house cost as little as £2,000. This was an incentive for the people in the old inner-town areas to move out to houses with modern facilities. Consequently, newcomers to the town could buy older properties for as little as £200 and £400, most of which was available on Council loan schemes. The local authority officials claimed that in the 1960s Rochdale was one of the most rapidly growing development areas for private house-building programmes in Greater Manchester.

At the same time, the local authority was also building a large number of dwellings, far in excess of the immediate demands of the town. This was done in order to facilitate slum clearance programmes.

Table 5 shows the number of council houses completed in Rochdale in 1963–71.

The figure of 3,777 represents a 45 per cent increase in the number of council houses in the town. The availability of houses attracted people from the nearby towns. This was particularly true in the case of immigrants, as the paragraphs below show, who were looking for cheap housing, near their work place. According to the Housing Manager of Rochdale there were approximately over 300 council houses vacant in the town in 1972–3, when in most other places there was an acute housing shortage.

Table 5

Council houses completed in Rochdale, 1963–71

Year	*Number completed*
1963	142
1964	12
1965	29
1966	932
1967	356
1968	316
1969	195
1970	700
1971	1,095
Total	3,777

Note; From 1972 to the end of the 1977–8 financial year, 1738 houses were completed in the public sector in the Metropolitan Borough of Rochdale. In addition 275 houses were completed by the housing associations in the same period.

Employment

The other reason for people moving from one area to another is the availability of jobs in the area. This was true of Rochdale as well. Out of Rochdale's 91,000 population in 1971,[10] 49,987 were 'insured'.[11] Out of this approximately 17,000 were working in textiles which was more than a third of the work force in the area.

There is, of course, also evidence of a lot of people, migrants, in particular working in textiles in Oldham and other nearby boroughs. But the point I am trying to make here could be supported by looking at the unemployment figures over the period 1960–73, because Rochdale's unemployment was relatively low compared to other areas and the number of jobs available was usually higher than the number of registered unemployed. This attracted migrants who were looking for jobs during this period.

Looking at the figures for those from the New Commonwealth in Table 6, we find that few were registered as unemployed. The reason may perhaps be that they accepted jobs or conditions which the indigenous workers would not, such as permanent night-shift and multi-shift work and heavy manual jobs. It is interesting to note that in 1973 out of the total figure for male unemployed there were roughly 2.0 per cent migrants registered as unemployed (these included mainly the recently arrived Ugandan Asians) compared with an estimated migrant population of 8 to 9 per cent in the

Table 6

Number of persons registered as unemployed, Rochdale Employment Exchange

Period		*Male*	*Female*	*Total*	*From the New Commonwealth* *Male*	*Female*	*Total*
1960	May	251	44	295			
	Nov.	222	39	261			
1961	May	203	32	235			
	Nov.	384	40	424			
1962	May	523	41	564			
	Nov.	717	73	790			
1963	May	813	78	891			
	Nov.	619	57	676			
1964	May	361	40	401			
	Nov.	234	39	273			
1965	May	175	21	196			
	Nov.	128	31	159			
1966	May	113	23	136			
	Nov.	272	57	329			
1967	May	610	170	780			
	Nov.	905	197	1,102			
1968	May	659	114	773			
	Nov.	678	115	793			
1969	May	656	114	770			
	Nov.	653	88	741			
1970	May	714	97	811			
	Nov.	822	105	927	24	—	24
1971	May	1,256	158	1,414	82	4	86
	Nov.	1,827	370	2,197	57	5	62
1972	May	1,983	352	2,335	36	3	39
	Nov.	1,601	258	1,859	31	—	31
1973	May	1,108	157	1,265	23	3	26
	Nov.	695	120	815			

Note: It appears that recently the unemployment rate among those from the New Commonwealth countries has gone up. For example, out of a total of 2,715 registered unemployed in Rochdale in November, 1977, 152 were from the New Commonwealth.

Source: Department of Employment. (No separate figures for people from the New Commonwealth were kept before 1970.)

town.[12] Throughout, the unemployment rate among the New Commonwealth citizens has been lower than that for the population at large.

Table 7 shows the approximate number of people employed in different industrial groups in the area. This gives an idea of the number of firms in any category and the ranking of the industry in the area.

Table 7

Firms and employees in major industrial groups

Industry	*No. of firms*	*No. of employees*			*Employees as percentage of total employed*
		Male	*Female*	*Total*	
Textiles	101	8,500	6,000	14,500	30
Engineering	127	7,000	1,100	8,100	17
Construction	23	1,700	140	1,840	3
Paper	8	500	300	800	1
Transport	36	1,800	200	2,000	4
Wholesale and retail distribution	138	2,000	3,000	5,000	9
Administration including Local Authority	7	4,000	7,000	11,000	25

Source: Department of Employment, Rochdale.

According to the Manager of the Rochdale Employment Exchange there were approximately 50,000 insured people in the area, of whom 57 per cent were categorized as in manufacturing in 1974.

Job opportunities and the availability of houses attracted people to Rochdale from other areas, and even from other countries. After the Second World War, the British government admitted about 350,000 displaced persons from Eastern Europe into the country and directed them to areas where the industries were suffering from a shortage of labour. Rochdale was one of the areas to receive them and they boosted the labour force in the textile mills. According to the 1951 Census there were already 2,258 aliens in the town. Until the early 1960s the number of New Commonwealth immigrants remained very small. After that time more started arriving, mostly from Pakistan. The survey, carried out by the author in two areas of immigrant concentration, shows that there were people of 24 nationalities living there. The largest immigrant group were Pakistanis.

The Local Structure of the Pakistani Population

Number and Distribution

There were 2,815 people whose birthplace was recorded in 1971 as Pakistan out of a population of 91,455.[13] Table 8 shows the breakdown by birthplace. The 1,035 Indians in Rochdale, at the time of the Census enumeration, include a large proportion of Pakistanis who were born in India but migrated to Pakistan at the time of the 1947 Partition.[14] These in terms of ethnicity should be included as Pakistanis.

Table 8

Rochdale census, 1971

Total population	91,455
Total born in the New Commonwealth	4,435
India	1,035
Pakistan (including Bangladesh)	2,815
Kenya	205
Nigeria	15
Guyana	10
Jamaica	45
Cyprus	35

Source: Census 1971, Country of Birth Tables, HMSO.

In fact, the estimated number of Indians in the area was not more than 300 in 1975 including the children born in Britain.[15] Such discrepancies exist elsewhere and are very misleading when different ethnic/national minority groups are under discussion for specific purposes in particular areas. For instance, out of a sample of 103 working Pakistanis from the Tweedale Street area, there were 77 who said that they or their parents had migrated from India to Pakistan at the time of Partition. (Also see p. 24.) Similar considerations apply to some Asians who came from East Africa to Britain and also to white people who were born in India and who are included in the India or Pakistani-born population.[16]

Another problem in using the 1971 Census figures is that of the distinction between Pakistanis and Bangladeshis. The 1971 Census figures show Bangladeshis as Pakistanis because the Census was taken before the creation of the independent state of Bangladesh. Therefore, the number of Pakistanis given in the table above includes Bangladeshis. In Rochdale, however, the estimated number of Bangladeshis did not exceed around 300 in 1974–5. They were mainly concentrated in the Wardleworth area and a survey done in the area in 1973 estimated the number of Bangladeshis to be 216. Pakistanis were, therefore, the largest ethnic group, particularly if the families who were joined by their husbands and fathers since April 1971 and the children born in this country were included.

Table 9 gives the number of children born in hospital in Rochdale to parents from the New Commonwealth for the three years 1971–3. As the estimated figure of Pakistanis in Rochdale was about 8,000 during this period the majority of the children under the New Commonwealth category were, therefore, Pakistani children. (The estimated figure of 8,000 was arrived at by the Community Relations Council by taking into account the migration of Pakistanis from other areas of Britain to Rochdale, dependants, who came since 1971 census and the children born to Pakistani mothers.)

Table 9

Births in the Rochdale area

	Total births	*New Commonwealth*	*New Commonwealth % of total births*
1971	2,230	223	11
1972	2,078	219	10·7
1973	2,073	207	9·7

Source: Birch Hill Hospital.

The survey data from two areas of heavy concentration show that wives and children had arrived in great numbers since 1971 (see pp. 37–8) due to the fear that the right of entry would be restricted by the Immigration Act, 1971. After Pakistan left the Commonwealth in 1973 and the Pakistan Act was passed the rate increased further. As a result of this Act a lot of Pakistanis were forced to change their nationality from Pakistani to British.[17] They also brought their wives and children to this country to make sure that they did not lose the right to register as British subjects. This surely increased the number of Pakistanis in the town and consequently there were more family units as compared with the single-people household situation during the 1960s.

Areas of Settlement

Looking at the distribution of Pakistanis in the town, we find that there are four main pockets of settlement. Tweedale Street area and Wardleworth have large settlements and Spotland area and Durham Street area have a relatively small proportion, but equally concentrated in a few streets. All of these areas are less than a mile from the town centre.

The Electoral Register can be used to check this statement because Pakistani names are identifiable. This does not mean that the figure for houses occupied by Pakistanis is correct, because a significant number of Pakistanis do not register as voters,[18] but it indicates concentrations in certain areas of the town. If we look at the smaller areas within the wards we find greater concentration of Pakistanis in these areas as compared with the ward as a whole.

Table 10

Number of New Commonwealth immigrants and houses occupied by Asians in four Wards of Rochdale

Name of ward (area)	*Total no. of houses*	*Houses occupied by Asians No.*	*%*	*1971 no. from New Commonwealth*
Central Ward (Tweedale St. area)	1,396	327	24	1827
Wardleworth Ward	1,243	245	20	1025
Deeplish Ward (Durham St. area)	2,712	139	5	410
Falinge Ward (Spotland area)	2,655	125	5	425

Source: Figures calculated from the Electoral Register, 1972. For the last column, ward data, 1971 census, has been used.

The other source which supports this point is the ward data.[19] These are included in Table 10 and confirm the concentration of Pakistanis in these areas. The estimated number of houses occupied by Asians (mainly Pakistanis) in the town was 1,200. These were mostly owner-occupied. Looking at the Electoral Register of 1961 we find there were only 169 Asian men living in 36 houses. This shows that the arrival of Pakistanis in Rochdale took place within a decade or so. Table 11, taking two examples of Central Ward and Wardleworth Ward, supports this argument.

Table 11

Total number from New Commonwealth and post–1960 entrants in Central and Wardleworth Wards

Area	*Total no. from New Commonwealth*	*Post-1960 entrants*	*% total from New Commonwealth*
Central Ward (Tweedale St. area)	1,287	1,153	89·6
Wardleworth Ward	1,025	890	86

Source: Census 1971, ward data.

There were not many Pakistanis, or for that matter Asians, living in council houses in Rochdale. In 1974 only 30 council-owned properties in the town were occupied by Asians. These were occupied mainly by the Ugandan Asians who had come in 1972 as a result of President Amin's expulsion order. They were settling down slowly and the trend suggested that most of them would buy houses eventually. In 1977 a re-check of these families showed that most of them had bought their own houses.

Very few Pakistanis had purchased houses on the new developments. A study of the Electoral Rolls of the town shows that the trend might be changing to a small degree. In two wards where there are a lot of new properties, the number of Pakistani-occupied houses had risen from 5 in 1970 to 12 in 1972, and to 16 in 1973. An analysis showed that the Pakistanis who purchased these new houses were professional or self-employed persons. These people were better equipped in terms of transport and found no difficulty in using the facilities available in the Pakistani community some distance away. They were also in a position to afford to buy these relatively expensive houses.

Year of Arrival

The household survey carried out in the Tweedale Street area and another survey carried out in the Wardleworth area,[20] in which 211 and 160 households were covered respectively, show that most of the Pakistanis came to this country, and to Rochdale, after 1960 and the majority of their wives and children after 1965 or even 1968. A sample of 112 women in the Wardleworth area revealed that 81 (74 per cent) of them came to join their husbands after 1968.

Table 12 presents the year of arrival in Britain and in Rochdale of a sample of Pakistani employees living in Tweedale Street and Wardleworth areas. This shows that a significant number of people came during 1960–71, most probably as a result of the Commonwealth Immigrants Act 1962. The significance of the period of entry, before and after immigration legislation, is also shown in the table. This was due to the fact that Pakistanis who were already here arranged work permits for their relatives and friends and sponsored them to come to Rochdale.

Table 12

Year of entry to Britain and Rochdale

Significant changes	*Year*	*Tweedale Street area* (N–354) *Britain*		*Rochdale*		*Wardleworth area* (N–216) *Britain*		*Rochdale*	
Pre-1962 Act	Before 1960	19	158	11	104	10	108	4	40
	1960 to 1962	139		93		98		36	
Pre-1965 voucher changes	1963	11	67	16	65	25	52	13	51
	1964–5	56		49		27		38	
	1966–7	55	120	51	143	29	52	30	104
	1968–71	65		92		23		74	
After 1971 Act	1972–4	9		42		4*		21*	
	Total	354		354		216		216	

*1972–3

It is because of this sponsorship system that those who came from 1964 onward mostly came directly to Rochdale. The Rochdale figures, particularly during 1968 and after, were higher because jobs and houses were in short supply in other areas and the kinship—friendship network was well established. Looking at the figures for the Wardleworth area, which is a predominantly 'Mirpuri' area, we can see that movement from other places (such as Bradford and Huddersfield) to Rochdale increased significantly after 1968.

The figures in Table 12 relate to workers only. When we look at the year of arrival of Pakistani dependents, we find that the wives mainly came in the late 1960s and early 1970s. It appears from the immigration figures that while the number of West Indian arrivals dropped off rapidly after the second Commonwealth Immigrants

Act in 1968, substantial number of Indians and Pakistanis continued to come between 1968 and 1971; from 1972 onwards, the flow was very much reduced. The explanation for the difference is that following the 1968 Act most arrivals were dependants of people already here, due to the longer waiting time to get entry certificates for the dependants. As the Asian migration and particularly that of Pakistanis (including Bangladeshis) had taken place later than the West Indian one there were more Asian than West Indian dependants still to come. Table 13 illustrates the late arrival of Pakistani wives and children.

Table 13

Year of Pakistani wives' arrival in Britain

Year of entry	*Tweedale Street area* (N–176) *Number*	*Wardleworth area* (N–112) *Number*
Before 1960	None	None
1961–5	20	11
1966	14	9
1967	17	9
1968	29	11
1969	23	16
1970	25	18
1971	17	17
1972	15	16
1973	11	5
1974 (first six months)	5	no figures available*
Total	176	112

Note: Three Pakistanis in the Tweedale Street area had English wives.
* Because this survey was done at the end of 1973.

The figures since 1971 have decreased due to long delays in granting entry clearance at the British Embassy in Pakistan. Although a number of Pakistani dependants applied for entry clearances, there was a two-year delay in getting interviews. In general the late arrival of the wives coming to join their husbands, has created an imbalance between the sexes among Pakistanis.

Sex Composition of Migrant Population

The 1971 Census shows that men in Britain form 48 per cent of the adult population. If we look at the sex balance within the ethnic minorities, we find that, among the West Indians, the balance between the sexes is much the same as among the general population, while among the Asians the proportion of men to women is abnormally high. Among Pakistanis it was 295 to 100 in 1971. It is worth noting that in 1961 the proportion of Pakistani men to women was 538 to 100. For Indians it was 124 to 100. Early waves of migration tended to consist mainly of men, and wives and dependants tended to join later. One reason for the balance of sexes among the West Indians is the greater independence and influence of women in West Indies than in Indian or Pakistani society. This may have accounted to some extent for the numerical difference, as some West Indian women came to Britain independently to work. Table 14 indicates the trend towards a more sexually balanced migrant population (some changes since 1971 are shown for Rochdale in Table 15).

According to the 1971 Census, 76 per cent of Pakistani adults were men. As far as Pakistanis in Rochdale were concerned the 1971 Census data show that out of 2,815 people categorized as Pakistani, there were 2,090 males and 725 females; that means one female to three males.

Table 14

Pakistani sex ratio

Census	*Males per 100 females*
1961	538
1966	354
1971	295

Source: Prepared from information in tables in G. B. Lomas, *Census 1971, The Coloured Population of Great Britain* (The Runnymede Trust, 1973), p. 80.

Table 15 compares the survey data of 1974 with the 1971 ward data.[21] This shows that the imbalance between the sexes among Pakistanis in Rochdale was even higher than the national average.

When the Tweedale Street area is compared with the Wardleworth area differences are revealed which are mainly due to differences in the regional composition of the two areas. Punjabis live in the Tweedale Street area and they tend to bring their wives over in contrast to the Mirpuris, the predominant group in Wardleworth area, who have a tradition of keeping their women folk back home. Many Mirpuris told me that they would not bring over their wives and young children if they were given the surety

Table 15

Sex ratio of Pakistanis in two areas

Survey area	*Total 1971 census ward data*	*Males*	*Females*	*Total Pakistanis in the survey area (1974)*	*Males*	*Females*
Tweedale St.	1,287	914	373	1,094	624	470
Wardleworth	1,025	799	226	853	618	244

that they would never lose the right of entry to this country. Every new legislation about immigration or a public debate on this subject increased their worry about losing this right. Hence when Pakistan left the Commonwealth in 1972 and when the 1973 Pakistan Act was passed more dependants from the Mirpur area applied for entry clearance to join their husbands because of the fear of losing this right of entry in the future.

The Bangladeshi group were also predominantly male; out of 216 Bangladeshis living in the Wardleworth area, there were 159 males and only 57 females including the children born in this country. In comparison, out of 988 white people living in the same area, 482 were males and 506 females. The figures for Pakistanis, as a whole and for the Wardleworth area in particular, indicated that there were still many all-male households in the area.

Age Structure

Many studies of migration have reported that there is a tendency to migrate at a younger age both intra- and internationally. The census material for Britain reveals that the age structure of migrants was significantly different from that of the population at large. Among ethnic minority groups there were comparatively large numbers of children and a very small proportion of old people. Table 16 shows the sex imbalance for Pakistanis and age distribution by sex.

If we take the 15–44 age group, 71·6 per cent of Pakistanis in Britain fall into this category, which means the Pakistani population is younger compared to the indigenous population. The ward data and survey data confirm the argument that the majority of Pakistanis (58 and 51 per cent respectively) fall in to the age category of 15–44 years. Only 6·3 and 6·8 per cent respectively were found to be over the age of 45 years.

Table 16

Age-specific sex ratio of Pakistanis according to 1971 census

Age	*Born in Pakistan* Male %	Female %	*% of total*	*Born in UK** Male %	Female %	*% of total*
0–4	2·9	6·2	3·7	60·5	56·3	58·2
5–14	13·6	18·2	14·8	22·2	27·5	25·1
15–24	23·9	21·9	23·4	13·0	8·3	10·4
	}72·2	}69·6	}71·6			
25–44	48·3	47·7	48·2	—	—	—
45+	11·3	6·2	9·9	4·3	7·9	6·3**
All ages	100	100	100	100	100	100
Thousands	95·8	32·5	128·5	18·5	22·9	41·4

* With one or both parents born in Pakistan
** Includes those whites whose parents were born in Pakistan
Source: G. Lomas, op. cit., p. 70

The Tweedale Street survey data show a percentual change on the ward data particularly in the 0–4 and 5–14 age group categories. This was due to the arrival of children as dependants since 1971. There were 306 children born in this country in the survey area. This indicates that the imbalance of age groups will be corrected as the present young Pakistani population grows older (see Table 17).

Table 17

Age structure of Pakistanis in the Tweedale Street area

Age group	*Ward data 1971 Number*	*%*	*Survey data 1974 Number*	*%*
0–4	241	16·3	219	20·0
4–14	281	19·0	242	21·4
15–44	859	58·2	559	51·8
45–64	91		73	
	} 95	6·5	} 74	6·8
65+	4		1	
Total	1,476	100·0	1,094	100·0

Level of Education and Language

For the Pakistanis as for many other Asians, the language situation is a matter of concern since those who learnt English learnt it as a second language. Furthermore, their native languages are very different from English and it is probably much harder for a Punjabi-

or Urdu-speaking person to learn English than, say, for a French- or German-speaking person, due to the initial obstacle of a totally different alphabet.

In Pakistan a literate person is one who can read and write in any language while in Britain literacy in English is the main criterion. It is important to know the educational level of the Pakistanis when we talk about communication problems with the indigenous population, and to decide whether it is the language barrier or other sociological factors which 'incapsulate' Pakistanis in the neighbourhood and at work. Nevertheless, the language barrier may be a contributory factor. The figures in Table 18 reveal the educational levels of Pakistani workers living in the Tweedale Street area. These figures show that over 22 per cent of Pakistanis were illiterate and had never been to school and over 31 per cent had either a limited knowledge of English or none at all. Most of the older and middle-aged Pakistanis did not get a chance to go to a school either because of their families' financial circumstances or in some cases because there was no school in the village. On the other hand, 46 per cent were educated up to matriculation standard and above.[22] This includes a fair proportion of young people who attended schools and colleges either in Pakistan or in Britain. For this reason younger Pakistanis are much more likely to be fluent in English than older ones. Also it is well known that older people are less inclined and perhaps less capable than younger ones of making the effort to meet

Table 18

Educational level of Pakistani workers living in the Tweedale Street area

N–354

	Number		*Percentage*
Illiterate and no schooling	79		22·3
1–5 years' schooling	49		13·8
6–9 years' schooling	62		17·6
Matriculation	98	(164)	46·3
CSE, 'O' level, 'A' level anf F.A.*	44		
B.A.	18		
M.A.	2		
Other (electrical engineer and motor mechanic diploma)	2		
Total	354		100·0

* F.A. is an intermediate stage between Matriculation and the Bachelor's degree. It is roughly equal to 'A' levels in terms of syllabus.

other people, learn the language and adapt to new social norms. A short exposure to English in youth appears to be more effective than a long exposure at a later age. I have observed that fluency in English tends to be age-related, whatever the explanation.

Employment

The employment of Pakistanis was predominantly in textiles. Table 19 gives the breakdown of employed Pakistanis from the Tweedale Street area and illustrates this point. Apart from 51 Pakistanis who were self-employed, 78·8 per cent of the others were in textiles.

Table 19

Industrial distribution of Pakistanis in the Tweedale Street area
(total Pakistanis in the survey area= 1,094)

Industry	*Number*	%
Textiles	239	78·8
Light engineering	15	4·9
Paper mills	8	2·6
Public transport	28	9·5
Working with Pakistani employers	8	2·6
Professional services	3	1·0
Others (one car mechanic and one taxi driver)	2	0·6
Total	303	100·0

They were mainly doing manual jobs.[23] The figures include 23 women working mainly as spinners in textiles. This is what we would expect on the assumption that cultural factors largely prevent Pakistani women from engaging in economic activity outside their homes although many work at home doing sewing for Pakistani manufacturers.

Pakistanis were employed mainly on shift work, with a high proportion of permanent night-shift work. This pattern was very uncommon among the general population. At the time of the survey there were only two unemployed Pakistanis (both had recently arrived back from visits to Pakistan) and only one retired person.

Most of the Pakistanis worked in Rochdale and adjoining areas such as Royton and Heywood—they worked in large numbers in a few mills. They were residentially concentrated in certain areas and also worked in segregated departments and shifts, which incapsulated them apart from the indigenous population. Therefore, the opportunity for developing inter-ethnic social relationships in their neighbourhoods and at work was limited. This aroused suspicion in the minds of the indigenous population, particularly as in all-male households the curtains were all drawn throughout the daytime because of the different shift systems and consequently different routines.

Rural—Urban Background

About 80 per cent of the population of Pakistan live in villages and only 20 per cent in urban areas. Many of those in the urban areas are first-generation urban dwellers and retain close and frequent contact with the villages from which they came and in some cases they still own property in the villages.

Not surprisingly, Pakistanis in Rochdale came mainly from rural areas. Out of 103 in the employment survey 95 came from villages and only 8 from urban areas. Most of these were from the peasant proprietor group. Even the small businessmen and others in occupations in the urban areas had some connections with the rural areas.

The migrants in Rochdale still retained close contacts with their original villages and relatives there, and I observed a lot of evidence to this effect. This was also confirmed by the relatives of the migrants when I saw them during my visit to Pakistan.

Area of Origin

The Pakistani population of the Tweedale Street area were predominantly Punjabis whereas those in the Wardleworth area were mainly Mirpuris (see Table 20).

Table 20

Area of origin

Area (Region)	*Tweedale Street Area* (N–211): *Number of heads of households*	%	*Wardleworth Area* (N–160): *Number of heads of households*	%
Punjab	201	95·2	49	31
Mirpur	4	1·9	106	66
Karachi	5	2·4	5	3
Quetta	1	0·5	–	–
Total	211	100	160	100

In the Tweedale Street area those from the Punjab came in the main from Lyallpur (79 households), Sahiwal (36) and Bahawalpur including Rahimyarkhan (21). Even those not from these three areas were in most cases related to someone who was. Punjabis in the Wardleworth area also mainly came from these districts. It is worth mentioning here that an in-depth analysis shows that most of the Pakistanis both from Punjab and from Mirpur came from very few villages within these districts in the two regions. Previously some migrants from these districts who had relatives in Rochdale had been scattered in other towns mostly in the North of England, but as jobs became available and they could obtain accommodation, they moved into Rochdale. This had resulted in a strong kinship—friendship-based ethnic community in the town.

FIGURE 2 *Map of Pakistan*

Ethnic Institutions

R. Breton noted that the range and variety of ethnic institutions may be taken as an index of 'institutional completeness'.[24] The ethnic facilities in Rochdale have an important bearing on the nature of the community and on the interpersonal relations there. Further, the ethnic facilities help to keep the Pakistani community a relatively close one as people can meet their basic daily needs within the ethnic institutions, except of course with respect to employment.

There were over 20 Pakistani-owned grocery/butcher and drapery shops (in 1974) in the town, as well as about 10 travel and shipping agents.

Although the men worked mainly outside the Pakistani community institutional structure this was not the case for women, who were mainly employed by the sixteen Pakistani manufacturers[25] (for details see pp. 130–35).

There were three Pakistani banks which were used by Pakistanis to remit money back home.[26] There were seven Pakistani cafés; motoring schools, launderettes, electric, radio and television shops and cinemas were also owned by Pakistanis to provide services to their community.

Some Pakistanis ran part-time taxi services to transport shift workers in particular factories to and from work. There were six Pakistani general practitioners in the town and Pakistanis were mainly registered with them. There were three Pakistani welfare associations, three religious organizations, three political organizations and one professional organization run by Pakistani representatives (see below pp. 174–80).

There were two Mosques and four centres for children to learn Urdu and receive religious instruction after school and over weekends. These were located in the areas of high Pakistani concentration.

To emphasize the point: participation in ethnic activities and utilization of exclusive institutions increases the Pakistanis' identification with their religion, traditional culture, language and national origin and is an expression of their ethnicity in this country. Consequently, this increases Pakistani 'incapsulation' and reduces the chances of interpersonal relations across ethnic boundaries.

The Survey Area

The area for the surveys was the Tweedale Street area known as 'Pakistani area' from the early 1960s, which forms part of the

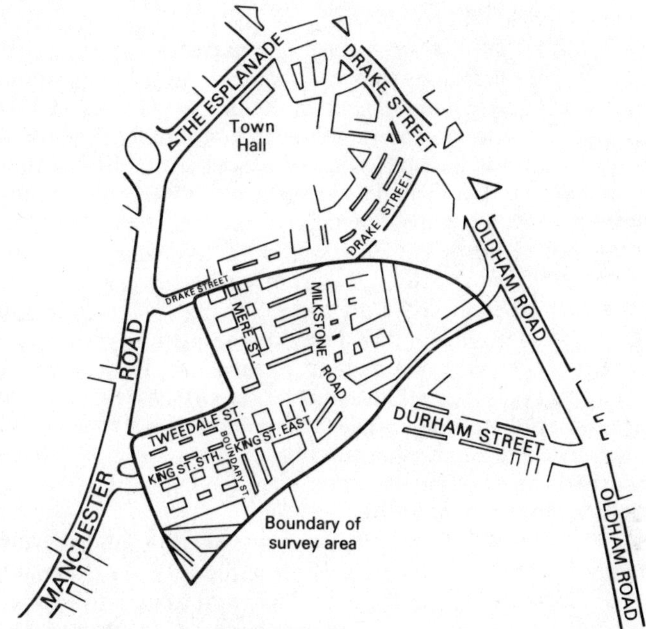

FIGURE 3 *Rochdale—Central Area*

Central Ward, as shown on the map in Figure 3. This is the area where the first house was owned by a Pakistani from the Punjab at the end of the 1950s. This house provided a base in the area especially for Punjabi settlement.

One still comes across a few dozen Punjabis who lived initially in this house. Slowly Punjabis started buying houses nearby and this process continues up to the present. Part of this area was declared a slum clearance zone in the early 1960s and part a General Improvement Area at a later date. Slum clearance indirectly forced the indigenous population out of the area to look for better housing. At the same time it provided an opportunity for Pakistanis to buy these houses at a nominal price usually with cash for the few remaining years of their projected life. Money was usually borrowed from kin or friends.

When large houses were purchased three to four partners sometimes shared the financial burden and responsibility for the house. Kinsmen and friends were taken as lodgers at a nominal rent and in some cases free. Cooking arrangements were usually shared. During 1974 Pakistanis could still live in Rochdale on £5 to £7 a week (£1.50 to £2.50 for rent, £3.50 for food and £1 for transport); in the case of a close relative rent was not charged, but gifts for the children and household goods were given by the lodger without any overt indication that this was a form of compensation for the rent. Elizabeth Burney mentions that the strongest attitude shared by all migrants is that no kinsman in need of shelter can be refused.[27] This attitude was very common among the Pakistanis in Rochdale.

Most of the ethnic facilities and services provided by the Pakistanis were based in the Tweedale Street area. Within the area there were streets which were predominantly Pakistani; Tweedale Street, Ellsmere Street, King Street East and South and Henry Street are a few examples. This provided Pakistanis with an opportunity to interact with each other on a daily basis. The life-style was similar to a village in Pakistan, except that there were more modern amenities in Britain. Visits to each other's houses were quite frequent. Living in a 'Pakistani area' they all knew each other at least by name, and people exchanged greetings and often stopped to talk to each other in the streets. The atmosphere in the area was usually friendly, particularly during the fine weather when the children played outside while the mothers chatted.

There was a sense of community among the Pakistanis. Mutual aid and physical and emotional support in times of need seemed to be part of the way of life in the area. Pakistani women usually kept an eye on each other's children, went shopping together and borrowed small quantities of food from each other when stocks ran out. Dishes of food were exchanged if something special was cooked. Similarly men helped each other with exchange of work and tools. Cars could be borrowed in time of need such as illness or bereavement, and so on. Lifts to and from work were quite common although in some cases a nominal contribution was made to cover the cost of petrol.

On a different level, Pakistani shops in the area acted as dissemination points for various types of information related to the community. They sold Pakistani newspapers and magazines, distributed leaflets regarding Pakistani religious festivals, meetings, and social and cultural activities. They also displayed posters advertising Pakistani films. For example, at election time or any other occasion important to immigrants the political parties and English officialdom, such as the Community Relations Council,[28] used the Pakistani shops as a distribution point.

Pakistanis also used shops as meeting points, leaving messages for each other there, and obtaining information about different activities in the community. News about a birth or a death, about people going to or returning from Pakistan was spread through Pakistani shops. During the field work it was found that a lot of discussions about immigration (particularly about entry certificate problems), politics in this country and back home took place while waiting at the butcher's or the grocer's. Information about troubles in the community travelled, therefore, through the kinship network and the shops in the area.

People who wanted to sell a house, or a car, used these shops to advertise and this was done by English people as well. This was noticed many times when English people came to Pakistani shops and asked the owners if they knew anybody who was interested in buying a house or a car and usually left the details with him. This was obviously done knowing that the Pakistani shops were a means of reaching Pakistanis. In addition it was a way to overcome the communication difficulties because the shopkeeper usually spoke English and acted as an interpreter if the need arose. This gave these entrepreneurs the opportunity to act as leaders and they were often able to mobilize public opinion in the Pakistani community through their contacts at all levels.

The other places of regular meetings in the area were the Pakistani cafés, cinemas and the Mosques. Among these, the Mosque as an institution and the religious leaders (including the *Imam*) played a very important part in the transmission of Islamic religion, culture, values and identity to the second generation. By so doing the Mosque is a significant factor in maintaining clear ethnic boundaries.

The situation as a whole led to multiplex relations and a close-knit community in the area. The need to deal with the indigenous people was not felt due to the availability of ethnic facilities, reinforced by a perception of external hostility which Pakistanis have to face. These facilities and feelings have an impact on the Pakistanis' ethnicity, lead to internal cohesion and reduce the chances of inter-personal relations across ethnic boundaries, thus contributing to their incapsulation.

4. Kinship Networks: The Family Structure and Functions

Kinship is a set of ties socially recognized as existing between persons because of their genealogical connections. It includes affinal relations created by marriage as well as those of descent. There has been much argument on the question of how far kinship ties are based upon a biological relationship. The classification of kin, the social categories and functions are of great significance and diversity and the biological referent is often indirect. In this work the concept of kinship is used to refer to both real or supposed descent and affinal relations of the kinship networks of Pakistanis. It is worth mentioning here that the kinship networks are a major element in the operation of the Pakistani community. In industrial societies among the ties of kinship those of the elementary family are primary.[1] In Pakistani society the extended family has comparable significance. The extra-familiar kin networks are also very important. These types of relationships are known as *Biraderi* in Pakistani society, and they affect the whole flow of goods and services. (See pp. 62–7.)

Relationships of Pakistanis interviewed in this work tend to be multiplex, within the kin-based 'clusters' (see pp. 77–82), and they incapsulate them from non-kin and the wider society. These may not be face-to-face relationships. Mitchell refers to such relationships as intense links with people at home maintained by migrants in which both sides continue to honour obligations. He argues that frequency of contact is not a significant criterion for the durability and intensity of such relationships.[2] The continuing ties with people at home (in Pakistan) are important to consider when describing migrants' relations. In this work the use of network approach is adopted to overcome the geographical boundaries.

Conceptual Framework

Studies of kinship in urban western society normally start from a consideration of the family. Sociologists hold different views on this subject. Parsons, Nimkoff and Goode, for instance, say that modern industrial structure favours the development of nuclear or independent families as opposed to the continued existence of joint–extended families. Industrialization and urbanization are believed to result in loss of function for the family.[3]

Durkheim, Simmel, Tönnies, Mannheim and many others have stressed that the family in urban society is a relatively isolated unit. In complex industrial societies members move where there are better job opportunities. American sociologists such as Linton, Wirth and Parsons support this notion.[4] The assumption is that the nuclear family developed in Western Europe and the United States as a consequence of the urban–industrial revolution. Its small size is ideal for meeting an industrial society's requirements for a mobile work force. This small-size family replaced the large rural one. This assumption is challenged by other theories regarding the family. Peter Townsend found it difficult to accept the idea that the extended family must give way to some variety of the nuclear family.[5] A study done by Greenfield of different societies reveals that industrialization and urbanization can occur with or without the small nuclear family.[6] Orenstein supports this by saying that if the size of the family reflects in any way the structure and characteristics of the joint-extended family in India, then few changes have occurred in this system during the period of industrialization in India from 1911 to 1951.[7] Another study of a Swiss town shows that due to the industrial revolution many fringe rural families were stabilized and further strengthened in their kin networks by earning supplementary incomes in nearby factories. Able-bodied members obtained work nearby and no longer had to leave the family unit in search of work.[8]

It is difficult to determine *a priori* if the new conditions during the transition from a rural to an industrial situation end the dominance of the traditional joint-extended family and replace it with a modified kinship network, or whether it is replaced by the nuclear one. It remains true, however, that the family network described variously as 'an emergent urban familism' or 'modified extended family' exists and functions in the modern urban industrial societies.[9] If by extended family is meant a group of kin of three generations or more with a fairly well-defined corporate linear character, involving co-operation in productive activities, common ownership of assets and recognized common responsibilities, such units are almost entirely absent from the modern urban industrial scene. But if extended family means in a very loose sense those extra-familiar kin who maintain a relationship of some intimacy with members of a nuclear family, then such groups do persist even in fully developed urban conditions. Whether or not kinship networks have been maintained or declined in urban situations, they have certainly changed.[10] The kinship networks and their functions of mutual aid have implications for the functioning of other sets of social systems in the society. The main activities using the kinship networks are mutual aid and social activities among the families involved in the network. This is more relevant for a migrant in providing the supportive functions related to accommodation, job and general settlement in the new situation. In this study Pakistanis were observed in this framework. The patterns of support take many forms in the new situation, including the exchange of services, gifts, advice and financial assistance. The question arises whether the links which are part of the Pakistani society persist in relation to the kinship networks in Rochdale. Kinship networks among Pakistanis are divided at two levels as follows:

1. Family: nuclear, extended or joint.
2. *Biraderi*, extra-familial kin.

Regardless of where Pakistanis live or what the composition is of the immediate residential group the structural rules for the Pakistani family are: (1) joint and extended-type family; (2) patrilineal descent group; (3) patrilocal residential rule; (4) patriarchal authority and respect related to age and sex; and (5) preferential marriage patterns which lead to kinship networks in the wider sense.

The question arises, what structural and functional changes have taken place in the Pakistani families in Britain?

Family Composition

Joint–Extended Family

The traditional family in the Pakistani society is the extended and joint type of family; a group of people living together in one house. The composition differs from one family to the other, due to different stages of the life cycle, i.e. parents with their children, parents living with married sons and their children, parents, children and their children, and so on (Figures 4 and 5 illustrate this point).

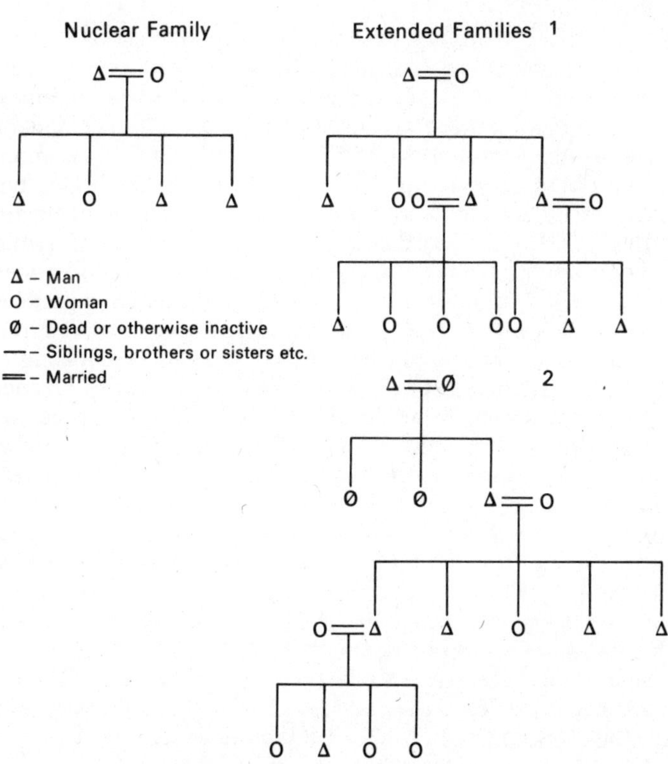

FIGURE 4 *Different types of families*

A family may consist of members of a conjugal family (husband, wife and children) if the married son lives apart from his parents and siblings. It may include all members of a joint family, i.e. the mother and father, their married sons, their wives and children, unmarried sons and daughters and occasionally a widowed daughter. It could be a stem family, the aged parents living with one of their sons and his wife and children, the other grown-up sons having established their own households. Another type is one where several brothers live in one compound with the married brother taking responsibility for their education and arranging their marriages. Married brothers may form separate households when their father dies, but keep their land and business in common.[11] The joint-family members usually pool their resources and have common property. There could be some absent members of the family who work in a city or live in another country, such as Britain, but have the same status. No doubt, family composition changes over time. It changes according to the natural cycle of any family; some members die, others are born, daughters marry out and daughters-in-law come in, as it is a patrilocal family structure. After the death of the parents, brothers may separate into new families, but work land together. Other changes may occur due to some members leaving temporarily in search of work, going with or without their wives and children, as is the case with many Pakistanis in Britain. This turns the joint household into separate entities, contributing labour, participating in the traditional gift exchange and attendance of ceremonies on their own behalf.[12] This joint household must be distinguished from the joint family. The members of a household form a joint family if their income is pooled and expenditures are made from a common purse, but the joint family does not necessarily coincide with the residential group.[13] Brothers may share land and other businesses and property, work together, and reside separately and divide the income. In some cases where one or two members of the family are working abroad, which is more applicable to Pakistanis in this country, and make remittances to the family, they still hold together and constitute a joint family.

Among Pakistanis in Britain extended families do not exist in such great numbers as in Pakistan.[14] The households are usually of two generations, compared to the three or more found in Pakistan. Grandparents are less frequently found in Britain, although sometimes they visit their children or come as dependants. When more families have grandchildren born in this country the composition of the household may change. Some households in Britain include unmarried brothers of the husband or wife, e.g. Mr X had his brother living with him as part of his family. In some cases married brothers live together and in fact pool their resources as a joint family. During the field-work several such cases were found. For

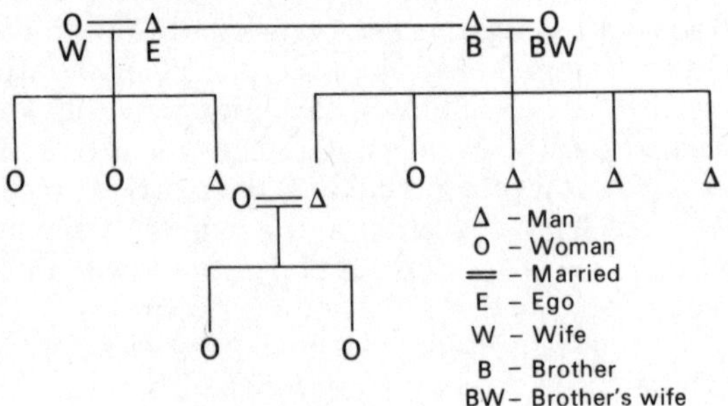

FIGURE 5 *Ego's joint family in Rochdale*

example, Mr M. S., a mill worker, and his brother Mr H. A., a shopkeeper, lived together and pooled their incomes jointly. One advantage they had was that their wives were sisters. Similarly, Mr M. A. and his brother, Mr Y. S., and Mr W. A. and his brother, Mr A.A., lived together as joint families (see Figure 5). In some cases cousins lived together in one household and shared the expenditure but kept their incomes separate. Mr C. S. and his cousin, Mr H. U., lived together but kept their investments separate. Sometimes nephews, cousins or other distant relatives who were usually single, lived as part of the family and participated fully in the activities of the household. They were usually younger than the head of the household who was likely to be in a position of authority and guardianship over them (see Figure 6).

Another type of Pakistani household exists in Britain where distant relatives or people from the same village or district live as lodgers. They are usually temporary members and leave to establish their own households when their wives and children join them. Particularly in the early stages of Pakistani settlement in Britain many single people lived together. For example, when Mrs S. joined her husband he was living with other relatives and friends and she cooked meals for everyone in the house. This situation is changing as more Pakistanis are bringing over their families to this country. Similarly, young men travel to Pakistan to get married, and return to establish separate households.

A 'nuclear family' in a city in Pakistan or in Britain may be a part of a joint family as mentioned above.[15] A joint family may consist of several branches living as separate households in different residences but pooling their incomes, all the major decisions relating to finance, ceremony performances and marriages, etc. being taken jointly. In addition, there could be some variation in financial commitments. If a Pakistani has his immediate family in Britain but still consults, and particpates in, his family in Pakistan and his sentiments and loyalty remain to the family there, his is still a joint family.

Some Pakistanis bring their families to Britain for economic reasons or for the education of their children. Mr M. A. said, 'I brought my wife and children to this country with the permission of my father for two reasons: one, that my wife could do some sewing at home like other Pakistani women in Rochdale and this would increase the income of the family. Secondly, for the education of my children. I regularly send money to my father to buy more land and to build a new *pakka* house (i.e. a house built with bricks and cement rather than with mud). I write and ask his permission if I have to take an important decision. I feel as long as my father is alive he is the head of the family and we all should obey him. I always feel that I am part of my family in Pakistan and I am determined to go back and live with them after a few years, once I have earned enough money. The happiness and prosperity of my family is my satisfaction.' Another two brothers whose parents were alive sent regular remittances to help and support their parents and unmarried brothers, sisters and some nephews. Their savings were being invested in buying land for the family as a whole. The material benefits were often kept common.

It is usual at the death of the father to divide the property among sons and daughters. Each son gets two shares and each daughter gets one, according to Islamic and state laws. In practice, daughters usually give their shares to their brothers and in turn receive gifts whenever they visit them. After the death of the father the factors which usually lead to the division of the joint family in Pakistani society are: hostility between the wives of the two brothers, or disagreement between brothers about the management of the property. When one brother is living in Pakistan and the other in Britain these situations can be avoided. This in practice supports the traditional joint-family system as one brother remits part of his earnings for investment for the whole family and the other brother(s) manage the family affairs in Pakistan. When the brother who lives in Britain visits Pakistan, he is treated with gratitude and respect by the other members of his family and *Biraderi* which indirectly encourages him to carry on discharging his responsibilities and to feel part of the joint family.

As a result of sponsorship and chain migration some joint families exist in Britain, who live in the same residential unit. During the field-work I came across several such Pakistani families in Rochdale. (Out of a sample of 211 households 121 were nuclear families, 58 joint–extended families and 32 all-male households.) (See Figure 6.) Many shared the residences but some of these families had split up residentially because it was difficult to get big enough houses. One respondent explained, 'I have to move out of my brother's house because the children have grown and they need separate rooms for their studies. We still treat each other as one family.' Others lived separately due to other reasons but still felt and functioned as one family. Mr G. R's wife did not get on very well with his brother's wife; it was a personality clash over authority in the decisions about housework. Mr G. R. decided to live separately as the disagreements could have an effect on the children. The two families were still one in every practical sense: all the important

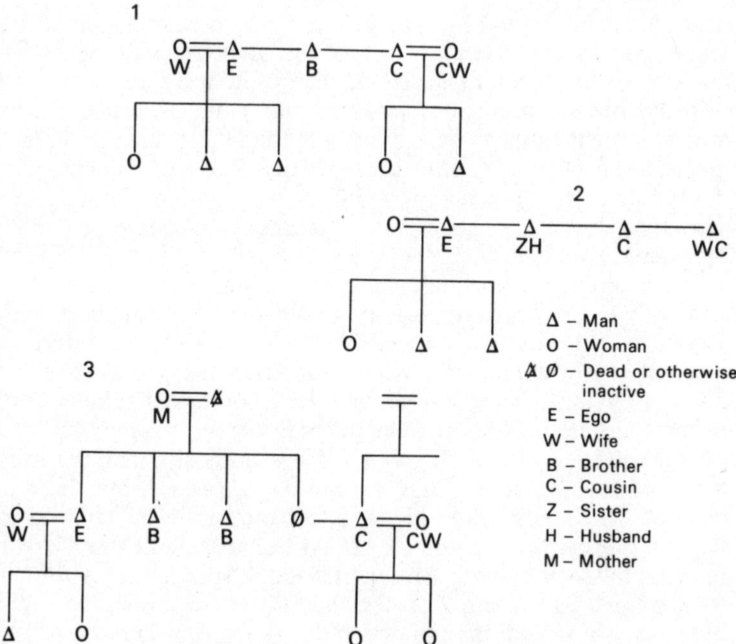

FIGURE 6 *Joint households in Rochdale*

decisions were taken jointly, including decisions about savings and investments. These examples show that in the new situation, Pakistanis continue to have a joint-family system although they adjust it to meet differing circumstances.

Authority in the Family

A Pakistani family is basically patriarchal. The authority in the family is with the head of the household who is male. It is also allocated according to age. The elders have more authority than the younger members of the family. The sex criterion can be seen to be of greater importance than age in practice. Age is more relevant in terms of respect, but not for decision-making, which affects the members of the joint family. For example, if the male head of the household dies, his eldest son (if he is grown up), and not his widow, assumes the status of the head of the household, although within the family the widow would have more say after the death of her husband. If the children are not grown up, the mother is usually the head of the household but an uncle or some other relative of the family will act as the spokesman of the family in relation to the outside world. Older members of the family have authority and respect from the younger members of the family as a rule. This is also true for the other relatives outside the family, such as *Mamu*, maternal uncle and *Phuphi*, paternal aunt. The elder members of the *Biraderi* who are usually distant relations and are joined in an active social network with a particular family are also respected by the younger members.

In the families in Rochdale, the patterns remained the same. Sex and age were the most important factors in a family network with regard to authority and respect. In nuclear families the authority was with the husband, who was the bread-winner and the head of the household. In joint families where two or more brothers were living together, the authority and decision-making power remained with the elder brother. The wife had less authority than the husband; he took decisions affecting the outside world, but she was head of the domestic household. If the mother-in-law arrived in Britain, then she was the female head of the household for domestic matters. Mr M. S. came to Britain first and he sponsored his brother to join him. The younger brother had some education and ran a business; but still all the important decisions regarding the family were taken by Mr M. S. When the other family members, wives and children, including his brother were in conversation or watching TV and Mr M. S. entered the room, they fell silent as a sign of respect. If other relatives asked Mr H. A. about something, he would say, 'I will let you know after consulting my elder brother.' If it was something relating to himself he would ask them to consult his elder brother. For example, when Mr H. A. wanted to visit Pakistan, all the family members agreed that he should go and buy some land there. Nobody dared to ask or suggest this to Mr M. S., the head of the household. They brought in a relative, Mr R. A., who indirectly suggested to Mr M. S. that it was time they bought some land in Pakistan as it was becoming more expensive day by day. Mr R. A. also suggested that it would be better if Mr H. A. went as the ladies of the household could look after the shop for a few weeks with his help. After some thought, Mr M. S. agreed to the idea and suggested that Mr H. A. should go to Pakistan and buy land with the help of a friend who happened to have good contacts. Everybody in the family was relieved and happy and started making plans about Mr H.A.'s journey. Once he was in Pakistan he continued to write and telephone Mr M. S. before making any decisions about the land they wanted to purchase. The two children of the family showed respect to all the other elder relatives in Rochdale. They called them *Chacha*, paternal uncle, and *Phuphi*, paternal aunt, or *Mamu*, maternal uncle and *Masi*, maternal aunt. This pattern of authority and respect was quite common among other Pakistani families in Rochdale.

Second-Generation Pakistanis

The children of Pakistani parents born or brought up in Britain are a generation caught between two cultures. They live in the culture of their parents at home, and are taught a different one at school, in the neighbourhood and at work. Their world is neither the 'old' nor the 'new' but both. They are in a difficult situation within the family; parents cannot fully understand their children; children in some cases are unable to understand their parents. This clearly could lead to increasing the generation gap and stress and conflict between the generations.

Pakistani children are usually introduced to their relatives when they come and visit the family or vice versa. One person, Mr A. K., was so concerned about this aspect of socialization that he actually gave lectures to his children how to respect their elders while he was giving them religious and *Urdu* language lessons at home. He explained, 'I do this because if we teach them from the very beginning with good reasons, they will respect us and follow the cultural values without questioning. However, if we leave it too late, they learn independence and other rude things at school and it becomes difficult to counter that influence at a later stage.' This attitude was quite common among my respondents. The main reason given was the need to keep the second generation under control so that they would follow the cultural values of their own society. This was, however, not true for all the families. I found some families where children had started questioning the authority of the parents. This was usually the case with families where the head of the family was not very strict or was absent for some time from the home. For instance, when Mr M. A. went to Pakistan with his wife and two children, aged four and six, two sons of twelve and sixteen were left with their uncle Mr A. A. because of their studies. Their uncle, who worked on night shift, used to sleep all day and did not get much chance to keep an eye on the children. Their aunt, the uncle's wife, did not say anything if the boys did anything wrong, fearing that she might give the boys and their parents the impression that she and her husband did not want to keep them. The boys were able to mix with other boys and really changed to become independent individuals, not bothering about their schoolwork, etc., so much so that the eldest boy gave up school and started working against his uncle's wishes. Their father wanted these boys to carry on their studies and was ambitious that one should become a doctor and the other an engineer. He was delayed in Pakistan for six months, due to family and business matters. When his eldest son, A. J., started work, another relative wrote to Mr M. A. telling him what had happened. He was so shocked that he booked his flight and was in Rochdale within a week, leaving his wife and other two children to follow. When he learnt about the independence of his sons and the irresponsible attitude of his brother, there was a big row in the family. When the father asked his son why he had started work without his permission, he gave as his reason that their uncle did not look after them properly and they needed some money to buy clothes, etc. This, in fact, was not true and Mr M. A. did not believe that it was so. There was a conflict in the family which took months to patch up. Mr M. A. said, 'I did try to see that my son started his education again, forgetting what had happened, but it was too late as he was under bad influences. My trip to Pakistan has ruined the future of my children. The younger one is following the elder. When I try to say something, he threatens to call the police. Now I have to be careful and keep my other two children under constant watch so that they do not get the bad influences from their elder brothers.' This example, given here in some detail, illustrates several points about the family relations and a growing pattern among Pakistani families in Rochdale. It shows the pressures on Pakistanis in the new situation.

I observed that there were, among others, at least three issues which affected the relationships between Pakistani parents and their children. These were: western clothes, particularly for girls, arranged marriages and the question of freedom. The situation seemed to be similar in Rochdale to what I found in a nationwide survey about the attitudes of parents and young people towards these issues.[16]

In this study I found, for instance, that 43 per cent of young Pakistanis did not see anything wrong with girls wearing western clothes. More than half (60 per cent) felt that more and more young people would rebel against the arranged marriage system. Also, a majority of 72 per cent felt that English people of their own age had a lot more freedom than they had, and 33 per cent clearly expressed that they would like more freedom than their parents gave them. At the same time, 32 per cent of parents and 47 per cent of young people admitted that they had family disagreements. The areas of differences seem very wide but the young people mentioned more frequently than their parents these issues: clothes, arranged marriages and freedom, 'things done in spare time/leisure'. It appears that the adolescent Pakistanis resent some of the restrictions imposed by their parents because of the social and psychological gap between them and their parents due to a different social environment and education. The world at home is different from that of school and community. Young people are a part of both worlds. As the example mentioned above illustrates, this situation increases the worry of Pakistani parents and desperate attempts are being made to keep young people within the family–kinship fold and culture. The case studies in Chapter 11 illustrate these points.

5. *Biraderi* and *Vartan Bhanji*: Institutions of Kinship Networks

Pakistani families seem to categorize kin and even to assimilate non-kin as quickly as possible into the kin-category networks. Terms of address illustrate this. Personal names are rarely used even for children. All older men are 'grandfather', all middle-aged men are 'father' or 'uncle' and all middle-aged ladies are 'aunts', and so on. The Pakistani kinship system is a 'categorizing system' as against the 'specifying system' usually found in industrial societies. There is, for example, the distinction between siblings on the grounds of their relative seniority and relative authority. The kinship system is basically an *authoritarian system*.

A Pakistani also has obligations to relatives and non-relatives outside the immediate family. These relationships or social networks are regulated by the institution of *Biraderi*.

The Concept of *Biraderi*

The word *Biraderi* is derived from the word *Biradar*, brother. Beyond the joint–extended family it is the *Biraderi* which structures kinship networks. (These sometimes include the non-kin as well in the Punjabi society.) *Biraderi* includes all the men who can trace their relationship to a common ancestor, no matter how remote.[1] It refers to both the whole group of those who belong to a patrilineage and any individual member of it.[2] The term *Biraderi* has several referents and its meaning changes according to the context in which it is used. For example, E. Blunt uses it to denote a group which does not mean a specifically located ecological or geographical group.[3] Korson states that it includes not only the blood relatives as Eglar has suggested, but other people as well.[4]

The descent group *Biraderi* includes all those who claim and can trace links of a common paternal line. As Pakistani society is patrilineal all the inheritance is through the male line and so is the *Biraderi*. Daughters belong to the *Biraderi* of their father but after marriage are also included in the *Biraderi* of their husbands. It is often difficult to draw the line where the *Biraderi* ends, as this depends on the person defining those he thinks belong to his *Biraderi*. In practice it depends on the contact maintained with each other, the degree to which endogamy is practised, the frequency with which members meet to take decisions which affect the *Biraderi* as a whole, or participate in ritual ceremonies and in *Vartan Bhanji*, an exchange of gifts and of a whole range of services.

Distantly related consanguines, those related affinally, or friends who have assumed either affiliation due to regular rituals or certain kinds of exchange of services may be incorporated into one's *Biraderi*. This type is usually called a 'fraternal *Biraderi*', and was found to exist among the Pakistanis studied.

Usually there is a difference in the use of the term *Biraderi* by the observer and by the participants. Wakil makes a distinction between 'general *Biraderi*' and 'effective *Biraderi*'. His distinction roughly corresponds with the wider definition of *Biraderi* as based on 'descent' and 'brotherhood'.

The effective *Biraderi* is a limited group; its boundaries are defined by degree of kinship, but may be altered through marriage, opportunity of contact—face-to-face or otherwise—previous obligations 'inherited' from parents, or any combination of these.[5] All members of the 'effective *Biraderi*' maintain the relationships of *Vartan Bhanji* with each other. Alavi uses the concepts originally used by A. Mayer for Indian situations.[6] Mayer distinguishes between two kinds of lineages in Malwa, Central India—the lineage of recognition 'based simply on recognition of a previous agnatic link' and the lineage of co-operation consisting of 'agnates who come to one's social functions'[7]—and Alavi adopts this distinction taking the *Biraderi* of 'recognition' in a more general sense as relating to descent and the *Biraderi* of participation in the 'fraternal' and 'effective' sense. The boundary of the *Biraderi* of recognition is defined by mutual knowledge of the actual links of common descent and is empirically determinable.[8] A *Biraderi* could be cross-caste and cross-village such as *Zamindar* (Landowners) *Biraderi* or *Kammi* (carpenters, blacksmiths, etc.) *Biraderi*. It is the *Biraderi* of participation which is more relevant in the British context where the members co-operate and interact in a new situation, sometimes cutting across the descent ties. This includes members of non-kin, who came from the same village or area and the other Pakistani neighbours. The specific meaning of *Biraderi* depends on the frame of reference and the levels of contact, such as an endogamous group, those who belong to one *quom* (sub-caste), those who became friends in Britain at the time of migration and settlement, those who live in one area, those who work together and so on.[9]

Biraderi in Operation on the British Scene

In order to understand social networks it is necessary to study the complete pattern of kinship networks and not simply the relationships within the elementary family itself. In the Pakistani kinship system the type of relationships and levels of contact, obligation and behaviour towards kin determine the flow of services. The social networks involving kin are found to be multi-stranded. The debate about 'descent theory' and 'alliance theory' in the interpretation of Pakistani kinship networks is also relevant.[10] From the point of view of choice of residence, job selection, reciprocal services and other related matters in Pakistani families, the *Biraderi* networks play an important role. In fact the whole way of life of Pakistanis is directly or indirectly related to this institution.

It is the function of *Biraderi* as a kinship and friendship group which is relevant to this study in the British context: how it helps individual Pakistanis in the process of migration and settlement through mutual support and how it forces them together and results in their incapsulation.

The role of *Biraderi* in the field of economic and political institutions will be discussed later. Also the process of migration and the *Biraderi* are discussed in the chapters on migration and case studies. However, it will be touched on in the following paragraphs as well.

W. H. Key shows that studies of migrants to the United States and geographical movement of families within the country illustrate that family members perform *invasion* or scout roles and then attract other kin into their communities and neighbourhoods.[11] Once new immigrants become established in the city in Pakistan or in Britain, they serve as informants, sponsors, innkeepers and providers for later kin and friends' arrival. Once these followers arrived there was a greater reliance upon kin and as their number grew, the kin group or *Biraderi* functioned most effectively to protect and acculturate their members in urban ways. The case material included in this work and the information on this aspect collected during the employment survey demonstrate this point. The professional Pakistanis who came either to improve their qualifications or to do a specific job, did not get much assistance from their *Biraderi*. Nevertheless, they used some sort of friendship contacts to feel their way in the new situation. One doctor came to improve his qualifications and told me, 'When I got the job in England I started looking for contacts. I used to spend almost every weekend with a close friend in the first few months after my arrival. To be honest, one feels frightened coming to a country where you do not know anybody, once you make friends it is all right'.

For workers it was different because they did not come to a specific job. Mr A. U. remarked, 'My uncle came to receive me at London airport. Everything was arranged for me in the house where my uncle was living with five other Pakistanis from the same area. They tried to get me a job, but it was very hard in those days. My accommodation and food were free. My uncle used to give me some pocket money so that I could move around to look for a job. I felt very upset when I could not get a job for three months. I used to cry and curse the agent who said that jobs were easily available. One day my uncle said that he had talked to his overlooker and he would give me a job next week. I started at £7 a week at night shift. It was hard, but satisfying that I was doing something. Then slowly I got used to things here. But it was with the help of my *Biraderi* that I stood on my feet, without this help one could go mad. Now we have quite a few relatives in Rochdale and I live life as we lived in our village, helping each other in any way.'

Mr M. S. who belonged to another *Biraderi* was sponsored by one of his relatives: 'I did not do anything, my relative Mr A. A. arranged my ticket through agents in Pakistan. He arranged my accommodation, food and job in the mill where he had worked for three years. Later my brother came to join us along with other relatives. We live like a *Biraderi*, as an extension of our *Biraderi* in Pakistan. This is the only way to be safe, successful and happy in this strange country.' (See Figure 7.)

Mr S. A. came here with the help of a fellow villager Mr B. U. who used to be in the Merchant Navy and then decided to stay here to earn some money. He arranged his passage, accommodation and a job for him. He said, 'I cannot forget the help I got from Mr B. U. in the early days. I respect him as a father; he has helped a lot of people to come and settle here without any self-interest. He is happy that people in the Pakistani community in this town look upon him as a father.' These examples illustrate the importance of *Biraderi* in the initial stages of migration and the continuing sense of obligation it engenders.

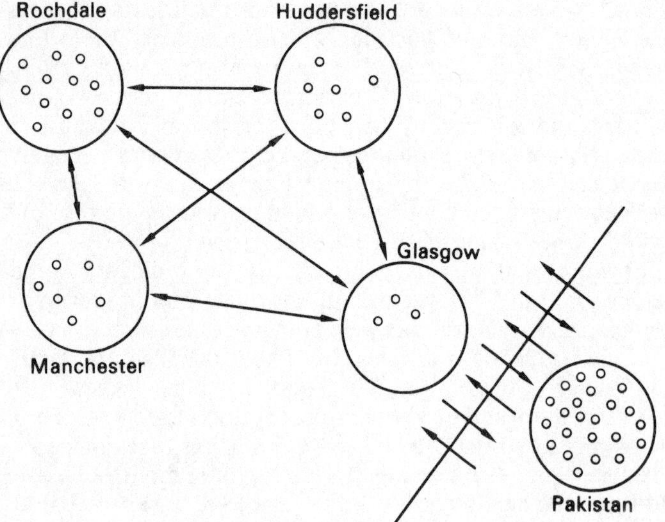

FIGURE 7 *A typical* Biraderi *network within and beyond Rochdale*

Major activities related to the Pakistani kinship networks, i.e. to *Biraderi*, consist of members giving each other financial aid and goods of value, and a wide range of services at specific times and under certain conditions. Kinship networks assist with the settlement, the achievement of status and occupational advance of member families and individual members.

Some services are provided by the *Biraderi* on specific occasions including births, circumcisions, weddings, deaths, accidents, disasters and personal troubles. A sense of moral obligation to give service or acknowledge one's kin in a manner appropriate to the occasion was found among Pakistanis in Rochdale. Turning to *Biraderi* when in trouble before using other agencies established for such purposes was the rule rather than the exception in Pakistani families. This pattern of help is found among kinship groups in other societies as well.[12] When asked, 'Where do you go for help if you need any?' a substantial majority of Pakistanis in the sample replied, the *Biraderi* or a friend. Table 21 illustrates this point. It shows that for financial and general help Pakistanis relied mainly on the *Biraderi* and friends. There were also those who used external agencies such as the bank and the Community Relations Council either exclusively or in addition to relatives and friends. This was usually done where the *Biraderi* or friends could not meet the need.

Table 21
Source of help when needed

N—103

	Financial help	*General help*
Relative/*Biraderi*	63	42
Friend	33	34
Pakistani organizations	—	23
Banks	15	—
Community Relations Council	—	15
Social Services Department	—	1
Solicitor	—	2

Frequent visits, messages and letters kept the *Biraderi* members in contact and up-to-date (see p. 88). Sometimes hundreds and, in the case of Pakistanis in Britain, even thousands of miles would be travelled to attend ritual functions of the close members of the *Biraderi*. Before demonstrating how the Pakistanis in our study fulfilled their obligations in the framework of *Biraderi* network, it would be useful to mention something about the importance of *Vartan Bhanji*, which outlines the principles of reciprocity for the Punjabi individuals and families within the *Biraderi* structure. However, to say that it exists does not mean that its structure will be the same as that of the 'traditional' version in the villages in Pakistan.

Vartan Bhanji: A Mechanism for Kinship Network

Friendship ties tend to rest on free choice and affection; neighbourhood ties on face-to-face contacts and kinship networks on relatively permanent relations. There is no reason why all these primary groups could not overlap—friends may be neighbours and kin members at the same time. As kin are treated as more reliable than mere friends, so close friends are generally sought from inside the *Biraderi*. This seemed the pattern amongst Pakistanis in Rochdale.

One system which extends to all these relationships in Pakistani society is the mechanism of gift exchange known as *Vartan Bhanji*, widely practised in the Punjab. The term means an exchange of gifts and also refers to the gifts so exchanged; likewise, it denotes the relationship between people established through this exchange.[13] Literally, *Vartan Bhanji* means 'dealing in sweets' and it has the extended meaning of dealing in 'relationships'. In Punjabi the word *Vartna* means 'to deal' and its derivative *Vartan* means 'dealing'. *Bhanji* means 'sweets' and it is also used with the meaning of 'relationship'. *Vartan Bhanji* involves exchange of sweets, fruits, food, money and yards of cloth; extending beyond material things, it includes the exchange of services, favours, like treatment, entertainment and participation in ceremonial events. In its operation this mechanism of exchange involves a wide range of relationships among the *Biraderi* and other groups who make up the Punjabi society. It is of vital importance to people as a means of achieving *Izzet*, prestige.[14]

Eglar makes it clear that although *Vartan Bhanji* is basically a relationship developing out of an exchange of gifts, the same term is applied to another kind of relationship in which no gifts need to be exchanged, but in which two individuals, two families, two villages, feel free to ask favours of each other.[15] This type of relationship is based on friendliness and on rapport and willingness to ask for and to grant favours. So in popular usage, *Vartan Bhanji* may have various meanings. It may mean the relationship, or the way of dealing, or the articles of exchange, or behaviour on certain occasions.

Vartan Bhanji transactions usually take place on specific ceremonial occasions such as birth, the circumcision of a son, marriage, visit to relatives, and death of an old person. Gifts may be given and received on other occasions—such as sickness and convalescence, departure for a pilgrimage to Mecca and, more relevant to Pakistanis in Britain, departure to and from Pakistan. *Vartan Bhanji* is usually on a reciprocal basis, symbolizing the roles of debtor and creditor. Alavi mentions that the exchanges of gifts are as transactions in a perpetual cycle of regular reversal of ritual debts between the households. Each payment, notionally, consists of two parts; one part extinguishes the pre-existing debt and another part creates a new debt in the reverse direction.[16] This two-way relationship puts an obligation on the individual and the household to reciprocate whenever a fitting occasion arises.

In practice *Vartan Bhanji* operates with reference to the *Biraderi* of participation as a whole, independent of effective relationships between particular households.[17] When two households are not on good terms, *Vartan Bhanji* continues unless either side wishes to terminate the relationship, which involves one party losing claim to membership of the *Biraderi* or both parties recruiting support and forming a cleavage within the *Biraderi.* Participation in *Vartan Bhanji* is an expression of alignment and solidarity with other households, so withdrawal from its membership means termination of such a relationship.

A major occasion such as a birth or a marriage, offers the chance of a detailed analysis of the transaction of *Vartan Bhanji*, but does not tell much about the important characteristics of relationships between *Biraderi* members. *Vartan Bhanji* is a source of financial aid system and a force in the social organization of *Biraderi* relationships.[18] There exists, however, an important classification of *Biraderi* based on duration and strength. It distinguishes between *Katchi* and *Pakki Vartan*, *Katchi* being weak and temporary and *Pakki*, firm and permanent. This in fact denotes the two types of relationships: one related to *Biraderi*, and the other to friendship and courtesy.

> The circle of households with whom these respective forms of *Vartan Bhanji* are transacted, and their modes of operation are different. It is only in *Pakki Vartan* that we see the full operation of the institution and its complementary mechanism of ritualised responses. It takes place only between households with whom permanent bonds exist. These are, above all, members of the *Biraderi* of participation.[19]

Alavi goes on to explain that *Katchi Vartan* indicates a courtesy relationship rather than permanent bonds. It takes place principally with friends and neighbours in the village who are outside the *Biraderi* of participation.[20] The relationship ends when one partner in the *Vartan* moves away from the area. This seems to be true as friendship ties may be much more vulnerable to breaks in face-to-face contacts than kin (*Biraderi*) groups because there are no institutional pressures, such as *Vartan Bhanji*, to maintain the relationship.

Vartan Bhanji in Britain

It is relevant at this point to demonstrate first, how the system of *Vartan Bhanji* plays its role as a force to strengthen the social networks among the Pakistanis in Rochdale, and, secondly, how a kinship network, i.e. *Biraderi*, acts as a support group in different areas of life and results in their incapsulation.

The need for and support of these relationships increase in Britain due to the absence of some of the kinship members. The other reason is that in Pakistan one depends on other kin members for a number of things; dependence on *apna*, own, relatives is the way of life of the Pakistani society, and this dependence increases in the British context due to the alien way of life. However, the *Biraderi* here is treated as an extension of *Biraderi* in Pakistan. As Mr M. S. explained, 'If we do not help each other here in Britain, life gets difficult and our wives get upset. The other reason is that if we ignore our relations in Britain where they need our help the word goes back to Pakistan and it affects the prestige of the *Biraderi.* We have to go back and we do not want to sever our *Biraderi* relationships while we are here. Instead, we are making them stronger and living like a big happy family.' This attitude seemed quite common among other Pakistanis in Rochdale.

The major forms of activities of the *Biraderi* network are inter-family visiting, participation together in recreational activities, and ceremonial behaviour significant to the *Biraderi* unity. Many Pakistani families who have their *Biraderi* in Rochdale visit each other almost every day. For example, when Mr R. A. went to work his wife and small children used to go to their relative Mr M. S.'s house. They spent the day together, sometimes joined by other relatives. Mr R. A. remarked, 'It is good because they can go shopping together and help each other with language difficulties and we do not have to worry when we are out at work. That is why I prefer to live near my relatives.' The people who worked on the night shift needed this type of support more than others. 'Relatives can keep an eye on the house. If something goes wrong my wife knows where to go for help.' This pattern was found to be quite common among Pakistanis.

When asked, 'If you had a choice of living in a largely Pakistani area or in an area where the majority of people are British—which one would you choose?' The majority of respondents gave their choice as the Pakistani area, as figures in Table 22 show. The reasons given were mainly to live near relatives and friends and the ethnic facilities such as Pakistani shops, etc. Language difficulties and preservation of culture were also mentioned as additional reasons for the preference to live in a Pakistani area.

Table 22

Preference for area in which to live

	N–103
Mainly Pakistani area	81
Mainly British area	15
Mixed area or either area	7

Those who gave as their choice a British area mentioned reasons such as 'clean and quiet area'; 'where others do not interfere'; 'to mix socially with British people and create better understanding'; and 'to remove misunderstandings'. These attitudes show that a minority of Pakistanis would like to live in other areas if they could, while the majority prefer to live with or near other Pakistanis.

Most of the relatives went together to the cinema on Sundays, a popular recreation for Pakistanis. Some professional people had started going out on picnics over weekends, but visiting each other, eating together, and talking about home (Pakistan) still remained the favourite activity. This visiting was not limited to *Biraderi* members only. Friends, neighbours or fellow workers also visited each other. These relationships overlapped. Mr S. M. worked with Mr M. A. as a television engineer, they were not *Biraderi*, but friends at work. They visited each other quite regularly and had established the pattern of *Katchi Vartan*. When Mr M. A.'s wife had a son Mr S. M. bought a lot of gifts for the mother and child. When Mr S. M.'s wife had son this was reciprocated. They exchanged gifts at *Eids* and on other occasions. When Mr M. A.'s mother came here on a visit, she was invited for a meal quite often to Mr S. M.'s house with other members of the family. She was given *jowras* (clothes) at her arrival in and departure from this country. This does not mean that Mr M. A. and Mr S. M. did not maintain relationships with other Pakistanis. Mr M. A. told me that when people came to know that his mother was going back to Pakistan they all brought gifts—so much so that it was impossible for his mother to take all those clothes and other gifts to Pakistan, due to the weight restrictions. She appreciated it very much, saying that it was just like Pakistan. She said she was pleased to know and experience the fact that people had not lost their values in this country and had not forgotten their moral obligations.

The *Biraderi* network also facilitated mutual aid. It was quite common to borrow money from *Biraderi* members if someone was buying a house or starting a business in this country or purchasing land in Pakistan. When Mr H. A. went to Pakistan to buy land, he collected about £6,000 from his relatives in Rochdale in just two days. This was not because he needed all this money but in case he was faced with financial difficulties in Pakistan. Part of the money was transferred to Pakistan and the rest was kept in a bank in Rochdale so that, if the need arose, it could be sent to Pakistan. It so happened that Mr H. A. did not use all the money. When he came back, the first thing he did was to return the money to his relatives and thanked them for their help. He said, 'I did not want to use this money for any other purpose because it would be cheating my relatives and losing their trust. The purpose it was borrowed for was served, so it was my duty to return it.'

Similarly, when Mr M. A. bought a big warehouse he obtained financial help from his *Biraderi.* It was quite common to borrow money when buying a house. Mr H. S. borrowed £2,000 from his relatives and friends to buy a house in cash. He explained, 'I did it for two reasons: first, because I knew that I could collect the money and save all the bother of surveys and mortgages; secondly, why pay so much interest on a mortgage if it is not necessary; thirdly, now it is mine and I can sell it when I want to. Also, I will be tempted to return the money to my relatives and for that reason will work hard to raise the money quickly, but this will be my net savings with no rent and no mortgage.' This attitude seemed common among my respondents.

During field-work and in the interviews carried out with Pakistanis, it was found that almost 80 per cent obtained help from relatives or friends either to pay the whole price of the house or to pay a substantial deposit to bring down the mortgage repayments. My observations lead me to believe that the private sector in housing among Pakistanis has developed with the help of this mutual aid. The transactions take place without any written document or receipts. They are always based on trust among the *Biraderi* and friends. A word is always given more weight (trust) than a piece of paper in Pakistani society.[21]

On ceremonial occasions, gifts are exchanged and sweets are distributed among the *Vartan Bhanji* members. A Pakistani marriage provides a good illustration of kinship—friendship networks in operation.

A Pakistani Marriage

The first Pakistani wedding to take place in Rochdale during the field-work was that between F. K.'s daughter and A. D.'s son, a *Biraderi* member. Both F. K. and A. D. came from Lyallpur district and belonged to *Arian Biraderi.* They worked as spinners on the night shift in the same factory. It was an arranged marriage. Neither the boy nor the girl was consulted, but the elders in Pakistan were asked their opinions. The final decisions about the engagement and the venue of the marriage were left to F. K.'s father, who was a farmer living in Pakistan. It was decided that to have the wedding in Rochdale would be easier and less costly than both the families going back to Pakistan to celebrate the marriage. Both families wrote to the relatives in Pakistan and Britain and personally invited those who lived in Rochdale. They knew that those in Pakistan would not be able to come, but it was their duty to inform them and invite them.

The groom was 22 years of age, working as a mechanic with the post office (telephones) and he had been in this country for the last six years. The bride had been in this country for three years and attended school here only for one year. She did not go out to work but did sewing at home for a Pakistani manufacturer as did her mother.

Vartan Bhanji plays a very important role in the ceremonies of marriage. This is an occasion when the relationships established by a household with its relatives, *Biraderi* and friends come into play. The celebration of a Pakistani marriage consists of several ceremonies. It starts with the *Gala*, the official opening of marriage ceremonies, and ends with the *Muklawa*, the consummation of the marriage, the three-day visit of the bride to the house of the bridegroom. Not all these ceremonies took place and others were modified because of the different situation in Rochdale.

A big community centre was hired for a Sunday to celebrate the wedding which was registered on the Saturday. Apart from the *Biraderi*, friends, workmates, the local officials, both Pakistani and English, were invited. Arrangements were made for two sections in the centre, one for the males and other for the females. *Nikh*, the religious marriage registration, took place as soon as the *Barat*, wedding party arrived. Food was cooked by the *Nai*, barber, and his family, according to the traditional way in Pakistan. It was served to the *Barat*, wedding party and other guests by F. K.'s close relatives.

The bride and bridegroom received many gifts, clothes, money, sweets and other goods. Those relatives from other parts of Britain who could not attend sent their gifts through other relatives. This applied only in *Katchi Vartan* because in the case of *Pakki Vartan* the presence in person and participation in the ceremonies are essential. The exchange of gifts and the attendance at each other's ceremonies symbolizes the support and solidarity expected between *Biraderi* members. The strength of these relationships is demonstrated by personal attendance at these ceremonies.

Those in Pakistan also participated emotionally by sending gifts with a relative who was visiting Pakistan just before the wedding.[22] They also sent greeting-cards. The two families related to the bride and groom celebrated the wedding-day in Pakistan by inviting *Biraderi* members for a meal and praying for the success of the marriage. News of the wedding was communicated to relatives in Pakistan by telephone, by letters and messages in person and pictures of the marriage ceremonies were sent as soon as they were ready. Details of all the gifts received from the *Biraderi* members were also communicated to the heads of the families in Pakistan so that they could keep a record of those giving presents for use on future occasions.

F. K. was offered and accepted all sorts of help in arranging the wedding ceremonies. Financial help towards the costs was given to him and many *Biraderi* members helped with the transport of guests and with serving the food at the centre. The basic rule for help was the same as in Pakistan, that is, a daughter of one person in the *Biraderi* is treated as a daughter of the whole *Biraderi* and this feeling is shown particularly at the time of marriage ceremonies. The official opening of the marriage ceremonies, the *Gala*, was performed by the bride's relatives but not the bridegroom's. *Maiyan*, when a knotted cord is tied to the wrists of the bride and of the groom, took place at both the houses. *Bid*, dried fruit and henna were brought by relatives to the house of the bride. Other ceremonies which took place on both sides included *Mehdi*, *Khara Lhai* and *Selami*, putting on henna, bathing, dressing and salutation of the bride and the groom respectively. *Meylis*, wedding guests, relatives and friends who came from other places also participated in some of these ceremonies.

The *Barat*, the wedding party, included the groom and his family and the guests as well, and *Mithyai*, sweets, were distributed among all the wedding guests. When the wedding party reached the community centre, the groom dressed in the outfit given to him by the bride's family in a room allocated for this purpose. The same ceremony took place for the bride in the women's section. The ceremony of *Laag*, money given to *Kammis* (those who work for *Zamindar*), was not applicable here in Rochdale because the *Kammis*, like the blacksmith, potter, waterman, etc. are not found here in their traditional roles. One *Kammi*, the *Nai*, however, was given some reward, as apart from his other duties during different ceremonies, he also acted as cook for the food served to the wedding guests. The ceremony of *Muklawa* also took place in the traditional way. The ceremonies were carried out in the spirit of the traditional marriage but some modifications were made due to the changed circumstances. For example, *Vag pharai*, the ceremony in which the groom's sister and cousins hold onto the bridle of his horse until he presents them with money, did not take place but it was symbolized by giving money to the girls.

Involvement in the rituals was evident in Pakistan as well as in Britain. The geographical separation was minimized as far as possible. The actual practices were modified only where necessary because of the difference in context. This shows that a Pakistani here still feels part of his *Biraderi* in Pakistan, where he intends to go back eventually. Therefore, it is quite relevant to study Pakistanis in the Pakistani and British contexts as one sphere of activities. This proves that the extended–joint family networks exist in the British urban industrial situation and proves also that isolated nuclear families are not the most functional type in the modern western society.

Biraderi and Other Aspects of Help

Biraderi networks are also used to find jobs. Almost 90 per cent of the people interviewed found their jobs with the help of a friend or a relative. The same was true of starting and running a business (see Chapter 7).

Services performed by the *Biraderi* members regularly throughout the year or on occasion included shopping, care of children, advice-giving, help after an accident, and the repair of houses, personal problems, etc. These services usually overlapped with help offered by other Pakistani neighbours and friends, for instance, the need to borrow a cup of sugar in the midst of preparing a meal, or have someone watch the baby for a few minutes while the mother ran out unexpectedly to the shop. Such emergency situations ranged from trivial mistakes to catastrophes.[23]

Inability to speak English creates added difficulties for Pakistanis, in particular for the women, in dealing with other people apart from close relatives. The role and status of women and the whole system of *Purdah* are discussed elsewhere in this book.

Reliance on neighbours is a natural result of the formation of ethnic neighbourhoods following chain migration. This is the pattern which exists in other ethnic groups as well, such as Italians in the United States. *Padroni* (bosses) played a very important role in the early days of Southern Italian emigration to the United States. The *Padroni* gradually lost their monopolistic power as the cluster of roles with which they had been vested was taken over by the close relatives and friends of prospective immigrants.[24]

In Pakistani communities, there appears to be an order of preference for appeal for help: family, *Biraderi*, fellow villagers, friends, neighbours, other Pakistanis and the rest of the society. For example, if one needed to fill in an official form or go to an office for some reason, one would look to one's family first. If nobody was able to help, one would consider the *Biraderi* members, and so on. The degree of dependence on other members of the Pakistani community increased due to the lack of education, unfamiliarity with the western way of life and the lack of confidence and trust in others. Women in particular depended on other relatives. When Mr H. S.'s wife took her two children to school she used to leave the other two little ones with her relative Mrs M. S., who lived nearby. Mrs M. S.'s two children of school age were also taken by Mrs H. S. Sometimes the two women took it in turns. One of the respondents described how when his wife was in hospital, his children were looked after by the wife of one of his relatives, who also cooked meals for them for about four months. Another respondent said that when his wife was pregnant and particularly when she was in hospital, his children were looked after by a friend's wife who was also a neighbour, for a few weeks. He explained; 'If we did not have this reciprocal help, we would not know what to do as our children could not stay on their own when most of us work on night shifts. They could not be looked after by English foster parents because of their different food habits and, in some cases, language difficulties.'

These examples demonstrate the dependence on other relatives, friends and neighbours here. Another respondent reacted, 'We are lucky that we have our relatives here, we live nearby, we help each other when the need arises, we do not feel lonely—sometimes I feel as though I live in my village. Due to these facilities, I have brought my wife and children to this country. Otherwise, I would not have done so because they would feel lonely.' This attitude was shared by some other Pakistanis.

Ties with other *Biraderi* members living in other parts of the town or other cities in Britain were kept alive by the use of cars and telephone. *Biraderi* members visited each other over weekends. Not all go on holidays, and visiting relatives was a common way of spending holidays. This helped to keep alive the contacts and the *Biraderi* networks.

To sum up, for most of the Pakistanis fulfilling their obligations to their *Biraderi* in Rochdale, elsewhere in Britain or Pakistan, was very important and self-satisfying. The role of their kinship network had not changed very much even in the new situation, but was modified due to the different context. It is in a sense the persistence more or less, of those links which is integral to the Pakistani society.

Numerical Analysis of Social Networks

Mitchell suggests that the analytical determination of the content of the network linkages is so crucial for the sort of network analysis that is usually attempted, that some involvement of the observer with the people he is studying is essential.[25] According to Max Weber's scheme of social action, to understand the conduct of others one must observe not only what they do but know what meaning they attach to their actions.[26]

Before the analysis of networks can become meaningful it is necessary to present the degrees of intimacy and obligations attached to different types of relationships. In this section the structure of the social networks of twenty 'research cases' studied, is presented, using numerical data.[27]

The research cases were chosen from five different occupational groups using the 'snowball' technique taking one person from each group as a starter. This gave us a cross-section of people from the community. The numerical data were collected towards the end of the field-work, to complement the ethnographic and social material. The results to be presented below are the numerical counterpart to the ethnographic and sociological data presented in this work.

Interactional Criterion—the Contents of Links

From a sociological point of view the most important interactional aspect of the links in a network is one which concerns the meanings which the persons in the network attribute to their relationships. The links between an individual and the people with whom he interacts come into being for some purpose or because of some interest which either or both of the parties consciously recognize.[28] This may be *Biraderi*, economic assitance, *Vartan Bhanji*, political or religious co-operation or simply friendship, neighbourhood or ethnic ties. Some of these characteristics have been previously discussed.

Similarly we have seen that the 'intensity' of a Pakistani's network with kin–*Biraderi* members is likely to be greater than that with another Pakistani who is not *Biraderi* but lives in the same street or comes from the same area in Pakistan. This is partly due to the obligations attached to the kin–*Biraderi* members in Rochdale, in other parts of Britain or in Pakistan. We have also seen that face-to-face interaction is not a necessary condition for the Pakistanis to honour the obligations attached to their *Biraderi* or *Vartan Bhanji* relationships. The relationships Pakistanis maintain with their relations both in this country and in Pakistan are one example of this.

The kinship—friendship networks are dominant in almost all fields of the Pakistanis' social interaction which sometimes cuts across the occupational groupings. A pattern of social relationships by matrix manipulation (see Table 23) could be drawn about the degree to which there appears to be a 'cluster' or 'clique' in the collectivity and to what extent every individual is linked to every other individual in the collectivity.[29]

Table 23

Original adjacency matrix

	1	2	3	4	5	6	7	8	9	10	11	12	13	14	15	16	17	18	19	20
1	*	3	3	3	3	3	3	2	1	3	1	2	2	1	1		1		1	2
2	3	*	3	3	2	2	3	3	1	3	1	2	3	2	1	1	2		2	1
3	3	3	*	3	3	3	3	2	1	3	2	2	3	2	2	1	2	2	2	1
4	3	3	3	*		2	3	2	2	3	1		2	1			1			
5	3	2	3		*	3	3	3	1	3	1	2	2	1	1	1	3	1	2	
6	3	2	3	1	3	*	3	1	2	3	2	1	2	3	1	1	[1]	1		2
7	3	3	3	3	2	3	*	2	3	3	3	3	3	3	2	1	3	2	2	1
8	3	3	2	1	3	1	3	*	1	2	1	2	2	1	2		2	1	1	1
9	2	2	2	1	2	2	3	2	*	3	3	3	3	1	2	2	2	1	1	1
10	3	3	2	1	2	2	3	2	3	*	3	3	3	3	2	1	3	1	2	
11	2	2	2		2	1	3		3	3	*	2	2	3	1	2	2	1	3	
12	2	2	2	1	2	2	3	3	3	3	3	*	3	2	1	1	1	2	2	1
13	2	2	2	1	1	2	3	2	3	3	1	2	*	3	3	2	2	1	1	
14	2	1	1	1	2	2	3	1	3	3	3	3	3	*	3	1	2	1	2	1
15	1	2	2	1	1	2	3	3	2	3	3	2	3	3	*	2	1	1	3	1
16	2	1	1		1	1	2	1	3	2	3	2	3	1	2	*	1	1	3	2
17	2	2	2	1	3	2	3	1	1	3	1	1	2	2	2	2	*	3	2	3
18	2	1	2	1	2	3	2	3	2	2	1	1	1	1	2	1	3	*	3	2
19	2	2	2		2	1	2	1	1	2	3	2	1	2	3	3	3	3	*	2
20	2	1	3		1	2	1	1	1	1	1	1		1	2	2	3	3	2	*

To measure the hierarchy of cliques, Hubbell's procedure was used.[30] This solution is based on coding from closeness to distance as 3, 2, 1 and 0 consecutively. The results give an idea of the *structure* of cliques in the group as shown in Figure 8. There are four clusters or cliques: (i) (1,2,7,10, 3,5,6,) (ii) (14,15,11,19) (iii) (9,13,12) and (iv) (17,18,20) and 4, 16 and 8 are marginals. If we take *Biraderi* of

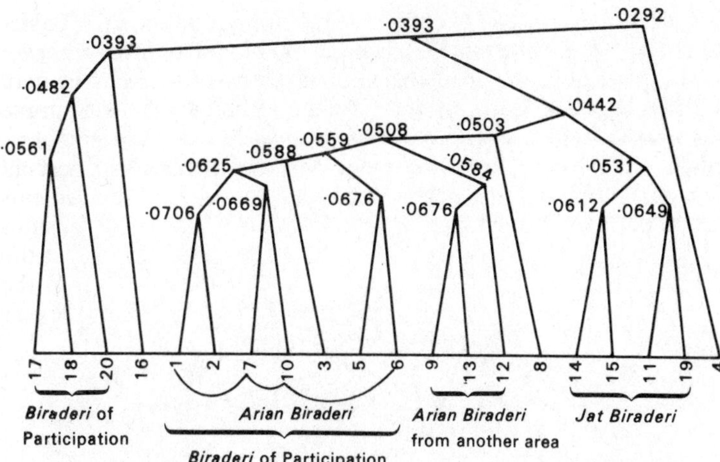

FIGURE 8 *Hierarchical clustering of perceptions of social distance between occupational categories*

origin and participation, these clusters can be explained. For instance, cluster (i) includes 1, 7, 10 and 6, who belonged to the same *Biraderi.* No. 5 is treated as *Biraderi* of participation, and 2, 3 were professionals as well as involved in the ethnic organizations, and so had developed links with others.[31] Cluster (ii) includes 14, 15, 11 and 19, all belonging to the same *Biraderi.* Although 14 and 15 came from Haroonabad and 11 and 19 from Lyallpur, they all came from the same area in East Punjab, India; and after Partition were given land in different places where they were now settled, and their families still have the *Vartan Bhanji* relationships. This *Vartan Bhanji* and other *Biraderi* obligations were prevalent in Rochdale.

Cluster (iii) includes 9, 12, 13, all belonging to the same *Biraderi.* Cluster (iv) includes 17, 18 (both *Kammi)* and 20, who were not related to each other; they all worked in public transport and had developed friendships and they usually visited each other and had established *Katchi Vartan Bhanji.* This shows that those who did not have their *Biraderi* members in Rochdale started in the new situation recruiting new members to their friendship groups to fulfil some of the needs of the *Biraderi.*

How are the marginals 4, 8, and 16 to be explained? For instance, No. 4 came from Karachi, he did not have any relatives in Rochdale, he lived in an area where there were not many Pakistanis and he was only friendly with a few people in *this particular network* like the doctors, teachers and the self-employed. This does not mean however he did not have friends outside this group of 20 people. Similarly, No. 8 came from *Gujrat* and did not have *Biraderi* members in this group. No. 16 also did not have many *Biraderi* members in Rochdale and none in this group. Although he came from Haroonabad together with other Pakistanis, he moved to Rochdale only in 1971 from Newcastle-upon-Tyne and although he had his own small *Biraderi* in Rochdale, he had not yet developed close links with many Pakistanis.[32]

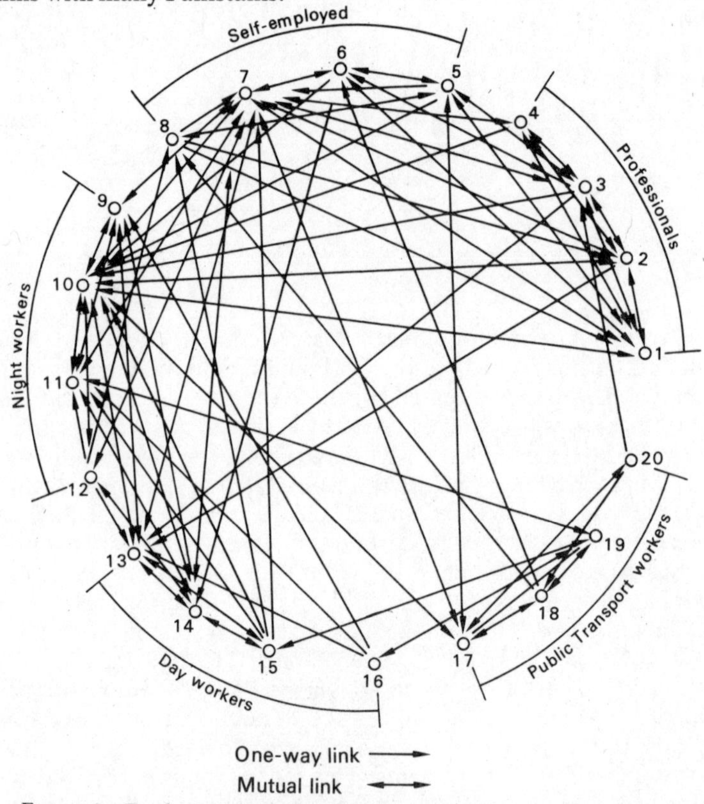

FIGURE 9 *Total network of the collectivity*

Figure 9 shows the total network of the collectivity, the links and the direction of the relationships in the network. Looking at it, we perceive clearly that the concentration of mutual links is on class and *Biraderi* lines. Some working-class people claim their close relationship with the people in the professional and self-employed category but this is not reciprocated. For instance, No. 15 claims his closest relationships with No. 7 and No. 8 which are not reciprocated, and No. 16 claims the closest relationships with Nos. 9, 11 and 13, which are not reciprocated. As No. 16 was newly arrived in Rochdale it is understandable that he was not regarded by Nos. 9, 11 and 13 in the same way. No. 13 who was involved with the Pakistan Welfare Association was regarded by Nos. 12 and 16 as being in a close relationship with them which he did not reciprocate. The same was true of the two doctors and the school teacher. Those who look for help to others, who are in a position of authority, treat these relationships as close but the authority figures do not reciprocate. Identification with those in a position of authority is a characteristic of Pakistani society.

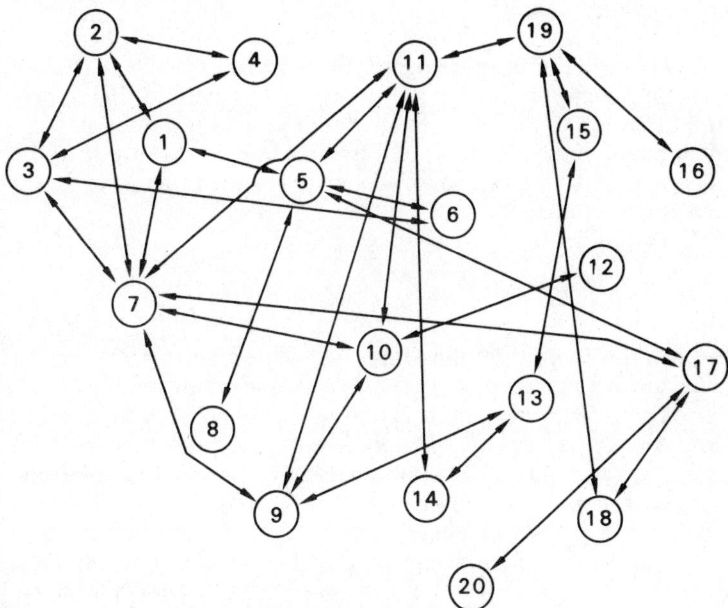

FIGURE 10 *Mutual connections in the collectivity*

It must be mentioned that the contents of the links or clusters in a social network are not automatically apparent but exist in the understanding that the actors have of their relationships among themselves. Let us see how many mutual connections these twenty people have. The analysis is based on Bernard and Killworth's *catij* technique[33]. (It is a technique to construct a sociogram by asking a respondent's choice of persons from a defined graph. It represents the number of steps i takes to get to j by the shortest possible path:

see Figure 10). One thing which appears from these data is that in most cases the mutual connections are on class and *Biraderi* lines. Figure 10 helps to show the direction of the flow of interaction. The Pakistani networks are in terms of kinship and friendships which Bott describes as areas of informal relationships. She contrasts them with the more specialized and formal relationships which are maintained with doctors, clinics, schools, and so on.[34] Therefore, we can hypothesize that the intensity of a Pakistani's relationship with his kin–*Biraderi* is likely to be greater than that of a relationship with other Pakistanis.

Morphological Criteria

In this section the morphological characteristics of the Pakistani networks which refer to the patterning of relationships in the network in respect of one another are outlined. The characteristics are 'anchorage', 'density', 'reachability' and 'range', but we shall be concerned only with measures which are relevant to the particular context of this analysis.

(1) *Distance or Reachability*

Reachability merely implies that every specified person can be contacted in a stated number of steps by any given starting person. If a large proportion of people can be contacted in a relatively small number of steps then the network is compact in comparison with one in which a smaller proportion may be reached in the same number of steps.

Mitchell writes, 'The degree to which a person's behaviour is influenced by his relationships with others turns on the extent to which he can use these relationships to contact people who are important to him or alternatively, the extent to which people who are important to him can contact him through these relationships.'[35] Table 23 on page 78 shows the minimum number of steps 'i' can take to reach 'j' using only the closest links, i.e. cell value 3.[36] The maximum finite distance in the group studied is 4 steps—the largest number of steps within which everyone can be reached. For instance, No. 16 emerges as relatively distant from the first six people which confirms what we saw above when looking at the 'clusters'. On the other hand, No. 7 is very close to the collectivity.

Looking at the compactness, i.e. a measure which reflects the extent to which people or the networks can contact one another, we find that for the Pakistanis, Index of Compactness is *0·9526*. This is a high degree of compactness as the Index of Complete Compactness would be 1.

The sociological significance of the notion of reachability lies in the way in which the links in a person's networks may be used to transmit information, to reinforce social norms of the society of origin and to mobilize support. It also provides us with a measure of the extent to which the network is close-knit or loose-knit. As Bott says, 'When many of the people a person knows interact with one another, that is when the person's network is close-knit, the members of his network tend to reach consensus of norms and they exert consistent informal pressure on one another to conform to the norms, to keep in touch with one another, and, if need be to help each other.' The case of a Pakistani mentioned below (p. 87) demonstrates this aspect. Bott goes on to say, 'When most of the people a person knows do not interact with one another, that is when his network is loose-knit, more variation on norms is likely to develop in the network and social control and mutual assistance will be more fragmented and less consistent.'[37] The close-knit network or high compactness in a group also incapsulates people from others.

A Pakistani could be in the company of other Pakistanis in different situations due to his *Biraderi* or friendship relations, in his neighbourhood, religious services and even at work. Therefore, it is by not establishing relationships in the wider society that Pakistanis retain a basis for close-knit networks, and by keeping the networks close-knit that they inhibit participation in the wider community.

(2) *Density*

Barnes uses density in the sense in which completeness is used in graph theory, i.e. the extent to which links which could possibly exist among persons do in fact exist. The links in the total network are dyadic relationships between persons, and one way of isolating a position or social locality in the network for closer study is to take a person and to look at the network from his point of view.[38] We considered the 'star' size of a person to the order of 1, 2, 3 and so on.

The 'primary' or first-order 'star' as Barnes refers to it denotes the number of people 'i' has direct contact with, i.e. the number of people put in the first category (first-step links); Table 24 gives the star sizes of all the people in the networks. It also presents the

Table 24

The morphological characteristics of twenty persons using order 1

Person's no.	*Star size*	*Zone density*	*Span*	*Median step*	*Index of centrality*
1	7	76·79	35·54	1·36	0·3919
2	7	67·86	31·40	1·31	0·4097
3	8	68·06	40·50	1·21	0·4286
4	5	93·33	23·14	1·50	0·3590
5	7	64·29	29·75	1·28	0·4266
6	6	73·81	25·62	1·39	0·3919
7	12	48·72	62·81	0·79	0·6296
8	4	75·00	12·40	1·55	0·3438
9	5	86·67	21·49	1·45	0·3919
10	9	56·67	42·15	1·06	0·5417
11	5	70·00	17·36	1·41	0·4097
12	6	66·67	23·14	1·34	0·4286
13	5	83·33	20·66	1·45	0·3919
14	7	76·79	35·54	1·35	0·4286
15	7	55·36	25·62	1·23	0·4922
16	4	55·00	9·09	1·79	0·3155
17	5	50·00	12·40	1·37	0·4286
18	4	35·00	5·79	1·50	0·3750
19	5	43·33	10·74	1·50	0·3750
20	3	50·00	4·96	1·65	0·3293

Note: When we use network as an analytical tool to explain sociological material we are interested in each person's contacts with others in the net. It is here that the notion of density or completeness appears. Following Barnes the next level of complexity would therefore be the set of all relationships between the persons in the 'primary' or 'first-order zone' of social relations.

structural characteristics of all people in the network, i.e. their relationships to each other as seen by them. To clarify further, I will illustrate by giving two examples, one of maximum contact and one of minimum contact (see Figure 11). Taking Figures 12 and 13 as examples I draw the primary or first-order zones of Nos. 7 and 20. (These are calculated taking the number of links a person has with others and the total number of possible links in that net.) Similarly, we can calculate and present the second-order zones and so on. These zones and stars are egocentric and not sociocentric constructs in the 'total networks'. The same procedure could be applied to 'partial networks', and it is here that these analytical tools are likely to be of more use. For example, in studying a *Biraderi* network of Pakistanis it would be useful to look at the first- or second-order zones of the partial network of these relationships and detect the potential deviants from the norms.

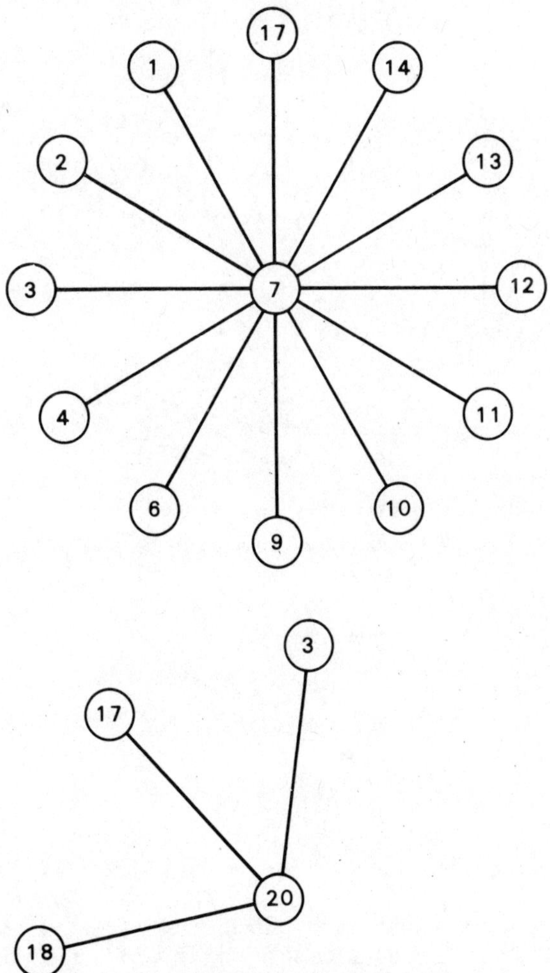

FIGURE 11 (a) *Primary Star Size of No. 7 (Star Size = 12)*
(b) *Primary Star Size of No. 20 (Star Size = 3)*

The overall density of the group is 31·84 per cent which is generally high.[39] But it is even higher when we look at individual network zone density (see Table 24). The 'span' i.e. the proportion of links captured by 'i' in his first-order zone could be shown. As in Table 24, No.7, a shopkeeper, comes out as the most centrally placed, whereas 20 is very weakly placed. This means that in terms

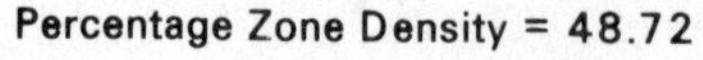

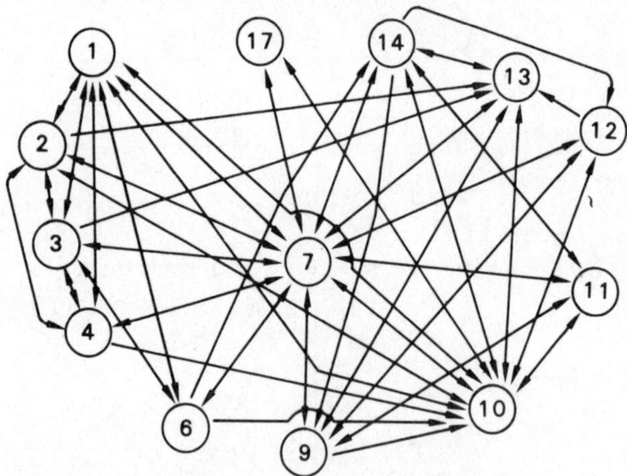

FIGURE 12 *Primary or First-Order Zone of No. 7*

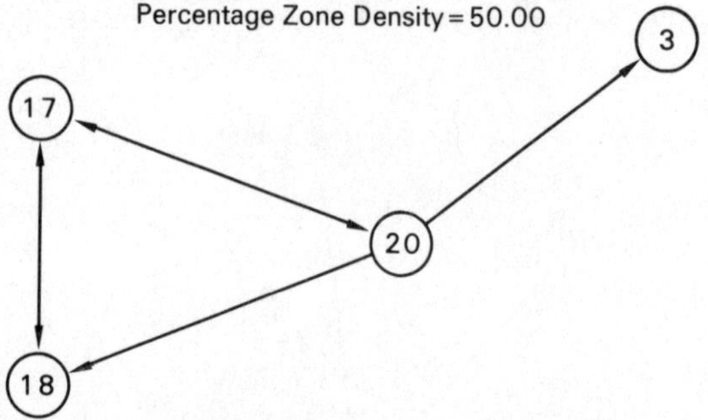

FIGURE 13 *Primary or First-Order Zone of No. 20*

of the flow of information or mobilization of support in this Pakistani group, No. 7 is in a better position. This, in fact, confirms the observations made on the basis of the ethnographic data. 'Median steps' in Table 24 refers to the number of theoretical steps each person must take to reach half the people in the network. This helps the mobilization of support in different situations, the flow of services, the seeking of general or financial help, and *Vartan Bhanji* in the network. We see from Table 24 that No. 7 emerges as being best placed and next comes his brother No. 10. Worst placed is No. 16 who is a new arrival in Rochdale and does not have any of his *Biraderi* in the network. Those who are better placed have an advantage in terms of manipulation of network over others.

We have seen that Pakistanis recruit other Pakistanis to networks on the basis of different relationships, and the types of relationships they use for recruitment to networks vary with their social situation or social position. For instance, it could be on the basis of *Biraderi* of origin or *Biraderi* of participation; or *Pakki Vartan Bhanji* or *Kachi Vartan Bhanji*. We saw that Nos. 1, 2, 3 and 4 (professionals) in many cases had relationships among themselves or with the self-employed (5, 6, 7). No. 1 had close relationships with No. 10 who was his *Biraderi*, and was also the brother of No. 7. Similarly, outside this group Nos. 2 and 3 had close relationships with No. 13 because they were both involved in ethnic organizations and so was No. 13, and so on. It is clear that to understand complex social relationships such as these, where the model of a functionally integrated social system has proved inadequate, analysis of the structure of social networks has proved most useful.

Such relationships help to explain the sponsorship and patronage existing in Pakistani community, which in practice recruit members to the networks and reinforce the kinship—friendship ties making the network close-knit and multiplex. This in turn helps in the settlement process of the Pakistanis and in keeping their activities within the ethnic boundaries, thus incapsulating them from the wider society.

British–Pakistani Context

In this section the ties which Pakistanis maintain with their kin group in Pakistan are considered. These ties can broadly be grouped as: (a) obligations which the migrants should fulfil towards their relatives in Pakistan, and (b) migrants' economic ties with Pakistan through property they own, which is mainly looked after by their relatives in Pakistan.

When a Pakistani comes to Britain he comes usually with the help, either of a financial kind or as a contact, of kin. In most cases his ties with kin in Pakistan remain active and obligations on both sides are met. In a few cases where this does not happen, relatives in Britain and in Pakistan condemn the kinsmen involved. When Mr L. A. started living with an English girl, his relatives openly criticized him and tried to make him feel ashamed and reform his behaviour. He was constantly reminded of the expectations of his family, children and other relatives at home. After a lot of pressure on Mr L. A. kinsmen ultimately threatened to ostracize him. But Mr L. A., instead of leaving the English girl, moved to another area to avoid their criticism. When I went to see his family in Pakistan they told me that they were very upset about his behaviour. They asked their relatives in Rochdale and other parts of Britain to persuade Mr L. A. to conform because his action had lowered the *Izzet*, prestige, of their kinsmen in Britain, as well as in Pakistan. They even requested me to help to persuade Mr L. A. to conform and they promised that they would forgive him for his wrong-doing.

The obligations of kinship in Pakistan extend beyond the man's wife and children, to include his parents, in some cases grandparents, siblings and even cousins, uncles and aunts (see Figure 14). The migrant is expected to earn, save and send money back to Pakistan to support his family and to invest. The majority of Pakistanis in this study supported their joint–extended families back home and had also invested in Pakistan—bought or built houses, purchased land and in some cases, started small businesses, usually power-looms or towel-making industries.

In most cases, the obligations were met in different ways and at different levels. A typical case was that of Mr H. A. who told me that he supported his whole family, i.e. joint family, in Pakistan which included more than twenty-five members. He also sent money to his sisters who were married and lived in other villages on occasions such as *Eid* or the birth of a child. He was very proud that by his hard work in this country he had purchased 50 acres of land and bought two houses in the nearby town. Another big house was built in the village. He thought that God had given him this responsibility to raise his family's economic status. He remembered when his father had to borrow money from his in-laws in 1961 to arrange his passage. He returned this money in the first year. He worked hard to earn more and save more so that he could go back to Pakistan quickly. His children and other children in the family were getting a good education and they had one house in the nearby town for their accommodation. He thought it was all due to his family's prayers for his success which was their success in turn. Pakistanis in Rochdale in almost all cases had chosen to invest savings in Pakistan. Relatives invested for them and looked after the property. This resulted in several types of ties back home. The feeling that Pakistan was the homeland persisted, and kinship networks continued to be active because the migrant planned to return home permanently. Pakistanis were reminded of this by the exchange of frequent letters and they were also expected to go to Pakistan whenever possible. It was found during the field-work that some Pakistanis had been to Pakistan three times or more since they first came to Britain in the early 1960s. Table 25 gives the frequency distribution of their visits. It is

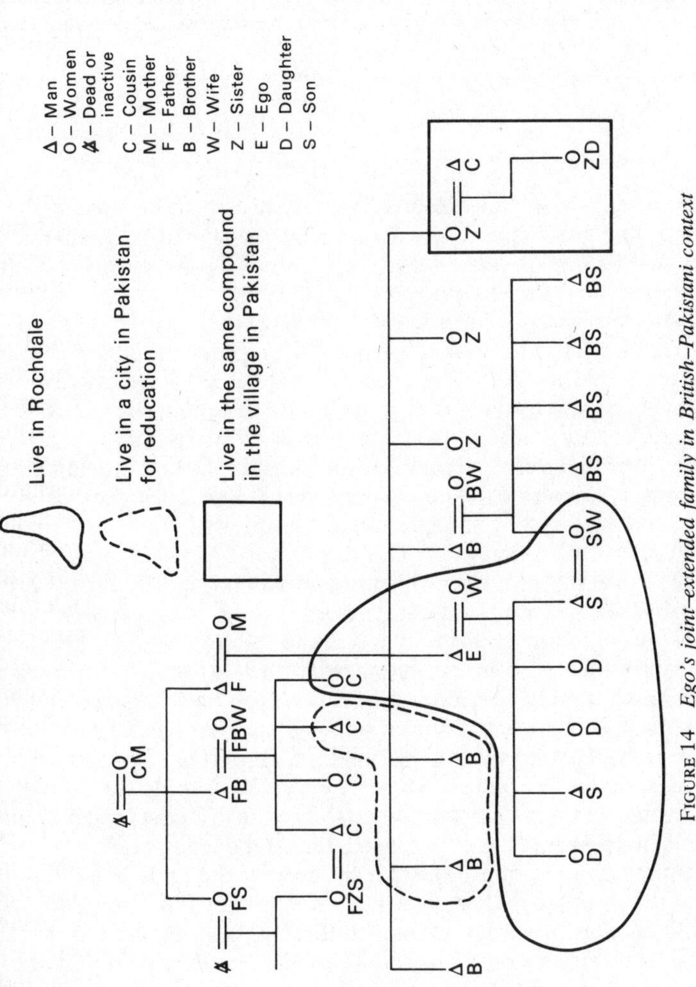

FIGURE 14 *Ego's joint–extended family in British–Pakistani context*

Table 25

Visits to Pakistan since arrival in Britain

N–103

Visits	*Number*
Once	39
Twice	30
Three times or more	16
None	18
Total:	103

worth noting here that despite their relatively short stay in this country and the expense involved in the journey, the number of visits to Pakistan is significantly high, which confirms the wish to maintain contacts back home.[40]

Those who had not been to Pakistan since their arrival tended to be recent arrivals either on work permits or as dependants.

Typical reasons for visits were the marriage of a relative, the death of a close relative, to bring the family and children over, to get married, to buy some property or for consultations and to keep in touch with the family and *Biraderi* in Pakistan. The maintenance of this contact was also expected by the kin at home. During my visit to Pakistan I was told by some relatives that they wanted their kin in Rochdale to visit them soon. This desire was expressed more often for the wife and children who were in Rochdale. Children were taken back to Pakistan for visits, to keep in touch with relatives back home because Pakistanis thought that the children would otherwise face difficulties in communicating with their kinsmen. Urdu and Punjabi was taught to children for this reason (see Chapter 9). Mr A. K. took his wife and children to Pakistan every three years for a few months. He told me that his children felt part of the joint family in Pakistan as they were always reminded by him that eventually they would settle in Pakistan. When they were in Pakistan they went to Pakistani schools and practised their language, which was an advantage. Some other Pakistani children of the same age did not know much about Pakistan. Mr A. K. thought Pakistani parents should take more interest in their children if they wanted to go back to Pakistan, otherwise these children would be misfits in that society. The longer Pakistanis stay in Britain, it appears, the more problems will arise in relation to their children settling when they return to Pakistan. Whether these people will go back or not is to be seen, but the typical attitudes mentioned above influence their behaviour in terms of contacts and settlement in this country.

Helping kinsmen is commonly found in other ethnic communities. One pattern among Jews seems to be for the successful individual to help not just his own children but nephews and sometimes nieces in their attempts to get on in society.[41] This was true of Pakistanis in Rochdale. They helped each other in this country and back home to raise the socio-economic status of their kinsmen. Social contacts were generally within kinship groups. This was particularly the case for Pakistani women, in particular those who were expected to observe *Purdah*, veiling, and did not go out to work. Their closest friends were usually their relatives—this pattern prevailed in Pakistan as well as in Rochdale. More than 80 per cent of the people studied had kin in Rochdale, except two (one had some relatives on his wife's side); all had kin elsewhere in Britain. The preferred endogamous marriage system strengthens kin ties. In the survey, out of 86 people married, 64 had endogamous marriages, many kin were therefore equally related to both the husband and wife.

There was a tendency for all major social ties to remain within a cluster of kinship networks. Only when there is no kin at hand do Pakistanis try to create comparable links with non-kin, and these were generally found to be in terms of *Katchi Vartan Bhanji*. The reason for this was that kin were the people to be trusted, as incomplete knowledge of the backgrounds and behaviour of potential friends necessitated caution, and because usually a Pakistani did not want to associate himself with 'bad' people who might dishonour the *Izzet*, prestige, of the kin group in Britain and in Pakistan. Therefore, it was only kin that one could trust, as the background of the people involved was known by the members. Once the trust was established it usually led to relations between the families of those involved in Pakistan as well. Similarly, we found that the criterion for forming one's kinship networks in Rochdale was established in Pakistan, thus making the kinship networks functional in the British–Pakistani context, so much so that the conflict between *Biraderi* factions and interpersonal conflict seemed to operate in this context.

Interpersonal and *Biraderi* Conflict

Due to the nature of *Biraderi* system and its obligatory functions the factions and conflict between individuals or *Biraderis* in Pakistan are reflected in the British situation and vice versa. There is a saying in Pakistan that there is always one of three causes of a dispute or conflict of an interpersonal nature or between *Biraderis*: *Zan*, *Zar* and *Zameen*, meaning women, money and property (mainly land) respectively. This is further illustrated by mentioning a few examples from the data.

Mr S. A. lived in Rochdale without his wife and children, but had some other relatives there. Mr Z. K., another Pakistani in Rochdale was from another *Biraderi* but from the same village. Mr S. A.'s father bought some land from Mr Z. K.'s uncle in 1964, after Mr S. A. remitted his savings back home. Up to 1972 Mr S. A.'s family was cultivating the land. At one harvest in 1972, Mr Z. K.'s relatives occupied the land by force. Mr S. A.'s father, being old, could not do anything as the rest of his family members were mainly women. He informed the village headman and the police but nothing happened. It was also reported that Mr Z. K.'s relatives insulted Mr S. A.'s family women, when they went out to get fodder for the buffaloes from their own land. When Mr S. A. learnt about this he contacted his *Biraderi* men in Rochdale who were furious after hearing about this unlawful and shameful act.

On one evening they (five of them) stopped Mr Z. K. in the street and asked him about what they had heard about the occupation of land by force and the insulting of their women. Mr Z. K. said that he did not know anything but Mr S. A. and his *Biraderi* men attacked him with hockey sticks. Within a few minutes Mr Z. K.'s *Biraderi* men who lived in the same house came out to help. There was a fierce fight and four men were slightly hurt. The issue did not stop here and led to another fight to take revenge after six months. Later the parties were brought together by the Welfare Association representatives.

Mr S. A. went home after some time to sort out the dispute about the land. I was told that when the news of fighting in Britain reached home there was a serious crisis in the village. Mr S. A.'s presence revived it and although the matter did not go to the court a lot of police activity was involved. In the end he came back, having spent a lot of money on police and other bureaucratic channels but he eventually got the land back. He said 'It was not money which I cared about, it is my and my *Biraderi's* prestige which was at stake and to save that I could do anything.' This case and attitude explains that Pakistan and Britain are treated as one for *Biraderi* activities, positive or negative.

Another situation which led to conflict between two *Biraderi* groups was created by the issue of a divorce. Mr B. A. left his wife in Pakistan and started making arrangements for marriage to a woman from another *Biraderi*. He sent the divorce papers to Pakistan through a solicitor. When his wife and parents-in-law came to know they contacted Mr B. A.'s parents in Pakistan who claimed they did not know anything. Mr B.A.'s parents wrote to him and their other *Biraderi* elders in Britain to put him right. The relatives of the would-be parents-in-law objected to Mr B. A.'s relatives' move. This in turn resulted in a conflict between two *Biraderis*, one trying to stop the divorce and the other encouraging it in their own interest. The matter was taken to the Pakistan Welfare Association. The Association could not stop the divorce but helped to reduce the tension with the plea that Pakistanis should not fight here as it gives the community a bad image in the wider society. One of the leaders attached to the Association said, 'This type of conflict has its roots in the villages back home. It is bad that we revive it here, where we need unity.' There was a lot of strife on this issue in Pakistan as well between Mr B. A.'s parents, parents-in-law and would be parents-in-law, so much so that his wife's parents and *Biraderi* threatened that if he (Mr B. A.) came to Pakistan to marry another girl they would make sure he was killed before he got married, for rejecting their daughter, who was innocent. This threat stopped Mr B. A.'s visit to Pakistan and he was hoping to get married by telephone and then to send for his wife. I was told by one of his relatives that he was facing some difficulties in getting a divorce because of the non-co-operation of his parents-in-law. This had made things worse and added to the tension between the *Biraderis* in Rochdale, though the persons directly involved in this issue were not very many. This example is related to the structural conditions of the Pakistani society which give rise to different forms of conflict.

The other type of conflict is the conflict between individual Pakistanis. This cannot be seen in isolation, as sometimes individual conflict leads to *Biraderi* conflict and so on. However, it would be relevant to mention the causes and processes of the conflict and its effects on the conflicting individuals. The basic causes seem to be again *Zan*, *Zar*, and *Zameen*, and a few examples are mentioned to illustrate the point, and the types of conflict which arose.

Mr F. A., a barber, and Mr S. K., a draper and part-time carpenter, started as partners in a shop selling fancy goods, etc. The building belonged to the barber and Mr S. K. carried out some alterations. Both contributed some cash and signed a contract for three years with a clause that if one broke the contract then he would pay £X to the other. Within a few weeks of the opening of the shop Mr F. A. accused Mr S. K. of fiddling the money. An argument developed and led to an open fight. The whole families of both men became involved in the fight and the police were called in. As a result the shop was locked and the keys were left with the solicitor. The matter went to the Pakistan Welfare Association and was also brought to the Community Relations Council. Mr F. A. also accused Mr S. K. of not telling him about the contents of the contract at the time. He thought (according to him) that these were papers to sign in order to open the shop. As he could not read, so he said, he was deceived. Well-wishers tried to solve the problem but did not succeed completely. The case went to court and Mr F. A. won the case although Mr S. K. was paid some compensation.

This again shows that one-time friendship could lead to enmity and conflict between individuals after suspicions developed about the dishonesty of one party. This means that the hostile relationships are seen to arise from certain interactions between individuals.[42]

Another type of individual conflict usually occurs over English (local) girls. This was more common with the single men in our study. One such incident explains the point. Mr K. B. and Mr P. N. lived in the same lodging-house. Mr K. B. had an English girl friend for a few months. They quarrelled and she left him. Slowly she developed a friendship with Mr P. N. who was known to her beforehand. When Mr K. B. came to know this, he warned Mr P. N. that if he did not stop, it could lead to serious consequences. He (K. B.) still thought that she was his girl-friend and would come back to him one day, although his efforts for a reconciliation failed. Mr P. N. decided to leave the house to avoid conflict with Mr K. B. as he wanted to continue the relationship with the girl. He started living in another house outside the central area. I was told that the English girl arranged his accommodation in an Irish lodging-house. Mr P. N. also left the night job where he worked with Mr K. B. and joined another mill at the day shift.

Mr K. B. was furious particularly when other fellow Pakistanis told him tauntingly that his 'darling' was living with Mr P. N. Mr K. B. took this as dishonesty and an offence against the friendship norms. One day he went with another Pakistani to the pub where this girl used to go and had a fight outside the pub with Mr P. N. I was told that the girl was involved in the fight too and she was the one who hit him hard with her shoes. Some other Irishmen became involved and hit Mr K. B. and his supporter, and the fight resulted in some injuries. Afterwards the girl, who accused Mr K. B. of raping and beating her while she was still with him, continued to live with Mr P. N.

This kind of conflict of course is common to many if not all groups but here there was an additional aspect which turned a conflict at an individual level into a wider one. After this case Mr K. B. wrote, acting in revenge, to Mr P. N.'s wife and parents telling them that Mr P. N. had married an English girl. This resulted in some angry exchanges back home between Mr P. N.'s family and his in-laws, who were from the same *Biraderi.* His parents and in-laws wrote to Mr P. N. and to relatives in Rochdale and Bury asking them to find out the truth. The relatives approached Mr P. N. and persuaded him not to behave like this and think about his wife, children, and family prestige. Mr P. N. conformed by moving to Bury with one of the relatives to ease the situation. He stayed a few months and then moved back to another house in the town, where, it was said, he continued his relationship with the girl.

These examples illustrate that the Pakistani proverb that *Zan*, *Zar*, and *Zameen* are the causes of hostility and conflict among Pakistanis seems equally to apply in the British situation.

It is also clear from the cases mentioned above that migration does not neccessarily detach the migrant from kin ties and obligations to them in Pakistan. Therefore, to understand the relationships and behaviour of Pakistanis in Britain it is important that the Pakistani end is brought into focus. Pakistanis in our study were preoccupied with their future plans, investments, status and children's future in Pakistan and not in Britain (see pp. 186–211). The obligations which migrants were supposed to fulfil and the regular contacts they kept with relatives in Pakistan through letters, messages and visits were a reminder of what their relatives expected of them. There was no discontinuity of relationships with Pakistanis beyond Rochdale. Consequently the myth of going back to Pakistan helped Pakistanis to maintain ethnic boundaries.

6. Economic Activity and the Role of Social Networks: Workers

Introduction

Most Pakistanis in Britain are economic immigrants. Economic activity affects not only life-styles but also social relations with family members, *Biraderi*, friends, neighbours and the wider community. It is shown in this and the next chapter how the Pakistanis in Rochdale are participating in economic activity and how in particular ethnic workforces and night-shift work help in their 'incapsulation'. In addition, the roles of village and kin *Biraderi* in finding jobs and in relationships at work are discussed. Some case studies of the firms where Pakistanis work help to explain these points. The particular questions which are dealt with are, how did the ethnic work groups emerge and what are their consequences in terms of social relationships? Wherever relevant some of the aspects of the work situations of Pakistanis have been compared with a study carried out in Bradford in 1966-9.[1]

Apart from observation and case studies a survey of employment was carried out in the Central Ward area of Rochdale to complement the material collected and to make comparisons with the Bradford stúdy. A separate interviewing schedule was used for the self-employed Pakistanis who were included in the survey. The primary group relations, as outlined in the previous chapter, continue to play an important part in sustaining the individual Pakistani, particularly during the initial stages following migration to British urban conditions. As a consequence ethnic communities or, as some people call them, 'Urban Villages' may be created slowly, with a degree of institutional completeness, in which the migrant continues to use his mother tongue, and to associate with fellow countrymen.[2]

The migrant may alternate between participation in the industrial sector of the society, where he is exposed to other nationalities, values, attitudes and expectations, and his own ethnic community in the urban setting. The next chapter about the self-employed Pakistani covers this point in greater detail. But first we look at the industrial scene in relation to Pakistanis.

External Constraints of the Labour Market

The position of immigrants on the labour market is the most important aspect of their position in the society. The type of work available to immigrants does not merely govern their incomes, it also helps to determine in what areas the immigrants settle, how they interact with the indigenous labour force and population, and their social status.[3] If immigrants are granted access only to a limited range of occupations upon arrival, there will be concentrations in certain factories and consequently in certain towns and regions.

The most recent comprehensive figures on economic activity of men and women of Pakistani origin are found in the 1971 Census. The results show that in 1971 there were 82,860 Pakistanis (76,930 males and 5,930 females) who were economically active (i.e. were already in or seeking employment). Their economic activity rate was 72·1 per cent.[4] The majority of Pakistanis who were economically active were employed in manufacturing industries. Table 26 shows that over 19 per cent of Pakistanis were in textiles, compared to 2·5 per cent for all economically active persons. The next group, about 16 per cent, worked in metal manufacture and metal goods industry. Pakistani males were more likely to be employed as labourers in textiles, engineering and allied trades than males from other groups and less likely to be working in administration, management and sales. They were found (with other ethnic minority workers) for the most part in occupations where earnings were low.[5] To earn more or to be at par with workers from other industries immigrants are forced to do overtime and night-shift work to earn premiums.[6]

The classification of Pakistani workers by socio-economic groups shown in Table 28 takes account not only of the occupations performed but also the employment status of the people concerned. Pakistanis were more likely to be employed in manual and, in particular, semi-skilled and unskilled jobs; 78·84 per cent were in manual categories and only 15·77 in non-manual. These were mostly in manufacturing industries and, in particular, in textiles.

One interesting sidelight on the position of Pakistani workers in the textile industry is given in a report by the Textile Council. A sample survey in the cotton industry showed that 15 per cent of

Table 26

Industrial distribution of economically active Pakistanis

Industry Order	Pakistanis				All employed persons,
	Males		*Females*		
	No.	*%*	*No.*	*%*	*UK-%*
1. Agriculture, forestry, fishing	60	0·08	—	—	2·7
2. Mining and quarrying	90	0·12	—	—	1·6
3. Food, drink and tobacco	3200	4·43	150	2·99	3·1
4. Coal and petroleum products	90	0·12	—	—	0·2
5. Chemical and allied industries	1010	1·40	50	0·99	1·9
6. Metal manufacture	6960	9·65	20	0·39	2·3
7. Mechanical engineering	3540	4·91	60	1·95	4·7
8. Instrument engineering	430	0·59	50	0·99	0·6
9. Electrical engineering	3580	4·96	320	6·37	3·6
10. Shipbuilding/marine engineering	240	0·33	—	—	·6
11. Vehicles	4280	5·93	80	1·59	3·3
12. Metal goods	5020	6·96	80	1·59	2·5
13. Textiles	13600	18·86	200	3·98	2·5
14. Leather, leather goods, fur	430	0·59	20	0·39	0·2
15. Clothing and footwear	2460	3·41	350	6·97	2·0
16. Bricks, cement, pottery, glass	1740	2·41	10	0·19	1·3
17. Timber furniture, etc.	980	1·35	10	0·19	1·3
18. Paper, printing, publishing	900	1·24	80	1·59	2·6
19. Other manufacturing industries	3330	4·61	100	1·99	1·4
20. Construction	630	0·87	20	0·39	7·0
21. Gas, electricity and water	120	0·13	20	0·39	1·5
22. Transport and communications	4830	6·69	190	3·78	6·6
23. Distributive trades	3730	5·17	520	10·35	12·7
24. Insurance, banking, finance, etc.	740	1·03	300	5·97	4·0
25. Professional, scientific services	2990	4·14	1420	28·29	12·2
26. Miscellaneous services	472	0·65	580	11·55	9·9
27. Public administration and defence	1170	1·62	250	4·98	6·6
28. Industry inadequately desribed	1190	1·65	140	2·79	0·7
29. Place of work outside UK	40	0·05	—	—	*
All industries and services	72100	100	5020	100	100

* = less than 0·05 per cent

Source: *1971 Census of population.* Data (10 per cent sample) were provided by Mr B. M. Deakin, Department of Applied Economics, University of Cambridge. I am grateful to him. (See Special Tabulations, DT 1240.)

Table 27

Occupational distribution of Pakistanis

Occupation Order	*Pakistanis* *Males* *No.*	*%*	*Females* *No.*	*%*	*Total*	*%*	*All employed persons, UK-%*
1. Farmers, foresters, fishermen	80	0·10	—	—	80	0·09	3·0
2. Miners and quarrymen	60	0·06	—	—	60	0·07	1·0
3. Gas, coke, chemical makers	550	0·71	—	—	550	0·66	0·6
4. Glass, etc. makers	630	0·81	—	—	630	0·76	0·4
5. Furnace, forge, foundry, etc.	1740	2·26	10	0·16	1750	2·11	0·7
6. Electrical workers	850	1·10	120	2·02	970	1·17	2·5
7. Engineering workers	11480	14·92	230	3·88	11710	14·13	11·2
8. Woodworkers	750	0·97	—	—	750	0·90	1·7
9. Leather workers	240	0·31	30	0·50	270	0·33	0·5
10. Textile workers	9670	12·57	180	3·03	9850	11·89	1·2
11. Clothing workers	1920	2·49	440	7·42	2360	2·85	1·6
12. Food, drink, tobacco workers	1880	2·44	90	1·52	1970	2·38	1·5
13. Paper, printing workers	530	0·69	10	0·16	540	0·65	1·3
14. Makers of steel products	3340	4·34	110	1·85	3450	4·16	1·3
15. Construction workers	150	0·19	—	—	150	0·18	2·2
16. Painters/decorators	510	0·66	—	—	510	0·61	1·2
17. Drivers of cranes etc.	1440	1·87	10	0·16	1450	1·75	1·2
18. Labourers N.E.C.	16730	21·75	90	1·52	1680	20·30	5·0
19. Transport, communication	4070	5·29	70	1·18	4140	4·99	5·7
20. Warehousemen	1900	2·47	150	2·52	2050	2·47	3·2
21. Clerical workers	1990	2·59	1300	21·92	3290	3·97	14·2
22. Sales workers	2920	3·79	330	5·56	3250	3·92	9·0
23. Services, sport, etc.	5080	6·60	480	8·09	5560	6·71	11·8
24. Administrators, managers	860	1·12	90	1·52	950	1·14	3·7
25. Professional, technical	3970	5·16	1320	22·25	5290	6·38	11·0
26. Armed forces	350	0·45	—	—	350	0·42	1·0
27. Inadequately described	3240	4·21	870	14·67	4110	4·96	2·6
All occupations	76930	100	5930	100	82860	100	100

Source: *1971 Census of Population*, Special Tabulations 1239, data provided by Mr B. M. Deakin.
Note: Figures and percentages in tables have been rounded and therefore totals do not necessarily add up to 100 per cent.

Table 28

Socio-economic distribution of economically active Pakistani males and females

Specified socio-economic groups	*Males*		*Females*		*Total*	
	No.	*%*	*No.*	*%*	*No.*	*%*
1. Professional	2,640	3·43	330	5·56	2,970	3·58
2. Employers, managers	3,170	4·12	210	3·54	3,380	4·07
3. Non-manual	4,180	5·43	2,540	42·83	6,720	8·74
4. Skilled manual, foremen	18,400	23·91	540	9·10	18,940	22·85
5. Semi-skilled manual	27,380	35·59	1,310	22·09	28,690	34·62
6. Unskilled manual	17,570	22·83	130	2·19	17,700	21·36
7. Armed forces and inadequately described	3,590	4·67	870	14·67	4,460	5·38
Total	76,930	100	5,930	100	82,860	100
Non-manual	9,990	13·00	3,080	51·93	13,070	15·77
Manual	63,350	82·34	1,980	33·38	65,330	78·84

Source: *1971 Census of Population*, Special Tabulations, DT 1241.
The socio-economic groups follow the classification used in E.J.B. Rose *et al*., op. cit. (pp. 1173–5) and are derived from the census categories as follows:
1 = Registrar General S.E.G. 3, 4
2 = Registrar General S.E.G. 1,2,13
3 = Registrar General S.E.G. 5, 6
4 = Registrar General S.E.G. 8,9,12,14
5 = Registrar General S.E.G. 7,10,15
6 = Registrar General S.E.G. 11
7 = Registrar General S.E.G. 16,17
Groups 1, 2, 3 are added together to form 'non-manual'; groups 4, 5 and 6 together make up 'manual'.

spinning workers and 10 per cent of the weaving workers were immigrants in November 1967. The immigrants staffed 59 per cent of the spinning night-shifts and 36 per cent of the weaving night-shifts.[7] Clearly Pakistanis being the predominant immigrant group in textiles got the jobs rejected by the indigenous labour. The percentage on night-shift work has increased in recent years as far as Pakistani workers are concerned.[8] This results in ethnic work groups.

A recent study outlines that there were 26 per cent Pakistanis working in the textile industry as against 2 per cent for the general population. Looking at the distribution of Pakistanis and the textile industry they found that in Yorkshire and Humberside and in the North West the proportion of the Pakistani population of these regions that is in textile industry is higher still (62 per cent in Yorkshire and Humberside, 52 per cent in the North West, as against 6 per cent and 5 per cent for the general population respectively).[9] Fairly small percentages are in construction, transport and the services. All immigrant groups are under-represented in the distributive trades, which form the largest single area of employment for the total population. Those who do have qualifications may find that these are not recognized in Britain. This is more relevant to Pakistanis, Indians and Bangladeshis than the West Indians. Graduates and teachers trained in Pakistan are working on buses or in factories. One group whose qualifications were recognized in Britain were Pakistani, Indian and Bangladeshi doctors. Recently the British Government has withdrawn this recognition and doctors are now expected on their arrival to pass a language and proficiency test before they can start work.[10]

There seem to be three reasons for this disadvantage in terms of jobs. The first is that the immigrants find it more difficult to get suitable jobs because of racial discrimination.[11] The second reason seems to be that the immigrants meet with special difficulties because they did not enter the British labour market at the best age.[12] The third general explanation is that the immigrants have less relevant experience of competence in the professional or managerial field than equally qualified whites. (There are no data to prove this notion except the observations and discussions which I had with managers and those who worked in the employment field.)[13] In a situation of this kind those Pakistani graduates who worked on buses or were doing manual jobs in the textile mills gave as the reason for their disadvantage the difficulty of getting a suitable job. One of the important factors for this disadvantage is discrimination against coloured workers which is widespread. The Race Relations Act 1976 and the White Paper *Racial Discrimination*, 1975, acknowledged this fact in the British society. The PEP reports of 1975 and 1976 proved this fact beyond doubt. The main findings of these reports were as follows: most employers in Britain only take an immigrant worker when no other labour is available. Immigrants are regarded as undesirable and their employment is merely an unfortunate necessity. 'The basic approach was to employ coloured people for a job only when it was impossible to recruit and retain white people at an economic rate.' This type of attitude means that immigrants are mainly employed in jobs rejected by the British workers. 'It is fair to say that coloured immigrants were often employed in one type of job as regards low renumeration, level of skill and interest, dirtiness and heaviness, and hours of work or type of shift, and where this was true it was the most menial unattractive type of job, for which it had been impossible to attract white labour.'[14]

A situation of this type, where immigrant workers get the worst jobs and are not regarded as suitable for better jobs, also affects their promotion. Up till now we have discussed the broader background, and now Pakistanis in the industrial structure of Rochdale will be seen against this background.

The Industrial Structure of Rochdale and Pakistanis

Out of a population of 91,000 (1971) there were 49,987 'insured' people in Rochdale and out of this working population, 57 per cent were categorized in 1974 as manufacturing population. This means that about 28,000 people were involved in manufacturing industry in the area. Out of 28,000 about 15,000 worked in the textile industry and 8,000 in engineering which is in most of the cases related to the textile industry.

This means that more than 50 per cent of the manufacturing population in the area worked in the textile industry, and another 30 per cent in engineering and only 3 per cent in paper industry. The textile industry's dominance in the area attracted Pakistanis, and their willingness to work at night and other difficult shifts explains their presence in this sector.

This was confirmed by the Department of Employment, although they did not have figures on the coloured immigrants in the industry. The firms I visited provided me with figures which did not cover all firms but related to the major firms employing Pakistanis. These figures support the hypothesis that those firms which employ coloured workers usually have continuous shift system. Sheila Allen also found this in Bradford where the highest proportion, 64·6 per cent, of coloured workers were found to be directly employed in the textile industry. 66 per cent of the firms employing coloured workers operated some sort of shift system, whereas only 12 per cent of those not employing them did so.[15]

The managers I talked to told me that in the textile industry, which is declining, it is very difficult to compete if they do not run the shift system to manufacture more goods and make them economical. They have managed to maintain a supply of labour due to the availability of migrant workers, in this case Pakistanis, who willingly work on permanent night shift and other difficult shifts rejected by English workers. As one employer put it, 'If there had been no immigrants available it would have made life a little more difficult for the management.' Another employer who has more immigrants in his firm admitted, 'Let us be honest, if the Pakistanis stop working at night shift and other alternative shifts or even overtime, we will have to close the firm because it is so difficult to compete in textiles these days.' These comments demonstrate that this pattern has developed due to the availability of the migrant labour. Since the social and familial demands on them were minimal when they first arrived and the financial reward of night shifts was slightly higher, Pakistanis were prepared to undertake work on this basis as a temporary measure. But they continued doing so even after their families joined them because of economic reasons.

The economic contribution of the Pakistanis was confirmed by the North-West Industrial Development Association in one of its reports: 'Pakistani immigrants have made a "significant contribution" to the local economy in Rochdale.' The report says, 'Their willingness to work on night shift has been of major importance in enabling firms in the area to operate continuous shift work.'[16] This report confirms what the employers in the area told me during my visits to the firms and in other discussions. However, the position of Pakistanis in the local industry will not be clear without the knowledge of the jobs they do.

Types of Jobs

In a broader sense employment opportunities appeared to be a crucial factor that would greatly affect the life-chances and life-styles of Asian and West Indian people in British society. This is not to say that there is a mechanical relation between the jobs people do and their housing, educational opportunities or the degree of social acceptance. But, in a negative sense, in so far as these groups are confined to particular levels of jobs within specific sections of the industrial structure their chances of, for instance, escaping from certain residential areas or of their children gaining access to selective forms of secondary or further education will be minimized. They may then be incorporated more or less permanently into a position of multiple disadvantage.[17] Out of 354 Pakistani workers in the survey area, 51 were self-employed, 3 professionals, 2 doing other work and the rest, 298, were almost all manual workers (see p. 43). The majority of Pakistanis are not only in certain industries such as textiles, but are also found within a narrow occupational range in these industries, as discussed above. In textiles they are mainly in spinning, winding, weaving and allied departments. The Textile Council report referred to above confirms this. This report found in 1969 that 59 per cent of immigrants worked on the spinning night shift and 36 per cent on the weaving night shift. This clearly shows that an overwhelming majority of Pakistanis are to be found in the manual grades.

Out of the three professionals, two were teachers, and one worked in a Pakistani bank as a manager. This pattern of employment of Pakistanis shows that the majority are concentrated in a narrow industrial field and are at particularly low levels of occupational status.

It has been mentioned elsewhere in this book that the majority of the Pakistanis have come from rural areas or had some sort of links with the villages before coming to Britain (see pp. 44–5). Accordingly, most of the Pakistanis did not have industrial experience and very few worked in the service sector in Pakistan before coming to this country, as is clear from Table 29.

Table 29

Occupation in Pakistan

Occupation	*Number*	*%*
Peasant farming	41	39·8
Business	17	16·5
Mill worker	4	3·9
Electrician/fitter	2	1·9
Driver (GTS)*	1	1·0
Government service	5	4·9
Teacher	2	1·9
Army/Navy/Air force	6	5·8
Student	17	16·5
Unemployed or no job	8	7·8
Total	103	100·0

* GTS—Government Transport Service

The majority had worked in agriculture or small businesses such as groceries or drapery shops while others were either in professions, or in the armed forces or still in full-time education. This contrasts with some other groups of migrants. For instance, some European migrants, particularly refugees, had training and high status jobs before migration. On the other hand, Pakistanis (and Indians) resemble many Irish migrant workers who also came from agricultural areas. Their reasons for migration were predominantly economic ones, as mentioned above (pp. 25–6). But such an overall picture of the industry and of occupational structure of the Pakistani community in Rochdale would not be complete without considering the formation and consequences of ethnic work groups.

Ethnic Work Groups

The data from the three mills where I observed Pakistanis working on night (and day) shifts reveal that over 90 per cent of night-shift workers were Pakistanis, most of them from Rochdale. The white staff was usually the supervisors and the mechanics to help with break-downs. In two cases the supervisory staff included 50 per cent with an East European background (later in one mill two Pakistanis were promoted as overlookers on the night shift). The Pakistanis mainly worked in spinning, weaving, blowing and labouring jobs. There were usually one or two people on the floor who could speak English fluently and usually supervisors used them as intermediaries for communication with their Pakistani workers.

(a) The Formation

Employers justify the segregation of Pakistanis into different departments and sections by referring to language difficulties. Segregation, they claim, makes possible efficient utilization of labour. Pakistanis are kept together and communication is through one English-speaking worker; a 'go-between', a Pakistani worker speaking both languages can pass on the foreman's instructions to his fellow Pakistani workers. I noticed that employers hire new Pakistani workers through these 'go-betweens' who, therefore, gain a position of influence on both sides, i.e. with management and workers. One of the informants in a mill was valued by the management for his skill in attracting workers who had good reputation as hard workers from other mills for shift work. He usually used his *Biraderi* contacts to reach these workers and gave these potential workers some financial incentive such as bonus payments or more overtime. After a few years' service for all the mills in the group, he was promoted to an Assistant Personnel and Training Officer. He was the first 'coloured immigrant' to reach that position in the group. I often found him working odd hours and approaching Pakistanis in their homes for overtime, change of shift or any extra jobs that needed doing. He sometimes used his position to convince Pakistanis that they must not give a bad impression by making too many demands or going on strike, and so on, and because he was an educated fellow-countryman they accepted his advice.

One possible explanation for the ease with which ethnic work gangs were formed is the pattern of migration to Britain, as discussed in Chapter 2. The Pakistani emigration to Britain was organized and depended on a system of sponsorship and patronage which made it selective and confined to some kin groups in a few villages in a few areas. These factors contributed towards the reciprocal relationships between sponsors and clients as an additional insurance for the immigrant against possible hardship, during his early days in Britain. I came across one Pakistani who had sponsored more than a dozen of his relatives and friends to come to Rochdale in thirteen years. This obviously leads to a need and desire to live with kinsmen and friends and to the emergence of village—kin networks and ethnic communities in certain towns and within certain parts of the towns as outlined above.

The effect of residence is reflected in the job situation. It was found during the field-work that many relatives were working together in certain firms, on certain shifts, in certain departments. The exception was where two working people from one household, say a father and a son, tended to work on different shifts, maybe in the same firm, so that one of them could be with the family. Usually in such cases the father worked at night and the son on the morning or evening shifts. Mr W. M. explained this arrangement, 'I work at night because I am so used to it for the last fourteen years. My son is young and he can visit other relatives and help the family with official form filling, etc. and shopping particularly when he is on evening shift. Secondly, night shift affects young people's health quickly. Our arrangement works very well and I can sleep all day without any interruptions.'

It is quite common and even obligatory among Pakistanis to help each other to find a job and to work together. In firm 'A' there were as many as 35 people related to each other and another 15 came from the same villages and mostly were related in some way. This came about through one kinsman who was appointed as an overlooker with special responsibility for migrant labour and for night shift. He gradually brought his kinsmen to work there. One of them told me, 'We work together, it is a good thing because we do not feel lonely. We talk about our relatives, villages back home and other topics of common interest. We feel that we work in our own factory as there is no pressure from the management at night, although we work hard because our overlooker should not be let down. Another advantage of working together is that we can travel together in cars and save time and reduce the expense, although in our case the firm provides transportation, but it gets inconvenient sometimes to go to a pick-up point.' This is a typical case and illustrates many points relevant to the Pakistanis who work in ethnic work groups and particularly on the night shift.

More money is obviously another factor mentioned. Mr I. D. said, 'I work at night shift for several reasons such as working together, no management and white people present so no communication problem, all of us work at night so for social reasons I will be left alone and on top of all this, I get 20 per cent more money.' He added, 'If you work at day it seems very long, if you work at night, it passes quickly. We are here temporarily so to earn more money is our aim and to get back as soon as possible.'

Apart from the money incentive for working at night, firms also encourage the concentration of Pakistanis in some special departments and on certain shifts. Firm 'B' brought an advertisement to me for translation which included an incentive offer for those who will bring other Pakistanis for spinning work at night shift. The incentive was £10 cash after the recommended worker started the job. This leaflet was distributed among the Pakistani workers in the firm. I was informed that the response was good.

The other reason for this type of encouragement which was observed was that a new Pakistani will usually be trained by another fellow worker. This was applicable to most of the firms I visited during the field-work. This means that the firms did not need a training course particularly for those who worked at night, and therefore the language problem was overcome. Even the firms which had a training programme did not bother to train Pakistani workers. Out of 103 who worked in the factories, only 9 said they had been trained for their present job by attending a training programme.

The situation discussed above shows that Pakistanis used their *Biraderi* and kinship networks to obtain jobs and worked with their fellow countrymen. It illustrates the way their networks function in the work situation.

Out of 354 working Pakistanis in the survey area, 298 worked mainly in industry and public transport and 201 of these were working on either permanent night shift (146), on multi-shift (21) or on an alternate morning and evening shift (40). Only 91 people worked on the day shift and this included 23 Pakistani women. Among the 68 men on day shift the majority were young people who usually did not like working at night. One of the respondents said, 'I hate working at night or even on shifts. You cannot regulate your life and it affects your health. I have asked my dad not to work at nights but he says he can earn more and work with other relatives which is easier to pass the time. If you work at night, sleep all day, there is no social life.' This view was expressed by other young people as well.

The ethnic work groups which have developed suit in general both the management and the Pakistanis. This is not, however, the whole story. What effect this arrangement has on the social relationships and life-style of the Pakistanis is discussed later. Ethnic groups can be seen to ease communication and to aid efficient production, but they have the side effect of segregating immigrants from other workers.

(b) The Effect of Ethnic Work Groups

Ethnic work groups lead to the segregation of immigrant workers from other workers. In the area of this study there is a lot of evidence to support this assumption. Pakistanis mainly worked on the night shift, multi-shift or double-day shift (see Table 30).

Table 30

Shift work

Type of Shifts	*Tweedale Street area (N–298)*	*Wardleworth area (Pakistanis and Bangladeshis) (N–212)*
Night shift	146	125
Multi-shift	21	8
Alternative shift (includes Public Transport workers)	40	21
Day shift (includes Public Transport workers and Pakistanis working with Pakistani employers)	91	58
Total	298	212

Table 30 shows that the majority of Pakistanis were shift workers. If we look at the composition of different firms where Pakistanis worked we find the pattern was the same in all of them. Out of 1,057 Pakistani workers in six firms, 970 (91·7 per cent) were shift workers (see Table 31 for details).

Table 31

Pakistanis working on different shifts in selected firms

Firm	*Night Shift*	*Double-day Shift*	*Day Shift*	*Total*
A	72	61	36	169
B	61	87	3	151
C	101	6	14	121
D	195	22	8	225
E	57	—	3	60
F	264	44	23	331
Total	750	220	87	1,057

In firm 'A' those (36 out of 169) who worked on day shifts only were concentrated in certain departments (see below, p. 111).

In firm 'B' out of 75 workers on the night shift, there were 61 Pakistanis, 5 Bangladeshis, 4 Poles and one Italian and 5 locals. The five locals were the supervisory staff and fitters. On double-day shift there were 87 Pakistanis, 24 others and 78 locals, mainly women, working the 6 a.m.–2 p.m. shift. However, on the day shift (7.30 a.m. – 4.30 p.m.) out of 323 there were only three Pakistanis who were trainee students. Among 86 office staff and 34 supervisors there was not a single Pakistani until 1974 when a Pakistani joined the staff to deal mainly with the Pakistani workers. The Pakistani labour force in this firm was more than 25 per cent of the total, but they worked overwhelmingly on the night shift and double-day shift (which changes every week).

Firm 'C' presented the same sort of pattern; out of a total of 239 workers, more than half were Pakistanis (121). Out of these 121 there were 101 working on the night shift and only 14 on the day shift and 6 (mainly students) on the evening shift (5 p.m. to 9.30 p.m.).

Other firms given in the table which I visited during the field-work presented the same sort of pattern. Firm 'D' had a total number of 1,517 workers. Out of these 225 were Pakistanis, and 195 worked on night shift. Firm 'E' had a total labour force of 300, 60 of whom were Pakistanis, all except three on the night shift. Textile firm 'F' was one of the biggest employers in the area and had a work force of about 3,000 people. Out of these, 331 were Pakistanis, 14 West Indians/Africans/Turks and 78 other nationalities, mainly East Europeans and Bangladeshi. On the night shift, there were 264 Pakistanis, 50 Bangladeshis, 19 Poles, 14 Indians, 10 West Indians/Africans and 10 locals. The Poles and locals were mainly supervisors and fitters.

The Assistant Personnel Manager of the firm said, 'They (Pakistanis and Bangladeshis) seem very concerned with overtime earnings and if the overtime is reduced the number of Asian employees is reduced.' Justifying the ethnic work group he said that in the late 1940s and early 1950s one whole department, except supervisor, was manned by Poles and Ukrainians. The problems with these nationalities have now gone as they have moved to better jobs after improving their English. He felt that the Pakistanis' language problem would disappear with the second generation. This view was shared by the management of other firms where Pakistanis work.

The ethnic work group system lessens the pressure for the immigrant worker to learn English and therefore slows down his participation in the wider society, because, if the immigrants are both isolated from the community at large and working closely with members of their own group, they will have fewer opportunities to learn or improve their English.

Looking at the situation irrespective of the reasons the fact is that 'ethnic work groups', and particularly night-shift work are incapsulating Pakistanis from the indigenous workers. Their work pattern affects their participation in the unions as meetings are held during the day and prevents them using other facilities at work, such as canteen, etc.

Those who worked on days only were concentrated in certain departments such as waste sorting and waste handling which involved dirty work. The remaining one or two Pakistanis working in other departments were usually labourers helping the local workers. Table 32 supports this statement.

The ethnic work group system offers possibilities of exploitation of workers unfamiliar with wages and conditions and rights of workers by using 'go-betweens' or 'straw bosses' who speak English. In fact, in some firms in Rochdale, the appointment of Pakistani supervisors for the Pakistani workers did result in more work and fewer demands.

There is also pressure from the white workers to put Pakistani (and other coloured) workers in separate shifts and departments. As one Pakistani, a foundry worker, explained this, 'The management gives the explanation to the white groups that we are lazy workers and we cannot work on the assembly line with other workers. Secondly, they justify giving us dirty jobs saying we do not know the language and we are not skilled. What in my view it boils down to is that they want to keep their white workers happy, and dirty jobs, which white workers will not do, to be done by somebody giving baseless reasons.' This comment raises the question of

Table 32

Ethnic composition of the work force

Firm A: Textile

	Shifts									
	Day			*Double Day*			*Night*			
Department	*P*	*E*	*O*	*P*	*E*	*O*	*P*	*E*	*O*	*Total*
Waste sorting and waste handling	18	–	–	2	–	–	5	–	1	26
Rag tearing	1	–	1	–	–	–	2	–	–	4
Blending	3	2	–	–	–	–	2	–	–	7
Cording	2	2	2	2	3	8	7	–	3	29
Spinning	–	–	–	33	4	7	31	1	–	76
Winding	–	5	–	19	15	13	16	2	–	70
Making up	–	–	–	1	70	20	–	–	–	91
Raising	–	7	4	–	–	–	–	–	–	11
Weaving	4	–	1	4	11	1	8	1	–	30
Transport	–	7	–	–	–	–	–	1	–	8
Despatch	–	6	–	–	–	–	–	–	–	6
Wet Store	6	1	1	–	–	–	–	–	–	8
Maintenance	–	18	–	–	1	–	1	2	–	22
Senior, Management	1	18	1	–	–	–	–	–	–	20
Cloth dressing	1	1	1	–	–	–	–	–	–	3
Office	–	45	–	–	–	–	–	–	–	45
Total	36	112	11	61	104	49	72	7	4	456

P = Pakistanis
E = English
O = Others such as Ukrainians, Poles, Bangladeshis, etc.

unequal treatment and the disadvantage Pakistanis (and other coloured workers) face in employment. It appears that the possibility of economic assimilation is remote and there is a danger of a continued two-strata labour force with a skilled local elite and an unskilled second-class Pakistani (and other coloured workers) labour force. This situation conflicts with integrationist policies in the workforce. However, ethnic work groups play another important role in terms of ethnic mobilization, namely to exert pressure on the management.

(c) Ethnic Mobilization

Ethnic work group organization gives an opportunity to unite and make demands on the management to improve work conditions either generally or for immigrant workers in particular. The action of ethnic work groups is usually drastic as it results in complete shut-down of certain departments or shifts. This has happened recently where Asians were involved in strikes such as the Imperial Typewriter dispute in 1974, and the Mansfield Hosiery dispute in 1972 in Loughborough. Other examples include the strikes at Courtaulds, and at Preston and Woolf's, Southall.[18] Both these strikes failed, as many do, partly because of the lack of experience of ethnic minority workers in industrial relations, partly through non-co-operation from the white workers and partly because of weak bargaining positions. However, it was demonstrated that the concentration of ethnic minority workers could lead to their mobilization for action.

During the field-work I observed one such strike in Firm 'B' where 61 Pakistanis who worked on the night shift were involved. Later they received support from a variety of other Pakistanis working on the morning and evening shifts as well.[19] There were a number of complaints but the main one arose when the management introduced 24 TS frames run using a 9½ inch pulley. This according to the Pakistanis slowed down the speed and as a result the wages were reduced because of the piecework system. Examples were given of night-shift earnings coming down from an average of £33 to £29. The other complaints included rate increase, stopped time not being booked, a method of doffing frames, as all these had an adverse effect on earnings. Pakistani workers also complained about the dirty stuff they were given to run off as against the white workers. In addition there was no dinner time allowed and the canteen was not opened at night. The strike was mainly led by the young educated Pakistanis.

When the strike started the workers involved approached their union, the National Union of Textile and Allied Workers, direct as there was no representative of the union on the night shift. They also approached the local Community Relations Council. The management tried to negotiate without the union but failed. Ten days after the strike a meeting took place between the strikers, management, the Secretary of Rochdale District Union and the author as a representative of the Community Relations Council. The spokesman of the workers stated their demands one by one in an articulate way. Then the Union spokesman presented his views and suggested a work study group to look into the problems of frames. He also asked the management to give rest breaks and record stopped time due to break-downs. The manager of the firm accepted these suggestions and requested the workers to go back to work. The strikers who were by that time supported by some white workers, mainly East Europeans, wanted to fix a time limit to meet their demands. The manager asked me if I could assure them that their demands would be met as soon as the results of the work study group were available. On my assurance then the workers went back to work. Two weeks later the report of the work study group came and then the management met the suggestions made. Other small difficulties about prayer facilities, etc. were also resolved.

This dispute was interesting in several ways. It showed how the workers' solidarity compelled the management to meet their demands. It illustrated the way in which ethnic work groups tended to isolate immigrant workers from their colleagues who might not be aware of their problems. The East European workers who joined the Pakistanis were the ones who were also affected on the morning shift. As a whole, cohesion through ethnicity was an important resource of the Pakistanis' unity. Conflict with the management united them.

The Pakistanis on the night shift were isolated not only from the union, but also from other groups of workers. The firm had a long-standing reputation for anti-union policies. The ethnic solidarity of the Pakistanis had helped them to organize the union in an active way. One problem which became evident in this dispute was the lack of mutual understanding between Pakistani workers and the trade union. But the lead given by some educated Pakistanis who were aware of industrial relations, created this understanding as a result of the dispute. I was told that similar moves took place in other firms as well which showed the ethnic solidarity of workers working in ethnic work groups.

The position of coloured workers becomes clearer only in local-level studies which give detailed break-downs of the jobs actually done by them[20] because the census does not provide this information.

To sum up, Pakistanis were employed in occupations rejected by the indigenous population. They were concentrated in certain industrial sectors, in this case textiles. These were the sectors which had either lowest pay or dirty jobs, difficult shifts and worst working conditions.[21] Overwhelmingly, the majority of Pakistanis are manual workers, usually unskilled or semi-skilled. Pakistanis also tend to be at a disadvantage in terms of promotion, the reasons given for this being their different qualifications and non-industrial background. In addition to these factors there is racial discrimination against Pakistanis and other coloured workers. For all these reasons Pakistanis, along with other coloured immigrants, form the lowest stratum of the British labour market, working in ethnic segregation which results in their incapsulation. It seems that they are likely to continue to do so, although the present situation sometimes gives them power to act together and mobilize support on ethnic lines.

Relationships at Work

Whether there are opportunities to communicate and establish relationships with other ethnic groups at work depends on the type of job and the type of situation. Ethnic work groups mentioned above are one of the sources of incapsulation of Pakistanis at work. One possible opportunity to create relationships across the ethnic boundaries could have occurred during meal breaks.

As the canteens in the three firms studied in some detail were closed at night there was no chance of meeting at meal breaks. In one firm 'A' there was a rest-room in the spinning department where there were facilities to make tea and warm up meals.

In the other two firms meals were kept near heating pipes in winter to keep them warm. Meals (chapattis and curry) were carried in tiffin carriers and tea or milk in flasks. In firms 'A' and 'C' Pakistanis usually ate in ethnic groups at about midnight. There was an arrangement whereby some would look after the machines while others ate. In firm 'B' there were no meal breaks. The strike mentioned above led to hard bargaining on this matter and a paid meal break of half an hour was conceded.

Those who worked on day shifts or on the morning shift usually had an opportunity to use the canteen as it was open at that time. Few Pakistanis went to the canteen, and they sat at separate tables. The meal breaks were mainly used as a chance for those in different departments to get together. Some Pakistanis sat with English workers but they were very few in numbers, and were usually charge-hands who sat with their supervisors. This was interpreted by other Pakistanis as an attempt to avoid them showing that they were getting 'big-headed' by associating with English workers. Mr X who worked in firm 'A' said: 'I cannot understand the mentality of Mr W, when he was an ordinary worker, he used to sit with us. Now, since he is promoted as charge-hand, he has gone stiff-neck and associates himself with the English people, because he belongs to *nai*, barber, caste.' In fact, there was some trouble about this charge-hand, and the management later removed him to one of their mills in another area to avoid factional conflict.

Many Pakistanis regard their work as temporary and the group pressure to conform and to mix with their group at work is strong. This behaviour is reinforced by the ethnic work group system. Those Pakistanis who worked in a situation where there were not many Pakistanis exhibited, however, different behaviour. Their number was very small and their personal characteristics differed. They joined their English workmates during the meal breaks and furthermore met them socially outside work. Mr Q. R. who was one of the four respondents who claimed to mix with English people at meal breaks worked in a television firm and was the only Pakistani in the firm. But he also saw this not simply as having no Pakistani to eat with since he felt that 'it is good to have a chat with English workmates in the meal breaks. It gives you a chance to get to know them and make friends. Although I work side by side with English people, this is not the case with many Pakistanis who work at night shift and there is hardly any English person to communicate with. The other difficulty they face is, if they get the opportunity, the language. But mind you the only way to create good community relations is to create social contact. I do not suggest that we should leave our cultural values but by meeting socially we can create understanding and goodwill which we need to remove stereotyping against Pakistanis.'

This answer raises several interesting points, one, that Pakistanis face language difficulties; two, they work mostly at night shift and thirdly, that to create social contact is to create good community relations. It is worth pointing out that a single, educated person like Mr Q. R. does not face the difficulties of language and working in an ethnic group. There are also fewer family and *Biraderi* pressures to conform to the community norms than for an ordinary Pakistani who depends on his family, *Biraderi* and community for several reasons.

Sheila Allen in her study also found that many Pakistanis did not use the canteen. One factor which she reported was that English workers did not like the smell of Pakistani food and they laughed at the Pakistani way of eating. To avoid this type of hostile tension and ridicule they sat in segregated groups in the canteen or stayed in their departments to eat with their own groups.[22] This was also the case with the respondents in Rochdale who had opportunities of eating in the canteen but perceived this hostile attitude of the white workers about their food and their manner of eating.

Sports activities also presented opportunities in some firms where inter-ethnic mixing could take place. In firm 'A' some of the young Pakistanis for instance, working on the day shift, played football on a nearby ground (owned by the firm) during their lunch breaks. This led to matches between Pakistanis and English workers, usually after working hours. This happened at least six times during the field-work. Later, an ethnically mixed football team and similarly a cricket team played for the firm. However, the two teams within the firm, one Pakistani and the other white, still existed and competed against each other. This had led to some friendships across the ethnic group boundaries. Management was quite pleased with this situation because it had helped to create a more friendly atmosphere in some departments where, they said, there had previously been some racial tension on the day shift.

Union Participation

The other area in which people get an opportunity to create social relationships at work is through participation in the union. In this section the question of Pakistani membership and participation in unions is examined.

First, a few general points concerning unions and migrant workers should be mentioned. There are several factors which contribute to the division between migrant and indigenous workers. The most important of these factors is that the two groups are generally employed in different types of work. This results in lack of contact and sometimes in different and conflicting interests. Other factors are differences in language and culture, which hinder communication and in some cases lead to differences in behaviour. There is also the problem of the indigenous worker's attitude to newcomers. According to some authors, working-class people who see immigrants as threat to their jobs have a strong traditional hostility towards immigration and this hostility divides workers.[23] In this situation immigrants appear as an alien and threatening work force to the other workers. The other important factor is the lack of contact between immigrant and indigenous workers because of the division of the labour force into incorporated ethnic work groups; we have seen this in the case of Pakistanis in this study.

Although the doctrine of internationalism is a strong tradition in the labour movement, unions oppose immigration because of the fear of disadvantages to the indigenous labour force. It is assumed that immigrants can be forced to work for lower wages and provide alternative labour in case of disputes. On the other hand, if the unions opposed immigration initially and continue to do so, they may find that the immigrants do not trust them and are unwilling to join. Where this happens, the unions lose on two counts.[24]

Looking at the attitudes of the unions towards immigrants in Britain, one finds that they have usually protected the interests of local workers. For instance, the European Voluntary Workers who sought employment in Britain between 1945 and 1950 faced these conditions: no EVWs to be employed where British labour was obtainable; foreign workers to be dismissed first in the event of redundancy, or to be replaced by British labour as soon as possible; there were maximum quotas of foreign workers, usually 10 to 15 per cent of the labour force; and foreign workers were not to be engaged unless they joined the appropriate union.[25]

In some cases there were formal or informal agreements restricting the promotion of foreign workers.[26] Thus the system of 'institutionalized discrimination' against foreign workers in Britain has operated to some extent with the explicit or implicit support of the trade union movement in the employment field.

As Commonwealth immigrants began to come to Britain in growing numbers in the early fifties, trade unionists became concerned about the possible effects on employment and conditions. On the other hand, the unions were in favour of free entry rights for Commonwealth citizens, at least until 1965. This was regarded as part of Britain's debt to her former colonies. Although trade unions in Britain opposed discrimination they took no special practical steps to stop it.[27] Immigrants who have gone on strike to fight for their own interests have, on the whole, received little support from indigenous workers and from the trade unions. Even where the issues involved were normal industrial ones of wages and conditions, there has been a tendency for employers, the press, and unions to label the disputes as 'racial'. At times unions asked for the dismissal of immigrant workers who would not join their union.[28]

There was a strike in 1970 as a result of a protest by 24 Indian workers in the Birmingham area that they were being discriminated against by the unions. In fact it was an inter-union dispute. When the 24 Indians went to the Transport Union, the Amalgamated Engineering Union complained of 'poaching'. The Transport Union then refused to accept the Indians' subscriptions. They refused to rejoin the Engineering Union and accused it of 'discrimination against coloured workers'. The case was taken to the Race Relations Board and to the TUC. Some of the respondents in Rochdale felt very strongly that the unions favoured the white workers and if immigrants were involved in a dispute the union officials took the management's side to defeat the immigrants' objective. This, they felt, increased the mistrust Pakistanis had towards unions.

No special efforts were made to overcome discrimination by the unions. For instance, a proposal to seek agreement with the engineering employers on a voluntary procedure through joint committees to deal with race discrimination was defeated 39—21 at the Blackpool conference of the Amalgamated Union of Engineering and Foundry Workers in 1970.[29]

Lack of union support for immigrants has caused several defeats and has led immigrants to feel that they are discriminated against. This factor affects their participation in the union activities and might lead them to form their separate unions.

It is still problematic how far the failure to involve coloured workers in union activity will encourage them to form separate organizations in attempts to obtain effective representation.[30] Ethnic mobilization along these lines has taken place but no permanent union organizations of these workers in Rochdale have yet been formed.

Talking to union officials in the Rochdale area in general and in the three firms studied in particular led me to believe that there had been little contact between management and trade unions about issues related to Pakistanis or other immigrants. The union officials did not know how many Pakistani members they had. Up until 1975 there were no Pakistani trade union officials. Apart from dealing with individual cases such as industrial accidents, trade union officials did not take any action to combat racial discrimination. One respondent said, 'Even the unions do not treat us fairly, if a Pakistani has an accident this case takes ages to get a compensation because the unions officials do not care about us. The compensation is usually low compared with an English worker who would get a decision quickly and receive more money. Sometimes I think why do we pay union fees if our rights are not defended properly, we might as well have our own union to defend our rights.' This comment raises the question of how Pakistanis feel about the unions.

When asked, 'Do you think a trade union based on an ethnic work force would be more helpful?' very few respondents thought that would be so. While about 25 per cent (23) did not give any opinion, only 12 out of 103 said that a trade union based on ethnic work force would be more helpful. Their reasons varied from personal experience where the union did not help, to strong feeling about the different problems and needs of Pakistanis because of their linguistic and cultural factors which the white union officials cannot understand. As one respondent put it, 'Apart from prejudice many of our problems are not understood and solved due to cultural differences and our own people will be able to understand problems better than others.' There were those Pakistanis who believed that unions should help impartially. One such respondent said, 'Anybody could be helpful, union should work impartially and look after the interests of its members.' Another respondent felt that management would not accept a union based on ethnic work force. Like some others who believed in the unity of workers he said, 'We should join the same unions and be effective as workers and not as Pakistanis or English.'

This means that if more interest were taken in the Pakistanis and in their problems, their confidence in the unions, and their participation, could be increased. One thing which emerges quite clearly from the responses is the different needs and problems of Pakistani workers within the British trade unions as a result of their cultural and language differences. The trade union officials' fear that separatist unions would emerge catering solely for coloured workers, has not been realized.[31] Given the attitudes expressed by the respondents and the unions' failure to meet the needs of the ethnic minority workers this fear does not seem surprising.

On the other hand the cultural and language problems could probably be overcome by encouraging Pakistanis (and other immigrants) to become union representatives, in that way contributing more through active participation. This brings us to our next point: union membership among Pakistanis.

Usually, the studies dealing with comprehensive membership figures or information on the participation of immigrant workers in union affairs are not available in great numbers. The little information that is available indicates a relatively low rate of membership and, in particular, a low level of participation in Britain.[32] This could be due to the unions' failure to defend immigrants' interests on different issues, and their lack of success in dealing with discrimination against them.

Out of our sample of 103, there were only 9 Pakistanis who said they were not members of any union. Four of these claimed that there was no trade union in the firm they worked for and the other 5 said they did not want to join. The membership percentage among Pakistanis in Rochdale in 1974 was, therefore, quite high if compared with the Bradford study in 1966–9. The Bradford study found trade union membership higher among the indigenous workers than among the coloured workers, 46 per cent and 16·2 per cent respectively.[33] We do not have comparative figures for white workers in the Rochdale area, however, and therefore our sample results should be treated with caution.

An interesting feature of the interviews was that almost a third of those who claimed to be the members of the union did not know the name of their union, but called it 'my union' or 'do not know'. In some cases the membership card was presented to check the name of the union and as proof of the membership.

The higher union membership of these Pakistani workers could be attributed to the fact that a larger proportion of them were manual workers, among whom union membership tends to be higher as compared with non-manual workers. On the other hand, higher union membership does not automatically mean greater participation. Out of the 94 Pakistanis in the sample who were union members only 4 had attended a meeting in the last year (8 others attended when they were involved in a dispute). The reasons given for not attending the meetings were that they had not been invited. As one respondent put it, 'I am never invited how can I attend the meetings.' This was a typical answer. Few others gave language difficulty as the reason. Shift work seems another obvious reason for lack of participation. One Pakistani who was quite aware of the union activities admitted, 'Let us face it, if Pakistanis work on the night shift how can they attend union meetings which are always held in daytime.' Those who worked in daytime did not attend for two reasons:

(i) that they did not understand English and
(ii) they felt if they attended the union meetings they might offend the management. (This means they are not fully aware of their right of participation in the unions.)

This shows the attitudes and limitations of Pakistanis in relation to their participation in the union activities.

As a whole this situation again incapsulates Pakistanis. They do not get an opportunity to create social relationships across ethnic boundaries by participating in great numbers in union activities along with white workers and thus taking part in a common fight against the employers.

The Effects of Night-Shift Work

As mentioned above, a large number of Pakistanis in Rochdale worked on night shift or on a multi-shift system. In this section we examine the effect of shift working on the family and social life and life-style of a Pakistani.

A Pakistani night-shift worker usually works twelve hours a night, that is from 7.30 p.m. to 7.30 a.m. The regular night shift is 10.00–6.00 a.m. but firms which do not have enough people for particular departments to work in either the evening or the morning shift encourage day-shift Pakistanis and other willing immigrant workers to work overtime up to 7.30 p.m. and then the night-shift worker starts his overtime at 7.30 p.m. This obviously varies from one firm to the other. All three firms studied had this flexible system of overtime to fill the gaps. In the morning some finished work at 6.00 a.m. where there was a double-day shift and others finished at 7.30 a.m. when the machines were taken over by the day shift workers. Those who left work at 7.30 a.m. returned home about 8.00 a.m. and then took their breakfast and went to bed. Most of the Pakistanis got up at about 5.00 p.m. and slowly prepared for the next night. If it was urgent some would make an effort to shop at a Pakistani shop. It was observed that some did shopping in the morning on their way back from work, when it was possible for them to buy an Urdu newspaper as well. They usually took this newspaper to work to read at night.

As far as family visitors are concerned they know that night-shift workers get up around 5.00 p.m. and that this is the time to call on them during the week. Even officials such as social workers or community relations workers are aware of this routine and they know when to call. A typical routine of a Pakistani night-shift worker is presented in Figure 15.

It is clear from Figure 15 that a Pakistani who works at night hardly gets any time for his family, leisure or any other social activities during the week. He also sleeps on Saturday until late afternoon and then spends the rest of the evening and Sunday visiting or receiving relatives and friends. In some cases night-shift workers work on Sundays in daytime to do specific jobs such as cleaning the machines or moving new materials from the warehouses to other places. Mr M. S. said, 'I always try to work on Sunday if there is work available because the wages are double for overtime on Sunday.' This attitude seemed common among other Pakistanis in Rochdale.

Those who were living as single people did not bother about time

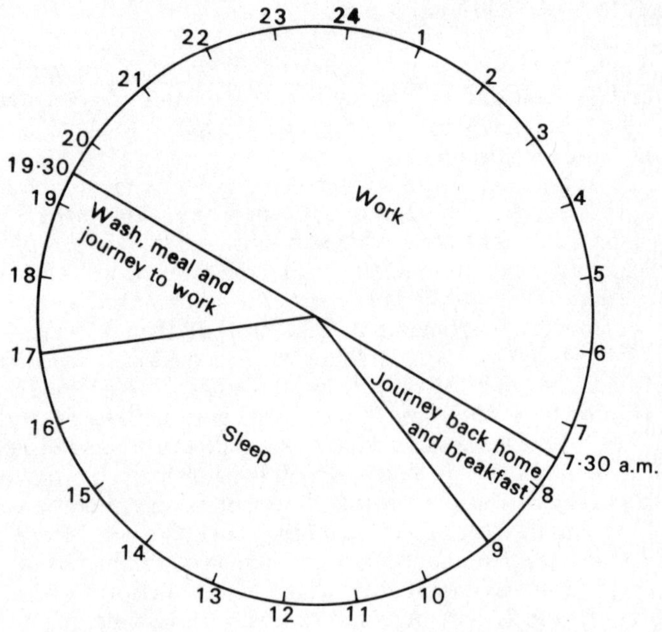

FIGURE 15 *Typical routine of a night-shift worker*

as they did not have family commitments. But for those who had their families with them night shift created problems as it affected the family routine as well. If the father worked on the night shift, the children usually saw less of him. During the school term there was hardly any contact on weekdays; when the father came back from work children were normally ready to go to school. In the evening when the children came back from school the father started to get ready for work. Their meal times differed and so did other activities. For instance, Mrs S. usually complained that her husband did not spend enough time with the children which was creating a gap in the father–children relationships. She did sewing for a Pakistani manufacturer and earned about £15 per week. She said, 'I started sewing so that my husband could work days and I can earn the difference. It is not fair on me and children to be on our own all the time. Even when my husband is here he is sleeping which is of no use to us in terms of help. It is too much.' She also shared the feeling with other Pakistani mothers that they and their husbands never went to parents' evenings arranged at schools. Children whose parents did not attend parents' evenings felt they were left out. Some of the respondents wanted to attend parents' evenings but could not attend because of night-shift work. Mr A. G. did not see a bright future for Pakistani children if they grew up here without any sort of paternal control. He believed the nature of his work and particularly the night shift did not allow him to keep in contact with the schools and with the family itself. Another factor, he added, was the language problem. The majority of Pakistani parents were unable to go and speak to the teachers or at least attend the parents' evenings.

Activities arranged by or within the Pakistani community were scheduled to take account of the pattern of shift working. Other socio-cultural meetings were usually arranged on Sundays, otherwise the majority of the Pakistanis would not be able to attend. Similarly, Pakistani films were shown on Saturday evenings and Sundays.

Night-shift work had given a kind of freedom to the youngsters in the Pakistani community. Some teenage children went out in the evenings once their fathers left for the night shift. Mothers usually hid this fact from the fathers because they knew that their husbands would not approve. On the other hand, mothers could not stop them as their role was usually a kind and protective one; and the final authority over children lay with the father.

Fathers came to know about the evening activities of their teenage children when they got into trouble. For instance, three Pakistani boys were caught by the police teasing English girls and their parents were contacted. This resulted in their getting a bad name in the community. Two of the fathers left their night-shift work immediately, and exchanged the shift with two other single Pakistanis on the day shift, who were looking for night-shift work, for the sake of their children.[34] In one case it was too late because the boy had had a fight with another Pakistani boy and was taken under the care of the local authority. This damaged the prestige of the family and acted as a warning for other parents.

Night-shift work also affects the relationship between husband and wife, because he is usually unable to fulfil his duties as a husband and father the way others do. On the one hand, the father's odd working hours bring more money and prosperity but on the other hand, lead to a constrained family and social life. This is even more difficult where Pakistani women observe *Purdah* and cannot go out shopping, and so on, on their own and their dependence on the husband increases. The wife and children have to be very quiet during the daytime so that the husband is not disturbed while he is sleeping. Sometimes unexpected relatives and friends come in during the day and it becomes obligatory to wake up the night worker. This affects his sleep and if done often, affects his routine for rest and consequently may affect his health and make him bad tempered.

When a family in Rochdale consisted of only husband and wife and children, the wife felt the lack of physical and emotional support when her husband was out at work[35] as in the family back home she was used to the company of other relatives. This lack of emotional and physical support was felt particularly at night. Living near their kin in the same area provided some emotional and physical support for their wife and children, and was mentioned by a majority of the respondents (see above, pp. 70–71).

Night-shift work affects the health of the workers, as sleeping during the day time is often difficult due to the light and household and traffic noises. This in turn affects the digestive system and consequently health.[36] One Pakistani doctor told me that working in textiles (and particularly dealing with dirty materials) and night work were affecting the health of Pakistanis beyond the point of recovery. He said this referring to the high incidence of TB and asthma among Pakistanis in Rochdale generally and among some of his own patients. There seems little doubt that night work has some adverse effects on health and has affected the health of many Pakistanis.

The social life of Pakistanis is affected by the night-shift work, particularly that of the women who (except for close relatives) do not go out to visit other people on their own. Visiting at night time may be forbidden by the husband, which leaves the wife and children dependent on the father's wish for outings, visits and other recreational activities.

Pakistanis who worked on night shifts had different life-styles from other Pakistanis. Their activities and social participation were restricted and this incapsulated them from the rest of the community along with the other factors outlined in previous parts of the book. This particular factor, however, is usually ignored by the community and race relations workers who are striving towards the integration of immigrants into British society. Before they start new projects and policies they rarely try to find out which factors incapsulate immigrants from the wider society.

7. Economic Activity and the Role of Social Networks: Self-employed Pakistanis

One way to avoid the difficulties and discrimination Pakistanis face in their work situation is to become self-employed. This also creates respect for the person concerned in the Pakistani community. It gives independence and, as one respondent put it, 'You are your own boss, no clock-in, clock-out business and no night shift, you are near home and close to your wife and children.' This is an alternative life-style to that of those Pakistanis who work in industry, particularly on night-shift work. A market trader said, 'My income is reasonable. It is more comfortable to have your own business, there is more rest and independence and more money and I am my own boss. It is daytime work and I can spend more time with my family. I am so independent that I went to Pakistan for six weeks in 1972 without losing any money as my cousin looked after my stalls. This you cannot do if you are working in a mill.' A manufacturer gave several examples of discrimination at work and said, 'That was one of the reasons I started my own business where I am my own boss, and nobody can order me or call me, "Oh Paki, do this or do that".' These comments show clearly that apart from the importance Pakistanis attach to self-employment in terms of prosperity, independence and respect, discrimination at work was a contributing factor. If we look at the case studies of those who were still working in the factories or public transport in many cases their ambitions included starting a business in Britain or in Pakistan, and they gave similar reasons for such ambitions.

Mr M. B. a day worker, put forward even stronger reasons for self-employment: 'The good future of Pakistanis in this country is only in their own business and unity as a community—Pakistanis in the town should help each other to start business. We should have a spirit of united action like the Jews. You cannot see a single Jew working in a factory on the shop floor. This is what I would like to see our community doing. If we are financially well off then we can have more community facilities to protect our culture and we will have more participation in the society and more power.' This attitude illustrates several points related to the importance Pakistanis give to self-employment.

The way Pakistanis start in business in this new situation is described in detail in Chapter 11. In this section we shall concentrate on the self-employed people in the sample, adding our observations and other related data wherever relevant.

Twenty-three self-employed Pakistani men were interviewed. The types of business and the number of men involved are shown in Table 33.

Table 33
Type of business of the sample

Type of Business	*Number*
Grocers and butchers	6
Restaurants and cafes	2
Personal services	3
General services	2
Manufacturers	3
Market stall traders	6
Electrical and radio	1
Total	23

Note: Personal Services include two hairdressers and one launderette, and general services include one travel agent and one school of motoring. The electrical and radio merchant was also a travel agent.

Out of these twenty-three respondents there were fourteen who had had some sort of business in Pakistan before coming to Britain. For instance, Mr C. H. who was an estate and travel agent had been a commission agent in Pakistan. Similarly, Mr M. T., a manufacturer of ladies' and children's garments, had had a grocery shop in Pakistan, but in Britain before he started his manufacturing he was a market trader for 6 years, from 1965 to 1971. Those whose business involved personal services had had experience and knowledge of that trade before coming to Britain; this was the case with two hairdressers.[1] There were those who did not have background experience in business but took the initiative and started off in business with the help of kin or friends. Mr W. K. was a mill worker and started selling radio and electrical goods in partnership with Mr A. S. After two years, Mr A. S. decided to start a shop in Manchester and withdrew his shares. Mr W. K. commented, 'I borrowed

£600 and a wholesaler in Manchester promised to give me some radios and other goods on a credit basis, so I took the risk. I did not know much about radios in the beginning that is why I asked Mr A. S. to be the partner as we were good friends and related to each other. Now I feel confident.' Other shopkeepers also started in partnership for several reasons:

(i) Lack of initial capital
(ii) Lack of confidence
(iii) Inability to speak English and consequent need for a partner to overcome the language difficulties
(iv) Ease of visiting wholesalers and carrying out deliveries without closing the shop
(v) Kinship–friendship ties

Partnerships did sometimes create problems and led to conflict situations in the Pakistani community between partners (see pp. 93–4.)

Finance was usually raised within the kin—friend group. Twenty out of twenty-three said that they sought financial help from within the community. This does not mean that they did not use any other source. The details of the sources of finance for twenty-three respondents are given in the table below:

Table 34
Sources of finance

Business	*No.*	*Own savings*	*Friends and relatives*	*Personal business contacts*	*Pakistani bank*	*English bank*
Grocery and butchery	6	5	5	—	—	—
Restaurant and café	2	2	1	—	1	—
Personal services	3	3	1	1	—	1
General services	2	2	1	—	—	—
Manufacturers	3	3	3	1	1	1
Market stall traders	6	6	4	3	—	—
Electrical and radio	1	1	1	1	—	—
Total	23	22	16	6	2	2

Own savings were mentioned 22 times and friends and relatives 16 times. This showed that friends and relatives were an important source of help when one made a decision to start a business. Sheila

Allen also found this in Bradford where out of 29 respondents 21 mentioned own savings and 21 again friends and relatives as a source of finance.[2] Combining the first two categories which may be regarded as 'informal' and personal sources these were the most frequently used as opposed to 'institutional' sources of finance. Only two respondents had used Pakistani banks and another two had used English banks.

When Mr M. T. started his business he initially borrowed some money from his relatives, although he later relied on banks. This pattern was quite common and as a consequence a network of capital-raising within the *Biraderi*—friendship groups had been set up.

Another source used to start a business was personal business contacts. These were usually Pakistani or Indian wholesalers in Manchester and other areas and in the case of market traders even the manufacturers in Rochdale. Mr K. got his business in radio and electrical goods off the ground with the help of a wholesaler in Manchester who gave him credit facilities. Similarly, Mr A. A., a market trader, bought from a manufacturer in Rochdale and paid him at the end of the week after selling the garments. He was also allowed to return the goods he did not sell. It was observed that this arrangement existed between other Pakistani manufacturers and market traders as well.

It has already been suggested that the banks were used as a source of capital once the business was established. There was a tendency to get external financial help to expand it. This was true of the café proprietor who used a Pakistani bank and of the manufacturer who used a Pakistani and an English bank to buy more machines. At this stage, it was possible in both cases to get money on the security of the business and the building.

Except for one manufacturer and the launderette owner who had some difficulty in getting planning permission, no other respondent mentioned any difficulty in acquiring a site.

It is interesting to note that none of the respondents started business immediately after his arrival in this country. All twenty-three respondents worked in factories from four to nine years. This shows that they first tried to save up and then started their business with their savings as the initial capital.

It is clear from the case studies and other information, that business ownership required initial capital and knowledge of the potential market. For instance, the emergence of grocers and butchers and those who provided services such as hairdressing was determined by the size of the Pakistani population in Rochdale. As the size of the population grew the business activity which served the community grew as well. This we can see by looking at the location of the Pakistani businesses. The vast majority of them were situated in the areas of Pakistani concentration, where Pakistanis relied on their own businesses to fulfil their daily needs for different goods and services.

Except the manufacturers, the launderette owner and the café proprietor, all others claimed that more than 80 per cent of their customers were either Pakistanis or Indians. One grocer/butcher said, 'Almost all our customers are Pakistanis and Indians. English people and Italians and Poles only come to our shops on Sunday if they need something urgently.' Another grocer put it differently: 'English people have started coming to our shops to buy things such as *Basmati* rice and spices which they use to make curry. Otherwise our customers are mostly Pakistanis.' This showed clearly that the businesses catered mainly for Pakistani customers.

The garment manufacturers, the launderette owner and the café proprietor appeared to be attracting customers other than Pakistanis. This was due to the nature of the business and service. But still the owners claimed that the majority of their customers were Pakistanis. One manufacturer said, 'English market traders come to us because we can provide the cheapest garments in the whole of the country. The other attraction is that we give credit facilities to those who ask for it.'

Apart from the manufacturers, the other businesses were mainly run by the owner, in some cases with the help of other family members or relatives. In grocery shops it was usually the wife or brother of the owner who helped. For instance, Mr H. A. had a lot of help from his wife. When he went to the wholesalers, slaughterhouse, or to do deliveries, his wife looked after the shop. In some cases children also helped after school and over the weekend. The tendency was for the business to be run by the family. When someone else was employed the person was either *Biraderi* or personally known to the family. This was the case for the Pakistani manufacturers who employed at least a close relative to supervise the work. They also relied heavily on the part-time work of Pakistani boys and Pakistani women, not necessarily related to the owner, doing sewing at home. Homeworking had expanded in recent years in Rochdale due to the arrival of Pakistanis on the scene. Therefore, the situation and the relationship of these two groups, i.e. the Pakistani manufacturer and the homeworkers, are outlined below.

Pakistani Manufacturers and Homeworkers

In the early days of Asian immigration to Britain 'peddling and hawking' was one of the economic activities of many Asians who were not used to industrial work.[3] This created a contact with the manufacturers and wholesalers particularly in the ladies' and children's garments trade. By and by the immigrants learnt about this trade and some took the initiative to start their own manufacturing and supply the wholesalers. This happened more in the Manchester area which was a centre for this trade. The trade obviously expanded when the families started arriving and women who otherwise were not allowed to go out to work in the factories were given this economic incentive of homework. This applied to daughters as well who would not go out to work in a factory. It is a classic case of a traditional occupation for new immigrants with a long history of participation by earlier groups of newcomers such as the Jews.[4] In the Manchester area the clothing industry was dominated by the Jews and now it is slowly being taken over by Asians as they can get the cheap homeworkers. Secondly, Jews have started moving to other trades admitting that they cannot compete with the Asians.[5] This could be due to the lower payments which Asian manufacturers make to their homeworkers.

Homeworkers are used in industries such as garment manufacturing or hat-making. Homeworking is an economic device for cutting overheads, therefore making the business more profitable and competitive. Manufacturers need a floating population of single operatives due to the seasonality of production as well. The operation of the homeworker system is an exploitation of cheap labour due to its informality, as there are no formal contracts between the manufacturer and the homeworker.

Those manufacturers who had their own market stalls as well, kept the profit at all the stages: manufacturing, wholesaling and retailing. This helped them to expand their business quickly. Looking at the case studies and other information collected in this field we find that the following were the usual stages of the process: factory worker or pedlar, part-time market trader (usually on Saturdays and sometimes on Sundays), full-time market trader when the business looked economically viable, and finally manufacturer and wholesaler. These activities usually overlapped.

In Rochdale Pakistanis entered the manufacturing business in the early 1970s when a Pakistani wholesaler and manufacturer from Manchester encouraged a Pakistani family to act as his agents locally. The wife was an educated woman and had had some experience of sewing before. She asked a few other Pakistani women to do homework to earn some extra money for their families. Her husband who was locally employed used to deliver and collect the garments. Then after a few months they started their own independent manufacturing. Then slowly the news of their success spread and two other market traders, Mr A. and Mr H. decided to follow. Then the manufacturers started up one after another and homework, as financial help to the family, increased. The supply of cheap labour aided the manufacturers and its use was facilitated by the ethnic affiliations of manufacturers and workers.

Once the Pakistani manufacturers got off the ground with the help of the wholesalers in Manchester and of their kinship—friendship networks, their business grew and they supplied garments among others to London and Ulster. One market trader claimed that the cheapest garments were available in Rochdale and that was why customers came from all over the country. I was told in 1976 that at least two Pakistani manufacturers in Rochdale were making enquiries to export garments to EEC countries and were looking for Pakistani contacts there.

The Pakistani workers who worked for these manufacturers were usually part-time. This did not mean that there were no full-time employees. Usually those who went out on the market stalls or had a lease were employed full-time. Pakistani teenage boys (some still at school) were encouraged to do part-time work such as collecting the garments and delivering materials to the houses, ironing, buttoning, and other small unskilled tasks. Cutting was usually done either by a full-time cutter or by the manufacturer himself with the help of somebody else trained to do this job.

The work force of three manufacturers is given in Table 35.

Reliance on part-time workers and on homeworkers for this trade in Rochdale is obvious. The other category of workers to note

Table 35
Work force of three manufacturers

Manufacturers	*Full-time relatives working*	*Full-time men and boys*	*Part-time men and boys*	*Full-time women*	*Home workers*	*Filipino girls*	*Total*
A	1	3	5	2	60	3	74
B	3	4	3	—	53	—	63
C	5	2	9	4	33	6	59

are the Filipino girls who were brought to this country by a clothing manufacturing firm as contract labour.[6] These girls were skilled machinists. They worked part-time with Pakistani manufacturers either in the evenings or over the weekends to supplement their income. As they were paid little by the contract firm and were in this country for a short time only, some Pakistanis helped them by providing accommodation nearer to their own factories in order to attract them to work for them in relatively skilled jobs. I was told that the output of the Filipino girls was twice as much as that of the Pakistani women who worked on the same type of jobs.[7]

Recently a few studies have attempted to explore the history and the conditions of the homeworkers.[8] The main conclusions of these studies are that homeworkers are usually women and they work for a manufacturer doing work traditionally done by women, e.g. sewing. Their rate of pay is usually lower than of those who work in the factories. Homeworkers supply their own machines and needles and are not compensated for machine repairs and the cost of electricity. In employing homeworkers the manufacturer avoids paying rent, rates, cost of the machines and supplying benefits and facilities which an employer would normally provide. All these items are hidden expenses to the homeworker. Homeworkers are not trained by their employers and they are used as seasonal labour to produce when there is demand for the garments. To put it another way, employers have no formal contracts and no responsibility towards the homeworkers. Homeworkers depend on the manufacturers or the agents for the work. There are neither unemployment and sickness benefits, nor holiday pay. These conclusions more or less apply to the Pakistani homeworkers in Rochdale.

Most Pakistani women homeworkers in Rochdale worked at home for the manufacturers and made ladies' and children' garments. Their rate of pay was lower than that of the factory worker. For instance, it was between 5p and 15p per garment in 1974 without hemming and buttoning etc., depending on the nature of the garment. It was observed that on average a Pakistani homeworker earned about £10—£20 a week. It would not be easy to calculate the number of hours a Pakistani woman would spend machining. What was observed was that after the household duties were done all spare time was spent on sewing. In some cases if there were more than one female in the house the time spent on sewing was longer. For instance, Mrs G. R. and her daughters spent long hours because they shared the household work. The two daughters who were both over 16 and had been to school for a few years in this country, did not go out to work and spent more time in sewing than their mother, who looked after the other children and usually cooked the meals.

This was typical of those who had grown-up daughters who were not allowed to go out to work. Mr M. G.'s family was another example where three daughters did home sewing. This meant that homeworking was a compromise between socio-cultural factors and the need to earn money. The manufacturers exploited this situation related to cultural factors and paid lower rates knowing that these women did not have a choice.[9]

The manufacturers did not provide the machines which were hired on a weekly basis from two firms (one Manchester-based). In a few cases Pakistani women had bought their own machines. The electricity and other costs were paid by the homeworkers. The women seemed to get a lot of work during the summer and not so much in winter months. Some manufacturers, who had their own wholesale business, changed the 'lines' quite often and women who worked for them were usually busy throughout the year.

The machines were usually set up either in the living room or in one of the bedrooms. I did not observe a single house where a special room was used for this work. The irregular hours of work sometimes created noise problems and led to complaints to the Public Health Department or to the local Community Relations Council. This affected the relations between Pakistanis and local people.[10] The officers of the Community Relations Council had to intervene in some cases to explain to Pakistani women that they should not use their machines early in the morning, late at night and over the weekend.

There is no formal training involved in homeworking. Homeworkers learn from each other as they would do in Pakistan. Pakistani homeworkers either learnt from other relatives or friends or spent a few days (a few hours each day) learning at the factory. Some Pakistani women were encouraged to work in the factory on more technical jobs so that the manufacturer or his wife could supervise it, but such women were very few in number. Those who went to the factory usually went in kin-groups and worked in all-women rooms. There were no figures available as to how many people worked for all the manufacturers and how many Pakistani women did homework. My own observations and dealings with Pakistanis over a period of about four years during which this business had expanded led me to believe that the majority of Pakistani women in Rochdale did homework.

In addition to the care of dependent children which was a common factor in all groups taking up homeworking, in the case of

Pakistani families there were other traditional factors keeping the women in the home. Homeworking was regarded as a way to avoid factory work which husbands disapproved of for social and cultural reasons. On the other hand, this work provided an extra income for the family.[11] Pakistani women claimed that they did this work for three reasons:

(i) that they could earn more and save more so that they could go back to Pakistan for a better life;
(ii) that their husbands could work shorter hours and particularly avoid night shift work which made the family and social life difficult;
(iii) that it kept them occupied and was a skill which they could use in Pakistan to start their own business.

For instance, Mrs S. said, 'I started sewing so that my husband could work days and I can earn the difference.' Mrs M. explained, 'We do sewing to earn extra money and as my daughters cannot go out to work they can earn to buy things which they would need to set up their own homes after their marriage.' Husbands also encouraged their wives to start sewing and some brought them over from Pakistan so that they could do this work and earn extra money. Mr M. A. said, 'I brought my wife and children to this country for two reasons: one that my wife could do some sewing at home like other Pakistani women in Rochdale did and this would increase the income of the family. Secondly, for the education of my children.' It is clear from the evidence that the economic necessity governs homeworking. But what are the effects of homeworking on the family life?

Due to homeworking in some cases the care of the children suffered. The mothers tried to spend as much time as possible sewing to earn money. Some women competed with each other to earn the most within the *Biraderi*. The women who earned extra money gained respect and felt proud in the *Biraderi* in the same way as a successful Pakistani businessman. This could lead to problems. Apart from the problem of little children who suffered from the time spent on sewing, the relationship of mother and children of school age was affected. Their needs such as clean clothes or dinners on time were sometimes ignored. This was also confirmed by some teachers and a social worker who said, 'First the night shift work done by Pakistanis was creating a gap between the Pakistani children and their fathers, now the homeworking is creating more problems and lack of attention by the mothers.' A health visitor had similar views and said, 'I was surprised to see mothers starting sewing a few days after the birth of a child. Apart from the fact that this could affect their health, the child's feeding time, etc. was ignored in some cases. Lack of the ability to communicate was creating enough problems. Now it is getting difficult to explain the effect of constant homeworking on their health and their children.'

Similarly, if there was only one woman to do everything in the house homeworking affected the preparation of meals, washing and cleaning the house, etc. It meant that she was doing a double day's work, as Pakistani husbands rarely helped their wives with housework.[12]

Homeworking was also contributing towards the isolation of Pakistani women. Like the night-shift workers the homeworkers did not get a chance to get out in the fresh air, and according to some doctors this was leading to ill-health and social isolation.

The crucial point is that the Pakistani manufacturers have provided homeworkers jobs and earnings where none might otherwise have been available. Homeworkers' legal position is 'self-employed', but whether deliberately or through ignorance, almost certainly they do not buy their insurance stamps etc. Similarly one wonders how many manufacturers, and Pakistani parents in this trade are breaking the law by using illegal child labour.[13] My conclusion is that as delivery boys are the backbone of a newsagent's life, Pakistani boys and homeworker women are the backbone of the Pakistani manufacturing business in Rochdale.

If one has a close look at the whole clothing industry in relation to Pakistanis in Rochdale one finds Pakistani manufacturers, Pakistani workers and Pakistani customers who are mainly market traders. The cloth is delivered usually by Indians or Pakistanis who are manufacturing it in Leicester or elsewhere. For other materials there is greater reliance and interdependence within the Pakistani or for that matter the Asian community. This has given rise to more Pakistani market traders as credit facilities are available. To put it in simple terms the whole industry follows the rule of scratching each other's backs. This helps to avoid the discrimination and formal work situation in the factory and provide self-respect and an 'informal relaxed atmosphere' as one respondent put it.

Looking at the whole situation there is no doubt that this economic activity within the community provides food for incapsulation particularly for Pakistani women who can play an important role in creating cross-ethnic relationships in the neighbourhood. This does not mean that the homework is the only factor responsible for their incapsulation but it is an increasingly important one.

8. Ethnic Group Mobilization and Political Participation[1]

Introduction

One area in which people use their links to mobilize support is the political process. In terms of ethnic minority groups in a country such as Britain, their participation in this process is an important indication of their involvement and integration in the wider society. This relates to aspects such as how aware ethnic minority groups are of the political process, their mobilization as voters on ethnic lines and their participation in electioneering. In this mainly descriptive chapter an account of electoral politics of Pakistanis as an ethnic group and of the way in which external hostility of the anti-immigrant candidates helped to create internal cohesion and reinforced Pakistani ethnicity, has been presented.

Commonwealth citizens living in Britain have a legal right to participate fully in politics. This includes the right to vote and to be a candidate in elections. Such participation in British politics is not a new phenomenon. At least two MPs from the Indian sub-continent have been elected to the House of Commons. The first was as long ago as 1892 when D. Naoraji was elected as Liberal for Finsbury Central. Mr S. Saklatvala was elected as Communist MP for Battersea North from 1924 to 1929. Both of these MPs were elected in straight fights with Conservative candidates.

Since the Second World War there have been no MPs of Indian, Bangladeshi, Pakistani or West Indian origin although there have been two West Indian members of the House of Lords, Lord Constantine and more recently Lord Pitt. There have also been a number of Parliamentary candidates. The most notable of these has been Lord (then Dr) Pitt who contested Hampstead in 1959 and Clapham in 1970 for Labour. Another Labour candidate was a Pakistani, Councillor Bashir Maan from Glasgow, who fought East

Fife in February 1974. The Liberals have put forward most candidates including Mr Preetam Singh (Sheffield Hallam), Mr Mihir Gupta (Smethwick), Mr Ghulam Musa (Bradford East) in 1970, Dr Dhani Prem (Coventry South East) in February 1974 and Mr Cecil Williams (Birmingham, Sparkbrook) in October 1974. The Conservatives have recently adopted their first candidate of New Commonwealth origin, Major N. Saroop for Greenwich. It appears that, slowly, political parties are encouraging candidates from ethnic minorities to participate in elections. Leaders from minority groups are trying to mobilize their groups to support the political parties.[2]

Politics and Race Relations

In the area of British political science little attention has been paid to race relations in empirical terms, apart from discussions of race in accounts of British Government and politics. In the last decade a number of studies have presented, in a rather cursory manner, the fact that immigration and race relations constitute an issue of high potential.[3] The focus of enquiry has been mainly upon the impact of ethnic/racial minorities on white electoral behaviour and upon the effects of the electoral mobilization of ethnic/racial minority voters. The main conclusions drawn from these studies are that 'while race relations present substantial political problems in Britain, these problems are not yet electoral, because of the overwhelming preponderance of the white population.'[4]

The political debate concerning New Commonwealth immigration has been a continuing one. Butler and Stokes showed that in 1964 and 1966 more than half of their sample felt 'very strongly' about immigration, and a further third felt 'fairly strongly'.[5] Another study demonstrates that 'a majority of the public has been consistently hostile to further immigration and a somewhat smaller majority has consistently favoured the repatriation of at least some of the coloured immigrants already in Britain.'[6]

The role played by the ethnic minority electors in British elections is still a subject of vague and tentative assertions. Deakin and Bourne indicated about the 1970 General Election that there was considerable swing towards the Conservatives in areas of substantial immigrant settlement.[7] There was also the view that ethnic minority voters usually support the Labour Party.

Other studies have shown that immigrants and, in particular, Asians do support other parties too.[8] These studies usually deal with race and local politics, involving the participation of ethnic minority candidates in local elections which provide an incentive for the mobilization of ethnic minority voters. But this is not the only stimulus which affects their mobilization, as shown in the following paragraphs, describing Rochdale Pakistani organizations and leaders and how the threat of anti-immigrant candidates in the elections helped create united action. This matter must obviously be discussed in the framework of the political parties. The period covered is mainly from 1972 to the end of 1974. Due to the different nature of local and Parliamentary elections they have been discussed separately.

Another type of political activity which must be distinguished from British politics is participation in the political life back home while living in this country. The Pakistan People's Party, the ruling party in Pakistan during the period of field-work, has its UK branch and organizations in several areas of Britain. Later other parties established similar branches of their parties in the UK although not on the same scale as the PPP. This type of political participation is discussed elsewhere.

Rochdale Elections

1. 1972 Local Elections

In the 1972 local council elections the Labour Party nominated Mr A. H.Chowdry, a Kenyan Asian, whose family was living in Pakistan and who spent some years there as a child, for the Central Ward. Mr Karim Dad, the President of Pakistan Welfare Association fought the Wardleworth Ward on the Liberal Party ticket. Both these candidates used the *Biraderi* organization to mobilize support. Meetings were held to discuss the strategy of campaign. Some supporters took time off to work for these candidates. Although British elections were new to some Pakistanis, elections and election campaigns were not. It appeared that the Pakistani turn-out was much higher in this election as compared with English voters. Mr Chowdry was elected while Mr Dad, though not elected, received a good number of votes. These candidates provided an incentive for participation for two reasons: one, that the Pakistani candidates knew how to mobilize their countrymen and secondly, that Pakistani voters realized that the time had come for them to have a representative on the local council to look after their interests. An early attempt on these lines was made in 1968 when M. Akhtar was nominated for the Central Ward by the Liberal Party.[9]

2. 1972 Parliamentary By-election

The 1972 Parliamentary by-election in Rochdale presents an interesting case of ethnic minority participation. The part played by the Pakistanis appears to have been a decisive factor in the election.[10] The election and its aftermath brought the social relationships of different ethnic groups into focus in a political context. The role of the candidate of the British Campaign to Stop Immigration, Mr Jim Merrick, which led to a social conflict had been given some attention. According to Coser, the study of social conflict is 'of central importance for an understanding of major areas of social relationships'.[11] This particular conflict united the Pakistanis. The presence of Mr Merrick and the nature of the campaign led ultimately to a realization among Pakistanis that they should act together. To follow Gerge Simmel's thesis, to understand conflict situations one should analyse the causes of the conflict and the mediating processes of conflict together with the immediate factors and effects which come into play.[12] Apart from Mr Merrick (BCSI) the other candidates were Messrs Cyril Smith (Liberal), Lawrence Cunliffe (Labour) and David Trippier (Conservative).

Mr Cyril Smith contested the 1970 General Election as a Liberal and came in second to the successful candidate, Mr J. McCann (Labour). After the death of Mr McCann he was the obvious candidate for the by-election. According to his agent it was the immigrant vote (mainly Pakistanis) which made the difference in the previous General Election. That is why, before he was officially announced as the candidate for the Liberal Party, he had held informal meetings with the Pakistanis. Other parties had not chosen their candidates up to that point. Mr Lawrence Cunliffe (Labour) conducted a short campaign and did not have much contact with the Pakistanis.

Mr David Trippier (Conservative) also did not appear to have much contact with the Pakistanis and on one occasion, offended them by saying that 'he was amazed to see the Socialist and Liberal candidates courting the immigrant vote: it is quite disgusting the way they treat Rochdale immigrants as political illiterates. It is quite like horsetrading rather than treating them as individuals. They are taking an amazingly patronising attitude towards them.'[13] On the other hand Mr Merrick's campaign had the effect of making the Pakistanis, the largest immigtant group in the town, take a more active part in the election and so counteract the racialist campaign.

The general view of the Labour Party workers was that Pakistanis usually voted for Labour candidates because most of them were workers and they thus identified themselves with Labour. But in this Rochdale election, this view was proved wrong, and the tradition of supporting Labour was broken, with a shift from Labour to the Liberals.

Sociologically speaking, Pakistani votes are usually mobilized and determined by the candidate's personal contacts, his understanding of the community's social and political structure and his personal links with the *Biraderi* leaders, formal leaders and associations. This was one of the main factors which resulted in the shift from Labour to the Liberals. The *Guardian* reported that 'Alderman Smith could win on the strength of a switch in support from Labour to Liberal by the Rochdale Asian community numbering about 6,000.[14] This view was also shared by most national and local newspapers.

Reasons for the Pakistani switch from Labour to Liberal were as follows:

1. The first factor was that the Liberal candidate was already known by many Pakistanis personally. He arranged meetings with and through their *Biraderi* leaders, and also approached some of them personally at a time when the Labour Party was still in the process of choosing a candidate, so assuring himself of many votes.
2. Labour's support for India at the time of the 1971 Indo-Pakistan war and especially Mr Harold Wilson's statement in favour of India hardened the Pakistani attitudes towards Labour. 'The Pakistanis, who normally support Labour, had been upset by Mr Harold Wilson's allegiance to India during the Indo-Pakistan war' reported the *Guardian*.[15] This was exploited by the Liberals to gain more support.
3. The Liberal candidate and the then party leader, Mr Jeremy Thorpe, who personally addressed and met the Pakistanis, explained their record and attitude towards Pakistanis and also promised to help in the release of the POWs held by India at that time. Mr Thorpe promised that, if successful, Alderman Smith would be sent to see the High Commissioners of India and Bangladesh, and the Ambassafor of Pakistan; he could fly to Asia for this purpose during the next Parliamentary recess. (However, Mr Smith did not go to the sub-continent due to health reasons.)
4. Another factor which seems to have contributed to the shift in support was the announcement by Mr Lawrence Cunliffe, the Labour candidate, that if immigrant organizations or individuals

wanted to meet him a meeting could be arranged through Councillor A. H. Chowdry. This arrangement was not liked very much by most Pakistanis. Although Mr Chowdry had been elected with the full support of Pakistani voters, he had apparently lost some of his popularity at the time of the by-election because of Labour's hostile attitude to Pakistan during the Indo-Pakistan war.

5. The President of the Pakistan Welfare Association had contested the local election in May 1972 as a Liberal candidate. Although he had lost the election he still supported the Liberals, together with the members of the Pakistani Welfare Association, whose paid-up membership was claimed to be over 700 at that time with many more adherents. He managed to get the maximum of votes from Pakistanis for the Liberal candidate.
6. The presence of Mr Merrick was a major factor. The Labour candidate kept fairly quiet on the issue of immigration, but the Liberal candidate condemned Mr Merrick's views at meetings with Pakistanis and publicly criticized his placing of agents at the polling stations to challenge the Asians' right to vote.[16] The only group other than the Liberals which condemned Mr Merrick openly was the small but lively Rochdale branch of the International Socialists.

Apart from meetings with Pakistani leaders, the Pakistanis were addressed by representatives from each of the three major parties. Special meetings were held in the local Pakistani cinema. Pakistanis working on night-shift in some factories were also addressed by the three major candidates. All three parties displayed and distributed election material translated into Urdu. Announcements in Urdu and Punjabi were made by loudspeakers with the help of Pakistani supporters, and interpreters were used during the whole election campaign and on election day to overcome communication difficulties, keeping in view the importance of the Pakistani voters in the election. On the other hand, Pakistani associations, in particular the Pakistan Welfare Association, held meetings with Pakistanis to make them aware of the danger of the British Campaign to Stop Immigration in general and for Pakistanis in particular. The Association asked the Pakistanis to support Mr Smith as he was more sympathetic towards their problems. Some Pakistanis were appointed polling agents and duties on a street-by-street basis were assigned to volunteers who made sure that the majority of the Pakistanis voted, a technique very much in use back home which resulted in maximum turn-out.

After a campaign in which one candidate had made a special issue of the immigration question in general and the Rochdale Pakistanis in particular it seemed likely that incidents would occur. These have been widely reported and the following account also draws on private observations.

Mr Merrick, the candidate of the British Campaign to Stop Immigration, appointed polling agents who were entitled to sit in the polling stations. If they suspected that someone had already voted or was trying to vote in someone else's name, they had the right to ask the presiding officer to put two questions to the voter. The questions are laid down in the Parliamentary Election Rules and have to be put exactly in the form given there.

Q1. Are you the person registered in the Register of Parliamentary Electors for this election as follows . . . ?

Q2. Have you already voted here or elsewhere at this election otherwise than as proxy for some other person?

At some polling stations, Mr Merrick's agents objected to all the Asian voters. Most of them could not understand the questions because of their inadequate knowledge of English. This worried Pakistani leaders and the other candidates because the Asian voters were becoming harassed and confused. This was the case paricularly at the Castlemere Street polling station in the Central Ward where queues began to form. The Pakistanis and the Liberal candidate protested against this, and the author was told that this led to an exchange of harsh words between Mr Merrick's supporters and Pakistani leaders. Mr Moore, the Town Clerk, intervened to ease the situation. At the request of the Liberal candidate, he also called the police to protect Pakistanis. The *Rochdale Observer* reported that both the Town Clerk and the Liberal Party leader, Mr Jeremy Thorpe had telephone talks with Home Office officials about the situation. Mr Smith stated after the election that he had himself been harassed by Mr Merrick's supporters; he could not get to his car and was literally manhandled when he asked for police protection for the rest of the day.

Some of the Pakistanis told me that in the evening, when most of the Pakistanis came back from work or were going to work on the night shift they were ready to face any situation whatever the consequences. This change of mood was noticed by Mr Merrick's supporters and they changed their behaviour to some extent. But the overall situation created tension and conflict.

The Liberal candidate won the election with a majority of over 5,000 votes over the Labour candidate. Mr Merrick polled 4,074 votes. This was a surprise for the political parties in a town that had prided itself on its good, even exemplary record of race relations. Mr Thorpe, the Liberal Party leader, speaking at Nottingham just after the election, alleged 'appalling intimidation of immigrant voters at the polling stations', but conceded that 'there was a need for more campaigning by all three parties on race relations.'[17]

On the other hand, Mr Merrick announced after the election results that he and his party would contest the next local elections in Rochdale. Mr Merrick's announcement worried the other political parties—'Act now or racialism will grow' was the headline in the *Rochdale Observer*.[18] Efforts began to be made to ease the situation. At the request of the new MP, Mr Smith, a meeting with the Executive Committee of the Community Relations Council was arranged on 19 November 1972. He offered to help in any way he could and asked the council to work hard, especially among working-class people to create good community relations in the town. As a consequence, the council formed a special sub-committee to formulate policies and take action on these lines. Later on Mr Smith was elected as Honorary Vice-President and Mr Lawrence Cunliffe as executive committee member of the Community Relations Council for the year 1973 to keep in touch with community relations work.

After the election Mr Cyril Smith went to the Pakistani areas to thank the people for their support. It was observed that Pakistanis also felt very proud of their support for Mr Cyril Smith.

This whole set of events changed the attitude of Pakistanis, who were to a certain extent divided before the election. They started a 'movement of unity' because they saw that if they were united they would gain more respect.

3. 1973 Local Elections

Mr Cyril Smith, MP, appointed a committee to advise him on race relations and to take positive steps to create harmonious relations in the town. This committee included representatives from the Pakistan Welfare Association. At its first meeting to which officers from the local Community Relations Council were also invited as observers, the committee mainly reviewed the by-election situation and other aspects of race relations in the town. The new MP also arranged a regular Sunday surgery once a month specifically for his Pakistani constituents. Two Pakistanis from the wards with the highest residential concentration, the Central and Falinge Ward and the Wardleworth and Newbold Ward, were nominated as Liberal candidates for the district council elections. This indicated that Pakistanis were seen not only as voters and vote-gatherers but as capable of being candidates as well. It was also a recognition of Pakistani support for the Liberals.

The Rochdale Anti-Racialist Committee was formed to counteract BCSI propaganda. This was supported mainly by the International Socialist Group, Pakistan People's Party, the Communist Party, Rebel Youth Group, Rank and File Teachers Group, Rochdale's Alternative Paper (RAP), and other trade unions and immigrant organizations and individuals. This Committee arranged public meetings before the county and district elections to expose the BCSI, using such slogans as 'The British Campaign Party's more Tory than the Tories! Racialists do the bosses' dirty work for them! Don't be conned by them . . . It's happened too many times before.'[19]

The local Community Relations Council decided to arrange neighbourhood meetings in order to assess feelings about the 'immigrants' and race relations in the town. Most of those who came to these meetings were found to have misconceptions and inaccurate information about the numbers and socio-cultural background of the immigrants. An interesting point which emerged was that those who expressed negative feelings towards the immigrants were those who had never had any informal contact with them, a fact that supports the view that knowledge about and acquaintance with members of minority groups make for tolerant and friendly attitudes.[20] Meetings of this kind were extremely useful in that they helped race relations workers determine the needs of a particular area and to act accordingly. For example, the Community Relations Council distributed more literature about the background of the immigrants and arranged tea afternoons in some areas to give English people a chance to meet the immigrants informally.

Once the two Pakistanis were nominated as Liberal candidates for the district council election action was taken to mobilize support for them and for the Liberal Party. The Labour Party nominated the sitting Pakistani councillor A. H. Chowdry from another ward where there were not many Asian voters. The Pakistani candidates for the Liberal Party were Dr S. H. Syed, a doctor, and Mr Karim Dad, the President of the Pakistan Welfare Association.

(i) *The Greater Manchester County Elections, 12 April 1973.* There were twelve candidates for the four Rochdale seats: Labour and Conservative each had four candidates, and there were two Liberals, one Communist and one BCSI candidate. Two Labour candidates, one Liberal, and one Conservative were elected.

Rochdale No. 4 Ward was contested by the BCSI candidate, Mr M. Sellors, but was won by the Labour candidate, Mr M. Matthews (Table 36).

Table 36

The results of the 1973 county elections

H. Matthews	(Labour)	3,310
J. A. Kielty	(Lib.)	2,725
J. E. Fletcher	(Cons.)	1,913
M. W. Sellors	(BCSI)	1,740

Mr Sellors was reported as saying that '[his] organization was pleased with its share of the vote. It was an encouraging sign for next month's elections.'[21] The percentage of votes cast for the BCSI had reportedly risen from 8·9 per cent at the time of the by-election to about 18 per cent. As the *Rochdale Observer* commented, Mr M. W. Sellors finished bottom of poll but he was within 200 of the 1,913 votes cast for Councillor Fletcher of the Conservative party.[22] It must, however, be pointed out that the BCSI's 18 per cent share of the vote was for one ward, which covered only part of the constituency. This election result was again taken as a warning signal by the immigrant population in general and Pakistanis in particular and by the three main political parties.

As far as the Pakistanis' participation in this election was concerned the representative of the Pakistan Welfare Association claimed that there had been maximum turn-out mainly in support of Liberal party candidates, not unconnected with the fact that two Pakistanis were nominated by the Liberal party for the district elections. Mr T. Chadwick, the Liberal candidate who was elected for ward No. 3 had a majority of 1,169. This ward included the Central Ward with about 958 Asian voters, mainly Pakistanis (30 per cent of the total electorate), and the Falinge Ward with about 335 (6·7 per cent of the total electorate).[23] This suggests that the Liberal party candidate might have received significant support from Pakistani voters. Pakistanis canvassed for the Liberal candidates during the election campaign. Leaflets in Urdu were distributed and meetings with the Liberal candidates were held to assure them of their support.

(ii) *Metropolitan District Council Election, 10 May 1973*. As far as Pakistanis were concerned informal campaigns for this election had already started. The BCSI nominated four candidates in two wards. As mentioned above the Liberals nominated two Pakistanis in two wards and the Labour Party one Pakistani in another ward. The number of candidates in wards contested by these candidates are given in Table 37.

Table 37

The candidates in the 1973 Rochdale council elections

Deeplish and Brimrod Ward		
Labour	3	
Conservative	3	
BCSI	3	
Liberal	1	
Central and Falinge Ward		
Labour	3	
Liberal	3	(one Pakistani, Dr S. H. Syed)
Communist	1	
BCSI	1	
Newbold and Wardleworth Ward		
Labour	3	
Liberal	3	(one Pakistani, Mr Karim Dad)
Communist	1	
Spotland Ward		
Labour	3	(one Pakistani, Councillor A. H. Chowdry)
Conservative	1	
Liberal	3	

It is interesting to note that out of 31 candidates in these wards there were only four Conservative candidates and in the two wards where Liberals nominated Pakistanis, there was no Conservative candidate at all. One could give the simple explanation that these were the predominantly working-class wards, and the Conservatives did not have much hope of getting enough support to win the seats. It means that in these wards there was a straight fight between Labour and the Liberals. At first the Pakistan People's Party chose in addition Mr P. Qureshy to contest the Central and Falinge Ward as an independent candidate, not realizing that another party was nominating a Pakistani for this ward. But when Dr Syed, the Liberal candidate from the same ward, learned about this, he, together with some other Pakistani leaders, approached the Pakistan People's Party and asked them to drop the idea because it would divide the Pakistani vote and undermine their unity. The author was told by the Pakistan People's Party representatives that they had dropped Mr Qureshy in order to show that the Pakistanis in Rochdale were united and would support a candidate who had been nominated by one of the three main political parties.

Meetings with Pakistanis were held at *Biraderi* level and volunteers came forward to help. Areas were assigned for canvassing and almost every Pakistani was approached. The understanding with the Liberal party workers was that first the Pakistani party workers should approach Pakistanis and white party workers should approach white voters; then at a later stage a combined door-to-door canvassing would follow. This method of campaigning was very much the same as that used during elections in Pakistan.[24] The Pakistani shops and cinemas were used for publicity, mainly in Urdu. Posters were displayed and distributed with pictures of Pakistani candidates and other Liberal candidates. All this helped to mobilize the Pakistani voters and made them take an interest and therefore participate in the election.

Lists were checked at the polling stations by the Pakistani agents and towards the evening those who did not vote were reminded by volunteers to come out and vote. This helped to get a maximum turn-out of Pakistani voters as against white voters.

As a result of the Liberal Party support and Pakistani campaign and unity Dr Syed was elected for the Central and Falinge Ward along with two other Liberals, Mr Cyril Smith, MP, and Mr R. H. Stott, and strong Labour candidates like Mrs M. E. Randle, Chairman of Rochdale Education Committee, were defeated in this ward. The results are given in Table 38. Mr Karim Dad, the Pakistani Liberal candidate for Newbold and Wardleworth Ward was not elected, but he came within approximately 100 votes of the last Labour candidate to be elected, and topped the list of the other Liberal candidates from the same ward. This is also given in Table 38. In Spotland Ward on the other hand, the Pakistani Labour candidate Mr A. H. Chowdry received only 558 votes out of an 5,675 electorate. All three Liberals were elected and no Labour or Conservative candidate got more than five to seven hundred votes.

The election of Dr Syed and the total votes received by the other two Pakistani candidates, Mr K. Dad (Lib) and Mr A. H. Chowdry (Lab), indicated that Pakistanis were being accepted as candidates and not just as voters and vote-gatherers. This augured well for the continuing contact between to two communities. One should not forget that this contact was mainly through the community and *Biraderi* leaders and there was not much contact between individual Pakistanis and white voters. Nevertheless this kind of common participation and co-operative action helps to create more under-

Table 38

The results of the 1973 Rochdale council elections

Central and Falinge Ward				
C. Smith	(Lib.)	1,789		Elected
R. H. Stott	(Lib.)	1,498		Elected
S. H. Syed	(Lib.)	1,280	(Pakistani)	Elected
Mrs M. E. Randle	(Lab.)	1,247		Not elected
P. Holt	(Lab.)	1,130		Not elected
J. Power	(Lab.)	1,067		Not elected
Mrs S. S. Sellors	(BCSI)	536		Not elected
P. J. Atkinson	(Communist)	156		Not elected
Electorate		8,137		
Newbold and Wardleworth Ward				
D. Walker	(Lab.)	1,108		Elected
K. Hernon	(Lab.)	1,072		Elected
G. Howarth	(Lab.)	1,064		Elected
K. Dad	(Lib.)	960	(Pakistani)	Not elected
H. Sunderland	(Lib.)	667		Not elected
C. Watts	(Lib.)	632		Not elected
C. S. Abendstern	(Communist)	76		Not elected
Electorate		7,282		
Spotland Ward				
Robert Scott	(Lib)	1,401		Elected
W. W. Jenkins	(Lib.)	1,308		Elected
N. Smith	(Lib.)	1,261		Elected
J. B. Haslam	(Lab.)	614		Not elected
A. H. Chowdry	(Lab.)	558	(Pakistani)	Not elected
E. F. Smith	(Con.)	475		Not elected
Electorate		5,675		

standing between members of different groups and to reduce hostility. As John E. Horrocks put it, 'essentially the reduction of hostility between groups is achieved by focusing the attention of each group on external, common goals that can be attained by co-operative action.'[25] Participation in elections is one of the areas where co-operation is possible. This is also Gluckman's thesis, namely that in a multiracial society, or one in which there are a number of ethnic minorities, opportunities for co-operative relationships generate cross-cutting ties which contribute to the cohesion of the society and reduce the probability of overt conflict.[26]

4. February and October 1974 General Elections

The Nuffield College Study of the February 1974 election notes that apart from a continued reluctance by electors to support black candidates of any party immigration itself seems to have played little or no part in the results.[27] However, as far as the National Front candidates who contested this election were concerned they made immigration one of their political campaign issues. One of these candidates, contesting the Rochdale seat, made immigrants and immigration one of the main themes of his campaign. The National Front candidate appointed polling agents who again intimidated Pakistani voters by challenging almost every voter.[28]

Both the Labour and Liberal party worked hard to gain Pakistani support. Meetings were held, literature in Urdu was distributed. But it appeared that Pakistanis supported in greater numbers the Liberal candidate, Mr Cyril Smith, who won the election. This was confirmed by Mr Lawrence Cunliffe the Labour candidate in this election, after the results of the election were announced: 'Alderman Smith, in the main, had increased his majority because he got 95 per cent of the immigrant vote.'[29]

Some people believed that Mr Cyril Smith's nationwide popularity and his television and radio broadcasts were also an advantage which contributed towards his increased majority at the February election. I observed that Pakistanis felt proud of their support whenever Mr Smith was on the television or in the news. He also maintained a close contact with Pakistanis, listened to their problems sympathetically at special regular surgeries and attended their social functions. Moreover, Pakistanis were sent to attend the Liberal Party Conference in 1974.

The October election was unique in a number of ways:

(i) It came after the shortest gap of the century between two general elections;
(ii) it had a record number of candidates (2,192);
(iii) there was a record number of voters (40 million);
(iv) and a record number of National Front candidates (90).

The view was expressed in some quarters during the election campaign that the immigrant vote as a whole, especially in some 'marginals'[30] such as Bolton, Gravesend, Preston, Nelson and Colne, Leicester, Nottingham and Bradford West, could be important for the candidates in particular and for the political parties in general. For example, the *Daily Jang* reported that the National Front campaign against the Pakistanis in Bolton had disturbed the atmosphere with its demands for the expulsion of all coloured immigrants and that the Pakistani vote could sway the election results.[31]

The *Morning Star* reported that the immigrant vote was crucial to defeat the Tories. 'Black and Brown people in Britain will play a decisive part in getting Labour back into power on 4th October.'[32] For example there were 16,000 immigrants in Leicester South, a constituency of 72,000 voters and immigrants' (mainly Asians') votes were very important in changing the February majority of 1,766 for the sitting Conservative MP.[33] Similarly, it was reported in the Asian press that the 10 per cent of immigrants living in Gravesend could play a decisive role in the local results, one which was regarded as an indication of results in the country as a whole.[34] This applied also to such places as Preston, Nelson and Colne, Bolton, Keighley and Bradford West. The concentration of immigrants in certain areas of course maximized their voting importance, particularly in the marginal seats where every vote counted.

The other factor which increased the importance of Asian voters in particular was their high turn-out as compared with the rest of the electorate. Dr Le Lohe found in Bradford that the Asian turn-out was always higher than that of the non-Asians.[35] For example, in the 1970 and February 1974 general elections in Bradford Asian turn-out was higher than the non-Asian[36] (see Table 39).

In the October election, it was again confirmed from checks at some polling stations in Bradford West and Rochdale that on average the Asian turn-out was higher than non-Asian: 64·6 per cent as against 57·3 per cent and 57·7 per cent against 54·6 per cent respectively. The high turn-out of Asians means that it is to the advantage of the political parties to take an interest in Asian voters.

Table 39

Asian and non-Asian percentage turn-out in the two General Elections

Polling Station	*Asian*		*Non-Asian*	
	1970 %	*1974 %*	*1970 %*	*1974 %*
KB	69·7	71·1	55·9	71·6
KD	71·9	83·2	48·0	61·5
LF	66·8	76·4	57·4	61·7
LG(BH)	67·2	75·3	46·3	53·8
LH(GF)	60·0	82·1	46·7	37·6
LD	—	70·5	—	60·7
KC	—	72·9	—	67·6

If we look at the history of New Commonwealth immigration and its relation to political issues in the elections, in 1964 no party thought the immigrant vote worth bidding for with the concomitant risk of losing native support. It was during the 1964 General Election, and in Smethwick in particular, that colour and race emerged as major factors in British politics. Ten years later, in 1974 all three main political parties did their best to win immigrant support in general, but also Asian votes in particular. The main concern of the candidates during the election campaign was with national issues such as inflation, the European Economic Community, etc. Most also had to adapt their campaign to some degree to take account of local conditions and issues. In the areas of high immigrant concentration such issues concerned immigration and race relations. This applied in particular to areas where there was a National Front candidate who was making a special issue out of immigration and race; one such area was Rochdale.

In their manifestos, the three main political parties did not give top priority to the question of immigration and race relations; the Conservative party was the only one which gave it a separate heading,[37] the Labour party mentioned that it would strengthen legislation protecting minorities and reform the law of nationality and citizenship[38] while the Liberal party issued a separate document *Immigration and Race Relations* which outlined its policy on the issue.[39]

During the election campaign the parties in general and candidates in particular sought to win the support of Asian voters. Certain policies regarding immigrants introduced by the Labour party during the six preceding months were to the advantage of Labour candidates. These were: reuniting the Ugandan Asian families, amnesty for those who were trapped by the retrospective clause of the Immigration Act of 1971, and equal rights for non-resident husbands and fiancés of women in this country.

At the time of this election all three party leaders sent messages which were published in the main Asian newspapers. These messages outlined their policies with regard to immigrants in general and Asians in particular. Many candidates, from areas of high concentration, also used the Asian press during the election campaign to win the support of Asian voters by listing what they and their parties had done for the Asians in their area and nationally. Furthermore, the Labour Home Secretary, Mr Roy Jenkins, the Conservative Shadow Home Secretary, Sir Keith Joseph, and Mr Cyril Smith, representing the Liberal Party, were interviewed on the BBC Television programme *Nai Zindagi Naya Jeevan* to explain the policies of their parties to Asian viewers.[40] This interview helped to clarify the present and future policies of the parties with regard to Asians in this country. All three spokesmen showed an awareness of the importance of the Asian vote.

As far as the participation of Rochdale Pakistanis in this election was concerned, full participation was urged by their leaders. There were 3,047 Asian voters (mainly Pakistanis) on the Electoral Register.[41]

As mentioned above, the Liberals had previously won Pakistani support in elections following the Parliamentary by-election of October 1972. The main rivalry was between Liberals and Labour and there was no boundary change. The Labour party had chosen a new candidate this time, Mr J. Connell. Mr R. Young and Mr W. Sellors were the other two candidates contesting for the Conservatives and the National Front respectively.

Mr Smith again appeared to be the Pakistanis' favourite. He maintained a regular contact with them through his surgery and helped many Pakistanis with their individual problems. The Labour candidate gained some support from Pakistanis due to the last six months' policies of the Labour government which appealed to them.[42] Councillor Bashir Maan from Glasgow, one of the Pakistani community national leaders, came to Rochdale and toured the local Pakistani community with the Labour candidate, Mr Connell. He said that the Labour party was the party most sympathetic to the problems of immigrants and one which insisted on the need for good community relations. Councillor Mann's presence might have contributed to the increase in support for the Labour candidate. The survey of 97 Pakistani voters shows that on the basis of recalled behaviour there was a net swing of about 6 per cent from Liberal to Labour in Rochdale.

Taking into consideration the importance of the Pakistani voters meetings were held with them in their houses at *Biraderi* level,[43] in cafés, cinemas, and in some cases at their places of work, particularly on the night shift. The Liberal candidate was quite aware of the community approach and used it. This approach was appreciated by the Pakistanis as offering a more informal and personal basis. Once again the election material was translated and distributed in Urdu. Pakistanis were encouraged to participate in the election campaign itself.

The National Front candidate in Rochdale and his supporters distributed and displayed literature which contained information about immigration and immigrants and stated the Front's policies toward immigrants. Posters such as 'Send them back, National

Front favours repatriation of all coloured immigrants', etc., were displayed. The National Front propaganda was counteracted by the distribution of a number of leaflets by the International Socialists and Rochdale Anti-Racialist Committee which exposed their fascist policies. One leaflet read: 'Smash Fascism, stop the National Front now.' The National Front propaganda, however, made Pakistanis take an active part in the election campaign.

On election day the National Front intimidated and harassed the Pakistani voters as they had done in previous elections since the 1972 by-election. Their agents at the Castlemere School polling station challenged almost every Pakistani voter in the afternoon. It was observed that this created panic, and the result was that a number of the Pakistani voters, particularly women, did not come to vote at all after hearing about the National Front's bullying tactics. This reduced the Pakistani participation, as one of the correspondents wrote in the *Rochdale Observer*, 'Fortunately, the police who were present and the Presiding Officer prevented the National Front members from physically assaulting or abusing voters, but they insisted on their democratic right "to challenge all immigrant voters" resulting no doubt in the word being passed around that anyone wishing to avoid being involved in an incident would be safer staying away from the polls.'[44] I observed that some supporters of the National Front candidate were making obscene remarks about the Pakistanis when they entered the polling station and at one stage the police had to interfere. The Acting Returning Officer confirmed that 'a very high percentage, approaching 100 per cent were challenged at Castlemere.' Mentioning the difficulties, he said that it took each voter five minutes longer than is normal to vote at Castlemere.[45] Apart from the Pakistanis the Liberal and Labour party workers were upset too, as Pakistanis were being forced into a situation where they were indirectly being deprived of their voting rights. It seemed that no one could stop the use of such tactics as long as they were legal. The Labour and Liberal party workers felt that there should be some sort of legislation to prevent this from happening.

The research in Rochdale and elsewhere has shown that Asian turn out is always higher than non-Asian in elections.[46] To measure the turn-out of Asians (mainly Pakistanis) against other groups at this election, three polling stations in the areas of concentration of Pakistanis were observed throughout the polling time. The polling numbers and ethnicity of those who voted were recorded. 2,501 people gave their electoral numbers as against 2,543 voters shown in the official returns, of these 2,501, 910 were noted as being

Asians, thus we had the electoral number of (and in the case of Asians ethnic origin) 98·3 per cent of persons voting. Inspection of the register showed that 1,585 of the 4,488 electors had Asian names. Since 910 of the voters were Asians, the turn-out rate amongst the Asians could be calculated as 57 per cent as Table 40 shows. Including the 11 Afro-Caribbeans observed to vote with the rest of the population, the non-Asian turn-out level was calculated to be 54·6 per cent.

Table 40

Asian and non-Asian turn-out in selected polling stations, October 1974 General Election

Rochdale	*Asian*			*Non-Asian*		
Polling Station	*Electors*	*Voters*	*%*	*Electors*	*Voters*	*%*
JA	316	230	72·8	397	241	60·7
JB	432	261	61·8	654	477	72·9
IB	837	419	50·1	1,867	873	46·9
Total	1,585	910	57·7	2,918	1,591	54·6

Thus the Asians (mainly Pakistanis) had a higher turn-out rate than other people in the area, but the gap between the two was not large. The results are somewhat at variance with the findings concerning local elections in the same area in 1968,[47] when the gap was considerably greater and overall turn-out higher than the level in this Parliamentary election.

It appears that Pakistani participation in this October election although marginally greater than that of other people, was lower than might have been expected from previous elections. The explanation for this as mentioned above is that many Pakistanis may have been deterred from going to the polls by the rather intimidating prospect of being challenged by polling agents of the National Front candiate. I came across some Pakistanis on election day and during the later survey, who did not go to vote for this reason, particularly women, although they had wanted to vote. This was confirmed by the Pakistani leaders (mainly Pakistan Welfare Association representatives) who were also acting as polling agents for the Liberal candidate. One of them said, ‘This is too much, our people cannot vote properly and they want to participate but feel frustrated when this intimidation takes place. Government should do something when this intimidation takes place, otherwise frustration may lead to aggression which will be no good for good community relations.' Another Pakistani felt that 'each time harassment of Pakistani voters has occurred in Rochdale, there has been some reaction expressed by our organizations, the interested political parties and some individuals who have written letters to the *Rochdale Observer* but it has never gone further than this, we feel that keeping in mind the increasing movement of the National Front and the repetition of the intimidation and harassment of Pakistanis at polling stations, there should be government action at a national level.' These comments give an indication of the feelings of Pakistanis on the issue of intimidation and harassment at the polling stations by the National Front agents. Some of them relate it to the fact of the 'discrimination against coloured voters because they are easily identifiable', as one respondent put it.

Mr Cyril Smith, the Liberal candidate won the election but reduced his majority from five thousand to about three thousand. This was the result:

Table 41

The results of the October 1974 General Election for Rochdale

C. Smith	(Lib.)	20,092
J. Connel	(Lab.)	17,339
R. Young	(Con.)	7,740
M. W. Sellors	(Nat. Front)	1,927
Liberal majority		2,753
Total electorate		67,014

The voting pattern of Pakistanis, both observed and found in the survey after the election, shows that the majority of them voted for Mr Smith (Liberal). Out of a sample of 97 Pakistani voters 17 respondents preferred not to reveal their preference, but 80 did give their party choice. Forty of these voted Liberal, 3 voted Conservative and 37 voted Labour. In the same survey on the basis of recalled behaviour about 19 February 1974 voting behaviour there were indications of a net swing of about 6 per cent from Liberal to Labour in October. It must be added that these figures should not be regarded as accurate not only for statistical reasons but also because this swing, calculated from a sample of voters' known allegiance, does not take into account possible differential changes in abstention. But it gives us an indication of movement between the two main political parties in a contest.

The possible explanation for this swing in Rochdale is Labour's local efforts to recapture the Pakistani vote. This was helped by the actions of the new Labour Government mentioned above. There was positive evidence that the new Government was more sympathetic than the one which it succeeded and this seemed to make Labour candidates acceptable, where previously they had not been regarded as such. Mr Maan's visit to Rochdale to help the local Labour candidate might have had some effect in gaining support from the Pakistanis.

The Pattern of Participation

To sum up; the pattern of voting in the 1974 General Election makes it clear that the complete ascendancy of the Labour and Conservative parties at Westminster is no longer assured. In the present politico-economic situation of the country, minor parties could well capture many more votes in future elections. In these elections the importance of ethnic minority groups' participation and of groups like the Welsh and the Scots as voters has increased. The Community Relations Commission's study of the October 1974 election, referred to above, shows that the ethnic minorities played a significant part in determining the outcome of the election.[48] This was due to the new Labour government's attractive policies for immigrants during the preceding six months. However, there is little evidence available that the Labour party has made any serious effort to recruit the ethnic minority members, still less adopt them as candidates. However, the evidence which I have presented above shows that the Labour party or any party will find it difficult to hold on to its immigrant vote. As compared with the early 1960s, political parties and candidates were able, in the early 1970s, to bid for immigrant votes openly without the fear of losing native support.

The mobilization of Pakistani voters in these elections in fact constituted an 'ethnic vote' situation. The entire situation also fits to some extent into the sociological theories of conflict, and in particular, the theories of Georg Simmel. His main concern was with the functions, rather than dysfunctions, of social conflict, that is to say with those consequences of social conflict which increase rather than decrease adaptation or adjustment of particular social relationships or groups. Conflict may contribute to interpersonal relations, and to the maintenance of group boundaries, and may prevent the withdrawal of members from a group. On the other hand, certain forms of conflict are destructive of group unity and may also lead to the disintegration of specific structures. The proposition that 'conflict with out-groups increases internal cohesion'[49] was demonstrated where the Pakistanis, having been threatened by anti-immigrant candidates, rallied together forgetting petty differences, participated actively in the elections and committed themselves to greater unity in the future. So the Pakistani response appears to fit the Simmel thesis about the functions of social conflict.

Their response shows that they have become more active in mobilizing support, organizing campaigns and in participating in the elections along ethnic lines. This means that to take more interest in Pakistanis and other immigrant groups is to the advantage of the political parties. Interest taken by the Liberals in Pakistanis in Rochdale, it appears, made Pakistanis both diligent voters and devoted Liberals. This also shows that the political parties cannot rely on immigrants for their support without giving something in return. As in all countries with an immigrant population, the concentration of new arrivals in certain areas of Britain has maximized their statistical significance as voters.

As far as the Pakistanis are concerned their mobilization as voters takes place through their *Biraderi* and friendship networks and formal leaders, following a pattern they are used to back home. In the British situation the need for this method of organization is increased because of the language problem. Therefore even though Pakistanis do participate in elections this does not bring them out of their incapsulation because most of the participation takes place on the ethnic community level and there does not appear to be much interpersonal contact.

9. Religion as a Binding Force

Background

One factor which affects the Pakistanis' relationships with other groups is their religion, Islam. A person who believes in Islam is a 'Muslim'. To a Muslim, Islam is a way of life, governing not only religious practice and morality but social relationships, marriage, divorce, kinship, economic and political relations. There are five pillars of Islam, or of Islamic belief. First, the declaration of faith (*Kalimah*): 'There is only one God and Muhammad is his Prophet'; second, five daily prayers; third, *Zakat*, alms-giving to the poor (2½ per cent of a man's yearly income); fourth, fasting during the month of *Ramazan*; and fifth, making the pilgrimage to Mecca. Discharge of these duties varies from one person to another and the degree of conformity according to the facilities and pressures on him, but the person who believes in these five imperatives of Islam is treated as a Muslim, for all practical purposes.

Islam has been codified into five categories of practical rules. These include: essential duties, acts recommended but not essential, acts lawfully indifferent, acts which are disapproved but not forbidden and acts forbidden with a punishment attached to them. In the first category come the five pillars of Islam mentioned above. The major offences, among others, include drinking spirits, using intoxicants, disobeying one's parents, eating the flesh of swine or animals that have died a natural death, delaying the time of prayers without proper excuse, breaking the fast in *Ramazan*, eating non-*Halal* meat and drawing interest on loans. The rules of Islam apply equally whether in Mecca, Pakistan or Rochdale.

A Pakistani practising his religion in Britain is in a different situation from his co-religionist in the villages or even urban areas in Pakistan. There, daily life is regulated in such a way that it fits in with religious observance, for instance, with regard to the timing of five daily prayers, and to observe the month of *Ramazan* special arrangements are made. In Britain a Muslim has to make an extra effort to comply with this religious routine. For instance, a factory worker might face difficulty in having a few minutes off to say his prayers.[1] Usually there are pressures from kin and the Pakistani community to conform, but for those who do not want to conform it is easier to find excuses. It is not my intention in this chapter to discuss how many Muslims in Rochdale conform or do not conform but to outline how religion plays a part in binding Pakistanis together and how mosques and religious instruction centres and religious organizations attempt to preserve traditional values and hand them on to the next generation.

One point which I would like to make here is that Pakistanis (particularly those who emigrated from India at the time of Partition in 1947) have had experience of being a religious minority in British India. This means that being a religious minority is nothing new to them. The experiences back home which led to Partition and the growth of nationalistic feelings are very relevant to their attitudes and behaviour in a foreign non-Muslim country, particularly so in their attitude to 'out-groups' and their struggle for the preservation of their values. Muslims in Britain usually quote the example of Jews in this country: as one respondent put it, 'If they [the Jews] can preserve their religion and culture and be successful in life why can't we do it.' It is interesting to note that while there is a lot of covert hostility by Muslims towards Jews their success in preserving their religion and culture is held up as an example by many Muslims in this country.

Islamic injunctions are apparent in many different spheres of life such as eating habits, dress, the relationships between the sexes and marriage, and obligations to relatives and other Muslim 'brothers'. The whole set of morals which is obligatory for Muslims is derived from the Quran and *Hadith*. 'For Muslims society exists so that men may live correctly and have a proper relationship with God in the ways revealed by the Prophet and the interpreters of his revelation as embodied in the religious law of Sharia.'[2] Pakistanis were used to this way of life in Pakistan, where every action was applauded or deplored in the light of Islam. When they migrated to Britain they were usually reminded by their *Biraderi* elders of the responsibilities they had as Muslims, particularly living in a non-Muslim country. Some of my respondents told me that they were given a copy of the Quran, a prayer mat and other religious books at the time of their departure. These things remind them about their religion constantly.

Usually when relatives or friends visit Pakistan, they are asked how far those in Britain are observing their religious duties. During my visit to the relatives of my informants, I was asked in particular about what facilities there were to practise religion. Several questions were asked about their relatives and especially about the children. One of their major worries centred on whether their relatives were fulfilling their religious obligations. One relative expressed it as follows, 'If they [Pakistanis in Britain] have to forget Islam and other obligations, particularly the transfer of religious knowledge to their children, then there is no use of such an economic gain, I would rather eat little and have few amenities in life but not sacrifice my religion, which is my way of life.' This attitude shows the importance villagers attach to their religion.

Religious Facilities in the Town

In Rochdale in 1975 there were two Mosques,[3] four centres for religious instruction and three religious organizations which ran different activities in this field. The two Mosques were used for the daily prayers and *Imams* also gave religious instruction to children, mainly in the evenings or on weekends. Mosques were also used for Friday afternoon prayers when most of the Muslims made an effort to attend. Those who worked on night shift got up early to participate. This way the Mosque served as a meeting place where the priest gave a lecture (sermon) on Islam and reminded Pakistanis of their obligations in terms of religion, family, country and other Muslims. Those attending were also reminded that they were living in a Western progressive society and that it was very easy for them to forget their religious obligations. In one of these Friday lectures the *Imam* explained the significance of teaching children religion as well as Urdu: 'To teach your children religion is a must but teaching them Urdu should be your priority as well. The reason for this is that if they know only English and can read Arabic but not Urdu, they will not be able to transmit this to the next generation properly. On the other hand, learning Urdu is important to communicate with other relatives and fellow countrymen in Pakistan. Without this they will not have patriotic feelings and will be misfits in Pakistani society.'

These Mosques are also used for meetings held by the Mosque societies, usually to listen to religious leaders visiting Britain from Pakistan for this purpose. The Union of Muslim Organizations in UK, a national body, also organizes religious meetings at the local level to explain to Muslims the significance of practising Islam in a foreign country. This body is also concerned with the religious needs of second-generation Muslims in this country, and is helping local Muslim organizations to start religious instruction classes.[4] Pakistanis also use the Mosque as a meeting point where they greet each other at least at Friday prayers if they do not meet frequently during the rest of the week.

Two big religious occasions which provide an opportunity to meet other Muslims are *Eid-ul-Fitre* which falls at the end of the month of *Ramazan* and *Eid-ul-Azha*, celebrated the day following the Pilgrimage at Mecca.[5] Pakistanis usually hired one or two public halls to say prayers at the time of these *Eids* and Mosques were used by women, who normally pray at home, to say their *Eid* prayers. Almost all my respondents attended *Eid* prayers.

Four centres which were run by the Mosque societies provided facilities for religious and Urdu instruction for children along with two Mosques. The estimated number of students in these centres and Mosques in 1975 is shown in Table 42. It must be noted that these numbers fluctuate: for instance, during holidays the attendance is usually highest. During the winter as it gets dark early few students attend. Figures in the table show that the religious instruction and Urdu teaching are taken seriously.

Table 42
Estimated number of students attending mosques and religious instruction centres in 1975

Centre or Mosque	*No. of students*	*No. of instructors*
Mosque I	150	2 (One *Imam*)
Mosque II	200	3 (One *Imam*)
Centre I	80	1
Centre II	100	1
Centre III	75	1
Centre IV	50	1
	655	9

Note: Figures were provided by two representatives of the two Mosque societies

Religious Leaders

The religious leader in this situation is the *Imam* or other religious *Ulmas* who do not have formal status but are effective in mobilizing support among Pakistanis. The *Imam* commands the respect of the followers of Islam and calls for active interest in religious issues by relating them to Islamic teachings. His role is largely of an intra-ethnic nature but there are times when these leaders act in inter-ethnic situations as well. For instance, an inter-faith dialogue was organized by the local Community Relations Council to discuss matters of common interest to Muslims, Christians and other religious groups in the area.

These religious leaders are mainly interested in the preservation of the Pakistani community and its religious and traditional norms and values. On religious issues they are instrumental in enlisting the backing of the community, and the formal leaders usually lend their support to them or act on their guidance.

Religious Organizations

There were three religious organizations[6] in Rochdale in 1975, of which the two Mosque societies ran the Mosques and the religious instruction centres. They also arranged meetings for visiting religious speakers. The big religious occasions were and still are: the celebration of the month of *Ramazan*, when special arrangements are made for the late evening prayers and the two *Eid* prayers. The birth of Prophet Muhammad (peace be upon him) was also celebrated, usually by a public meeting to which a guest religious leader was invited to give a lecture on the life of the Prophet. The meeting, however, did not have exactly the same form every year.

The Rochdale Muslim Society, dominated by doctors, had only a few members but all were educated ones. They usually met in each other's homes whenever needed to discuss policies in terms of religious activities. The society was concerned with the wider religious issues, for instance it tried to get *Halal* meat for the Muslims in the hospitals and dealt with the question of school uniform for Pakistani girls. It also negotiated the purchase of a piece of land for the new Mosque, from the local authority, and the Secretary of the society was the Chairman of the Steering Committee for the new Mosque which drew membership from all the Pakistani organizations and included some influential individuals. The role of this committee was to discuss the plan of the new Mosque, to raise funds and supervise the construction.

It was understood that whenever large sums of money were needed the members of this society, who were doctors and other professionals, could convince and collect money quickly because of their contacts with Pakistanis through their occupations and influence. For instance, the society arranged a charity dinner to raise funds to provide a cardiac care ambulance for the Birch Hill Hospital, Rochdale.[7] I was told that this was done as a sign of goodwill from the Pakistani community and 'an act which we as Muslims should do'.

The officials of the society were usually regarded as spokesmen of Pakistanis on religious matters. The Inter-Faith Conference arranged by the Community Relations Council was supported by the Muslim Society. A large number of Pakistanis from the town attended the conference at the request of the society. The conference had two speakers, one Muslim and one Christian, and lectures were followed by group discussions. The society also negotiated the question of dress for Muslim girls in the schools, as mentioned above, and persuaded at least one headmaster of a senior school to allow children time off to say Friday prayers.

One aspect which these representatives of the religious organizations made clear to me was that while they would co-operate with other Pakistani organizations on matters of national and religious interest they would not take part where the interests clashed within the community over leadership or power struggles. One of the Mosque societies, however, became involved in the leadership struggle over the issue of the *Imam*. The conflict was interpreted in some quarters of the community as a conflict between Punjabis and Mirpuris. The incident is recounted in some detail below, to illustrate the need for the religious organizations to keep aloof from internal power struggles.

The Golden Mosque Society drew its membership from both Punjabis and Mirpuris. The Executive Committee usually reflected the strength of both groups. Customarily if the President was a Punjabi the Secretary was a Mirpuri and vice versa. In the society's 1973 elections a Punjabi became President and a Mirpuri the Secretary. The *Imam* was a Punjabi also. In the meantime a Mirpuri was appointed to one of the religious teaching centres in the Wardleworth area to teach children Urdu and Arabic. I observed that there was a move afoot to replace the *Imam* of the Mosque with this man.

The differences between the Mirpuri Executive Committee members and the *Imam* became more evident when he was accused of helping the Punjabi candidates in the society's 1974 elections. The Mirpuris exploited this accusation and asked the committee to dismiss the *Imam*. The members of the Rochdale Muslim Society and the then Pakistani Councillor, Dr S. H. Syed, were invited to conduct the elections and investigate the charges. There was a lot of ill-feeling and at one stage it almost came to blows. There were accusations and counter-accusations. The election did not take place because the Mirpuris walked out in protest. Another election date was fixed, and a lot of independent negotiations took place. Mirpuri leaders from other areas were invited to deal with the deadlock, because unity was needed for building the new Mosque. Mirpuris claimed that they themselves did not have any quarrel with the Punjabis, it was just the *Imam* who was responsible. But there were obvious differences between the leaders of both sides, based on self-interest. By the next elections, some Punjabis were so weary of the situation that they did not take part and the majority elected on to the Executive were Mirpuris. A few days after the election the Executive asked the *Imam* to leave and he in turn told this to some of his Punjabi followers who advised him not to comply. It was reported that five Mirpuris went to the Mosque at midday a few days later and pushed the *Imam* out and locked the Mosque. The news spread among the Punjabis like wildfire and meetings were held to discuss what action to take. The matter was reported to the police who invited the Community Relations Council to solve the problem which could lead to serious conflict.

In the end the Punjabis decided not to reinstall the *Imam* to the Mosque, but instead took the case to the county court. A decision was given advising both parties to reach an agreement. The whole case affected the unity which was needed to build, and get concessions from the Local Authority, for the new *Jamia* Mosque. After negotiations a basis of common interest was established but the incident left some bad feeling at least between the leaders on both sides in this dispute. The conflict was clearly a leadership issue, but based on grievances relating to regional identity in which the *Imam* was used as an excuse. Later the Punjabi group bought a new building and started a Mosque and religious education centre and the *Imam* was asked to look after it.

It must be added that the appointment of an *Imam* in this country usually depends on the wishes of the Mosque societies which makes the *Imam* dependent on leaders and, therefore, less powerful. In contrast, in Pakistan *Imams* are usually appointed permanently and have more authority in community affairs. On the other hand the *Imam* in Pakistan is part of the local community while in Britain all people do not come from one area and the *Imam* could become a target of regional divisions as the above incident illustrates.

The leaders of these societies were mostly educated Pakistanis with a conservative outlook. The activities mainly were intra-ethnic. Except for the Muslim Society which had few members, elections in the other societies took place regularly. There were active volunteers to collect membership fees and contributions to funds from Pakistani shops and in factories. The salaries of the *Imams* and other instructors and the maintenance of the Mosques were met from these funds. Balance sheets were displayed in the Mosques and Pakistani shops at regular intervals. Similarly announcements of the activities of these societies were made through the Pakistani shops. Religious books and other literature were also sold by some Pakistani shopkeepers on behalf of these societies.

There was no evidence of Pakistani women's involvement in any of these societies. The only time women took part was on religious occasions such as *Eids* or the birthday of Prophet Muhammad. This was in accordance with the pattern which exists in Pakistan.

Pakistani Women's Situation

Muslims face special difficulties arising from certain rules of social behaviour laid down by their religion. To preserve traditional customs like *Purdah* can be very difficult. For instance, the majority of Muslims do not allow their wives and daughters to work or have contact with the outside world. Apart from veiling in the traditional sense, back home *Purdah* also refers to restrictions on the physical movement of Pakistani women. This means that except from close relatives women keep other men at a distance. They do not normally go out of the house without their husbands unless it is absolutely essential. In some cases they do not leave their house at all except in the company of their husbands. Those who are educated and 'Westernized' are more liberal in this sense as are upper-class women in Pakistan. Middle-class people are more conservative in their outlook as far as *Purdah* is concerned. Lower-class women in Pakistan go out to work in the fields but usually in sex-segregated groups which still comply with the rules of *Purdah*. In Britain there is more liberty. My respondents felt that according to their religion women's place was in the home. Therefore, they felt that women must observe *Purdah* with regard to all men not related to them, and particularly to other Pakistani men. Their argument was that Pakistanis were in Britain to work and did not wish to change their culture. In Pakistan there is usually a lot of *Biraderi* pressure to conform and the kinship—friendship networks established in Rochdale act in the same way in terms of social control.

When girls reach puberty, they are discouraged from going out to work. Those 23 women who worked in the factories were working in all-women work forces, and a close male relative was usually to be found working in the same firm. All but two were working in three mills. They mainly came from *Kammi*, artisan classes in Pakistan. For a middle-class Pakistani it is demeaning to send his wife or daughter out to work.[8] This unwillingness of Pakistanis in Britain to permit women to take up employment outside the home is not unique. Other Muslim groups such as Turks in Germany and North Africans in France who came to Western Europe a decade or more ago, behave in the same way.

Women also find it difficult to participate in literacy and language courses, because they are not allowed to leave their homes and to participate in any kind of social life.[9] This increases the need for a meeting place for Pakistani women. A home tutoring scheme to teach English to Pakistani women at home on one-to-one basis was started by the local Community Relations Council to overcome these difficulties. Some respondents told me that although it was useful for their women to learn English there was no real need as they would be going back to Pakistan (women feel more strongly about going back as they miss their relatives rather more than the men). In addition the men feared that these English ladies might teach their women about liberty and other permissive ideas in Western society which would threaten men's authority over women. This attitude, I was told, created difficulties in finding enough Pakistani women willing to learn English with the permission of their husbands. No doubt, all this leads to the incapsulation of women.

Attitude of the Parents

Pakistani parents felt it was very important for their children to obtain religious instruction, and there was a lot of parental co-operation in running the religious instruction centres. Part-time instructors were hired and four houses were used for this purpose. Two of these were rented, one was owned by the Mosque Society and one was the office of the Pakistan Welfare Association (part of the house was used for this activity). As mentioned above, children attended after school hours for one to two hours, and longer over the weekend.

At home mothers also play a very important role in transmitting religious beliefs and values to their children by teaching them the Quran (if they are educated) and telling them stories related to Islam. Children also learn prayers from their mothers at least by imitating when they pray. One can see a child of two years sitting with his father or mother, bowing himself on the prayer mat in submission to God. This becomes the routine and slowly children learn in the home environment about religious and moral values.

The parents, and their relatives in Pakistan, were worried about the British co-educational system[10] and the permissive atmosphere which was seen as a threat both to morals and to Muslim (Pakistani) culture. It was normal therefore to express the need for extra care. One of the respondents explained, 'I regret bringing my children to this country, because with television and the school situation, it is very difficult to keep control. I make sure that my children go straight to school from home, and return straight home from school. They also go for religious instruction. But how could we stop what they learn and see? I brought them here so that they could get a good education but schools do not have any control. I have a feeling that they would be spoiled irrespective of our precautionary measures, as some situations are out of our control; that is why I am seriously thinking of taking them back to Pakistan before they are too old.' This feeling was shared by other Pakistanis as well.

Mr M. R., a night-shift worker, whose family was still in Pakistan, related the lack of parents' attention to children to night-shift work. He explained, 'If we forget Islam and Pakistan, as this is happening with some families who do not take a keen interest in their children, it will be a disaster. Those who work on the night shift get less time to spend with their children. When my family comes I will not work on night shift and I will spend more time with my family.' He also advocated that the Pakistani community as a whole should act as a pressure group and keep Western elements out of the young generation, giving them religious and Urdu instruction and telling them what is moral and what is immoral. Another respondent suggested, 'I would like to see the children getting education but having no social mixing with British people at individual level.'

These examples illustrate why parents want their children to learn about the religious and cultural values in which they themselves were brought up and the effort they as parents and as a community are making in order to preserve and transmit these values. Those who were not discharging their parental duties properly were treated as irresponsible. As one doctor argued, 'Long hours and night-shift work affect family life and control and looking after the children. In this country, to bring up your children you need extra care as there is no control in the schools like you have in Pakistan.' Dr I. N. was of the view that the community leaders should bring the consequences of this lack of interest to parents' notice. He himself spent a good deal of time with his two daughters who went to school. They used to go to a Mosque to receive religious education in all-girl classes in the evening. Since they had moved to the suburb they only went over at weekends and during holidays and recited the Quran at home with the help of their mother on other days.

Pakistanis considered the work of the religious organizations of immense importance in preserving the religion and moral values, transmitting them to the next generation and binding Pakistanis together. One respondent said, 'Under the circumstances these organizations were doing a very good job. People should not expect miracles, it takes time to adjust in the new situation and provide facilities but the basic responsibilities lie with Pakistani parents.' Religion is one of the most important areas of agreement, on matters of belief, and where the opportunity for united action does exist.[11]

The attitudes mentioned above show that the first-generation migrants see themselves as guardians of their Muslim culture in this country. One respondent told me that he spent two hours daily teaching his children Urdu and Arabic. He worked in public transport and admitted that seeing how English children behaved increased his worry about his own children. As a consequence he usually declined overtime and gave preference safeguarding his children's future.

Pakistanis in Rochdale contribute generously towards religious activities. Apart from collections through Pakistani shops and some work places, gatherings at Friday prayers and *Eid* prayers provide additional opportunities to raise money for these activities. I was told by the people who ran these activities that there was adequate financial support and they were thinking of expanding them. One area in which they were planning to take some action was in providing a meeting place for Pakistani women.

The Pattern: A Binding Force

This type of organized religious activities provides an opportunity for the cultural awareness of the members and binds the ethnic group together. This pattern is not peculiar to Pakistanis. Jews have used their synagogues as a major institution for identification with Judaism. Poles in Britain belong formally to separate Polish Roman Catholic parishes. The Irish in Britain follow the Roman Catholic Church and this has played an important part in preserving Irish tradition among the immigrants.[12]

The pattern of the religious activities in the community seemed to maintain a separate Pakistani cultural existence in Rochdale.[13] As religion is the whole way of life so it affects individual social relationships across the ethnic boundaries thereby leading to Pakistanis' incapsulation. If you can keep your distance and avoid personal relationships, and if you are a good Muslim in a foreign land, it is appreciated greatly by the kinship—friendship groups and by the Pakistani community at large, and also by relatives back home.

Some of the religious activities of Pakistanis are seen by the indigenous community as alien, due to differences in outlook and behaviour. Such behaviour sometimes appears as the cause of conflict with indigenous people. Problems relating to Pakistanis have arisen in terms of worship and burial facilities[14] and in connection with dress, habits of hygiene and eating habits.

The aim of the efforts made by the religious leaders and organizations seemed to be to stress the values of Islam to Pakistanis and to emphasize the importance of its practice, continuance and transmission to the next generation as it regulates the whole way of life. The majority of the first generation seemed to be more committed to religious allegiance and observance, and therefore more orthodox in response to 'Western' values. Whether the second-generation Pakistanis will continue to behave in an orthodox way will need investigation in the future.

10. The Structure of Leadership and Ethnic Organizations

Introduction

I have outlined above how *Biraderi* networks continue to remain a source of security by satisfying primary contacts and needs, and how they play their part in the whole way of life of Pakistanis in Britain. I have also discussed how residential segregation, ethnic community and ethnic activities play an important role in reinforcing the traditional links and cultural values. In this chapter I shall focus on the Pakistani ethnic organizations in order to determine their significance and role in the process of adaptation, as channels of communication; as culture-sustaining agents and as buffers. I shall deal, in addition, with activities relating to the intra- and the inter-ethnic relationships which involve the leadership of these organizations.

Pakistani Leadership and the Wider Context

Leadership in the ethnic community is as important to study as the areas of kinship, employment and housing. The problem here is what resources leaders have in different situations and how these are being used. My assumption is that ethnicity has social significance in structuring wider authority relationships between groups in Britain and is significant not only for the patterning of authority relations within a given group. The question is what are the conditions under which ethnicity becomes socially significant and gains relevance for structuring inter-ethnic authority relations.[1]

Through their ethnic organizations the leaders might find ways of promoting the integration of their community into British society by helping individual Pakistanis to understand British institutions and by providing community facilities for this purpose. These ethnic organizations might also act as symbols of the unity and identity of the Pakistani community. But do Pakistani leaders assist the integration of migrants into British society? Eisenstadt argues that this depends on what kind of leaders we are talking about. The leader who will be most effective in assisting such an integration will be the one who wishes 'to perform definite roles within his group and to combine these roles with new ones related to the absorbing society . . . . he becomes by his very nature a channel of communication with the wider society, its values and symbols . . . . they may serve . . . not only as general symbols of identification and transmitters of values, but also as guides towards specific problems and role performance.'[2]

In contrast insofar as the leaders' attachment to their groups of origin is only superficial, i.e. shown in visits, vague friendly relations, and so on, without their performing any definite roles in relation to these groups (such as professional advice, leadership or formulation of views on matters of common interest, etc.) it seems that they may have a somewhat negative effect on their group's degree of social participation. The groups may seem in this way to lose some of their channels of communication with the wider society and its values, and very important gaps in their communicative hierarchy may occur.[3] The other empirical question is how far leadership is differentiated between various functions and the extent to which these functions are performed by few people whose influence extends through all sections of the community.

Here I shall concentrate on the structured situations of Pakistani ethnic leadership and the power relations in British society which affect minority—majority ethnic groups. Three situations will be examined, those in which poly-ethnic factors are present, the inter-ethnic situations, and thirdly, the minority ethnic—majority ethnic situation. The use of the term 'majority—minority' signifies a power relationship where the majority group is in a position of dominance.[4] These situations are not conceptualized as being rigidly demarcated because both ethnic groups and the structures in which leaders operate overlap.

In the Pakistani community the leaders who represent the community through the ethnic organizations to the wider community have limitations and constraints upon them. This in turn has consequences for ethnic mobilization in different circumstances at the national and at the local level.

The question of leadership cannot be understood unless the divisions within the Pakistani population are grasped. The degree of interaction among Pakistanis in their organizations at national and local levels reflects regional, urban/rural and *Biraderi* divisions, although, at the same time, the situation in Britain is making new demands for co-operation beyond these divisions. This brings us to a point where we can distinguish between different types of leaders in the community.

Formal Leaders[5]

A group of kinsmen and friends who come from one area in Pakistan may decide to form an organization and then announce their aims. These organizations are usually led by educated professionals or prosperous Pakistani businessmen. The leaders may have come from a rural area in Pakistan but because of their education and the nature of their occupation they had lived in urban areas of Pakistan before coming to Britain. Their knowledge and contacts give them more of an opportunity to lead other Pakistanis in Western situations. They usually act as spokesmen to the outside world. If we look at the composition of community relations committees and councils in Britain, we find that the Pakistani representatives on these councils are usually the professional, educated people rather than the ordinary working-class migrants. Some observers have argued that this is because of language problems, although there are enough Pakistanis working on the shop-floor and in public transport who could communicate quite well. My observations lead me to think that formal leadership in the Pakistani community depends, apart from the factors mentioned above, on one's occupation and the status attached to it in British society. Other factors are relevant, such as whether they work on night shifts and whether they can contribute financially to the running of the organizations. As spokesmen to the wider society they may reap additional rewards such as becoming a Governor of a school or a JP or being selected as candidates to contest local elections. This holds for other ethnic minority communities in Britain as well. On the other hand, businessmen help these organizations by financial contributions and therefore attain some power to influence decisions. In some cases, I noticed, businessmen used their position in these organizations to promote their business. This applied mainly to the travel and estate agents who were involved in the organizations.

The role of the formal leaders is mainly in inter-ethnic situations. One thing was clear, that the activities and support from other Pakistanis for the formal leaders was greater when there was a threat to national or religious identity. This was evident when demonstrations were organized in London at the time of the Bangladesh issue in 1971, and thousands of Pakistanis gathered from all over the country to show their unity and support their Government's action. However, the support at local level was still enlisted through the *Biraderi* elders who were regarded as traditional leaders.

I have observed another type of leader who did not represent any organization but was treated as a spokesman for the Pakistanis by the wider community. Commenting on this type of leader Hill and Issacharoff write, 'It does not seem unreasonable to suggest that in the majority of cases those Pakistanis involved in the community relations committees through their own initatives are those with the greatest possible chance of absorption into middle-class patterns of life in England.'[6] This type of leaders included the Pakistani social workers, community relations officers, etc. These people could be categorized as 'integrationists' because of their education and urban background and a wish to integrate. They were usually criticized by the traditional leaders, in particular by the religious leaders who were conservative in outlook and opposed integration because of their fear of losing the traditional values and the religious observances of Islam. On the other hand, those who categorized themselves as 'integrationists' labelled the religious leaders as 'segregationists' and 'separatists' because of their conservative outlook which, as one of the respondents put it, 'should be modified in the British situation'.

Sometimes the different outlooks of Pakistani leaders made the nature of representation to the wider community problematic. This might happen to such an extent that contradictory viewpoints could be presented by the 'conservative' and 'progressive' leaders from the same community on the same issue. For instance, when the issue of 'single-sex schools for girls' was being discussed in Rochdale by the local Community Relations Council with the local education committee, the leaders of the Pakistani organizations were represented at the discussions pleading on behalf of the Pakistani community for this facility to continue. Some individual Pakistani professionals who did not represent any organization expressed the view that the demand for single-sex schools for girls represented the traditional outlook and was not relevant in the British situation.

Pakistanis in supervisory roles such as overlookers or supervisors, who acted as 'go-betweens' between the employees and the management in order to overcome language difficulties had also gained influential roles among the Pakistanis both at work and in the community, like the *Padroni*.

Traditional Leaders[7]

The traditional leaders who draw their support from their *Biraderi* members are more powerful and maintain their power through the kinship groups. Traditional leadership depends on age, length of stay in this country and the number of relatives sponsored and patronized. The traditional leaders usually play their part in intra-ethnic situations and formal leaders depend on their support in an inter-ethnic situation, because the former are more effective in mobilizing support. For instance, if a professional Pakistani who was an official of a welfare association contested a local election on a political party ticket, he would contact the '*Biraderi* elders' to mobilize support for him. This pattern of support was followed also on behalf of a white candidate in an election.

There is one noticeable difference in the Pakistani leader—follower relationship in Britain and in Pakistan. In Britain the 'traditional' leadership pattern is the same as in Pakistan. However, as far as the contact between a formal leader and an ordinary Pakistani is concerned there is some difference. For instance, contact with a doctor in Pakistan is more remote and may be described as a superior official—common man relationship. In the British context in his double role, as a doctor and a community leader, he comes into closer contact with ordinary Pakistanis. His welfare role makes Pakistanis think of him as 'one of them' who helps them through his contacts with the problems they face in the wider society. This does not mean that his life-style is the same as that of an ordinary Pakistani. He is still treated as the one who belongs to the upper middle class and lives somewhere in the suburb of a city in his detached house. Pahl has mentioned that 'the constraints of locality are less, the higher an individual is placed on the occupational heirarchy.'[8] This was so in the case of Pakistanis. I observed that Pakistani organizations were dominated by middle-class or more prosperous working-class people who lived outside the inner area of the town where most of the Pakistanis lived.

Ethnic Organizations

In my time in Rochdale there were eleven Pakistani organizations[9] which could be classified in four broad types in terms of their functions: (i) welfare, (ii) religious, (iii) political (mainly concerned with politics back home), and (iv) professional. There were three organizations in each of the first two categories four in the third and one organization in the fourth. The religious organizations have been discussed above (see pp. 161–4) and here I deal with the remaining three types only. The information presented in this section is based on observation and intensive informal interviews with the people who ran these organizations. I also read their reports, constitutions and attended meetings and functions held by these organizations during my field-work.

Welfare Organizations

The adaptation of migrants to a new country involves the adjustment of old ways of life to the new environment. The migrants need some help from those who understand the functioning of the institutions in the society of their residence. Pakistani organizations met some of these needs by helping with form filling, tax problems and other day-to-day official matters brought to them by individuals.

The Pakistan Social Circle was founded in the late 1960s by one man with the help of some friends who then started *Tehrik-i-Istaklal* and lost interest in the Circle. It appeared to be a paper organization although the Chairman and founder, an insurance agent, claimed that it helped Pakistanis a great deal. I could find little evidence to substantiate this claim. The Chairman attended meetings such as those of the Community Relations Council representing the Circle. On the basis of his position he was nominated,[10] on the recommendation of the Community Relations Officer, as a member of the North-West Conciliation Committee of the Race Relations Board. His lack of grass-root support among immigrants in general and Pakistanis in particular was pointed out to the local Community Relations Council and the Race Relations Board in early 1970s by the representatives of the Pakistan Welfare Association, but without any success.

The Pakistan Welfare and Information Centre, set up in 1969 by a group of Punjabis, was active in helping Punjabis with their official problems during 1971–2. The majority of the members were Punjabis and all the dominant positions were held by Punjabis.

In 1973 the Rochdale branch of the Pakistan People's Party was formed by those who were running this Centre. Although the officers claimed that the two bodies had different roles and were fulfilling these separately it was in many senses one organization and certainly the officers were the same. In two years (1973–74) they did not call a single meeting of the executive committee of the Centre. There were no elections. The Secretary who was also press secretary of the Pakistan People's Party, spoke for the Centre on the local Community Relations Council and other bodies where it was represented.

He also continued helping Pakistanis on an individual basis using both the Centre and People's Party name. He worked with the Department of Employment as a clerk and had a travel agency which he ran as a part-time activity. He also acted as an agent to a dry-cleaning firm and sold records and other electrical goods on a small scale. The people he helped in his capacity as an officer of the Centre or the Pakistan People's Party bought goods from him and booked air tickets through him. He clearly had an interest as a businessman in using his position as a member and officer of these organizations to obtain custom for his various business activities.

One activity which the Centre arranged with the co-operation of the newly formed Rochdale Branch of Pakistan People's Party (UK) was a *Meena Bazaar*[11] in May 1973. This was to raise funds in response to the local Ronald Gorton Centre appeal for elderly and physically handicapped people.[12] The organizers of this *Bazaar* claimed that they wanted to demonstrate that the Pakistani community was part of the wider community in the town and therefore participated in both the appeals. The *Bazaar* was visited by English people as well. This served two purposes, the raising of funds and an opportunity for Pakistanis and English people to meet socially. It is argued by some that this sort of social interaction tends to reduce prejudice, leads to tolerance and greater mutual understanding in inter-ethnic situations.[13]

The Pakistan Welfare Association which was founded in the late 1960s did mainly welfare work and mobilized and helped Pakistanis as a community. In 1973–4 its paid-up membership was 700. It arranged a public meeting and a dinner or variety show annually in August to celebrate Pakistan Independence Day. It played an active role during and after the Bangladesh trouble, and demonstrated against the Indian invasion of East Pakistan. There was also a demonstration for the release of Pakistani prisoners of war. This demonstration was led by the then newly elected MP, Mr Cyril Smith. The Association also played an important role during the Rochdale by-election in 1972 (see pp. 139–43). At the time of the publication of the Pakistan Act 1973 the Committee members also approached the MP and other officials to ask them to press the British Government to recognize Kashmiris as Pakistanis. As many Mirpuris were affected by the situation they made several representations to the Pakistani Embassy and to the Home Office.[14] Such activity was obviously linked to the fact that the Association drew about half of its membership from Mirpuris.

The Association played a particularly active part during the period when Pakistanis were applying for British nationality. A solicitor (Liberal Councillor and JP) came every Saturday to the Association's office to sign all the applications without any charge. This was because of the Association's contacts with the Liberal Party and in recognition of mutual support between the Party and the Association.

It usually welcomed the representatives of the Pakistani Government and arranged meetings for them and responded to any appeal made by the Pakistani Government such as that for funds at the time of floods in Pakistan in 1973.

The Pakistan Welfare Association was the only organization which had an office in the centre of the Central Ward. After the executive committee election in 1973 when Mr K. D. was elected president and Mr M. P. secretary for the Association, contributions were raised by the membership to buy an office.[15] This office was partly used for the religious instruction of Pakistani children.

There was a close relationship between the local MP and the Association such as that the surgery which the MP held once a month for Pakistanis was usually attended by the officials of the Association who acted as interpreters and helped to explain the cases to the MP. The day-to-day activities included general advice and form-filling.

This Association also co-operated with the Community Relations Council to arrange neighbourhood meetings to assess people's feelings about the immigrants and race relations in the town. They did it as part of their 'unity movement', after the Rochdale by-election and intimidation by the British Campaign to Stop Immigration on polling day. There was close co-operation with the Community Relations Council in terms of community/race relations work. However, there was no separate effort made by the Association to combat racial discrimination in terms of jobs or in other fields.

The officers of the Association were mostly professional and business people. For instance, the President 1971–3 (a Mirpuri) was a successful businessman who was closely involved with the Liberal Party and contested the local elections twice.[16] The General Secretary was a teacher. There were at least two executive committee members out of six who were in working-class jobs; one worked on the day shift in a textile firm and the other as a driver in public transport. Meetings of the executive were held fairly regularly and elections took place after every two years. The case studies also show that the Association was regarded as helpful by the Pakistanis in a variety of ways.

However, in general I was told by the committee members of

these associations that they believed in meeting English people on a community level socially, but in the preservation of their cultural values as well. They emphasized, as one of them put it, 'We representatives are the educated ones and the responsibility lies on our shoulders to protect our community from western influence. We have to work hard to convince the authorities of our cultural needs and to get the necessary facilities. For this we have to act together.' He added further, criticizing the branches of Pakistani political parties in this country, 'I hope that we do not waste time in organizing meetings for the representatives of these political parties, this should be done in Pakistan. We should concentrate on the problems of Pakistanis in this country and unite as a community to protect our religious and cultural values. We should participate in the wider society as a Pakistani community as we did in the elections in Rochdale.' This comment clearly raises the question of unity in the community.

Political Organizations

The four political organizations mentioned above represented four political parties in Pakistan. Pakistan People's Party, the ruling majority party in Pakistan at the time of this study encouraged its extension to UK. A senior Cabinet Minister was sent to Britain to open the first convention of the UK branch in 1972. Since then branches have been formed in most of the areas of Pakistani settlement. A campaign for membership was launched in 1973 throughout the UK and Rochdale was one of the areas to respond by forming a branch. This lead was followed by the Opposition parties. The Chairman of *Tehrik-i-Istaklal* came to Britain to start a branch of his party. The Chairman of the Pakistan Social Circle responded by forming a branch in Rochdale. Similarly, some old followers of the Muslim League, the Party which struggled for the independence of Pakistan under *Quaid-i-Azam* Muhammad Ali Jinnah, the first Governor-General after Independence, started a movement in the UK to form a branch of this party. The Vice-President of the Pakistan Muslim League was invited to start the party branch in Britain. A branch was formed in Rochdale.

The fourth party, the Kashmir Liberation League, which has as its object the liberation of Indian-held Kashmir, also has a branch in Rochdale. The Chairman of the Pakistan Welfare Association was its national chairman in Britain in 1972–3.

The purpose of these political parties was, and still is, mainly to arrange meetings for politicians from Pakistan when they visited

Britain. The policies of the parties were put forward to the membership which in most cases was small. The parties did not usually take part in the political processes of this country, although some of their leaders mobilized support amongst Pakistanis for certain candidates in their other capacities. In contrast the representatives of the Pakistan People's Party have contested elections in other areas of Britain such as Bradford.[17]

There was a great deal of feeling amongst some Pakistanis about whether the political parties of Pakistan should have branches in this country. A correspondence column in the Urdu newspapers *Daily Jang* and weekly *Akhbariwatan* was devoted to this issue in December 1975 and in June 1976. Arguments for such branches were put forward, such as the nature of the Pakistanis' stay in this country and that as the migrants intended to go back so they should take a greater interest in politics back home. Others argued that as they were living in this country Pakistanis should be united and the political differences which existed back home should not be introduced since they would divide the community. The Standing Conference of Pakistani Organizations in UK (SCOPO) asked Pakistanis to stop the formation of branches of Pakistani political parties in this country and to concentrate on the problems they faced in Britain. There was favourable response to this appeal in the correspondence but this was not followed through.[18]

The competition for the leadership of these organizations sometimes led to conflict within the organizations. For instance, the competition for leadership in the Pakistan People's Party at the national level reached a crisis after its annual elections in 1974 when the party was literally divided into two factions. As a consequence a senior Cabinet Minister came especially from Pakistan to resolve the matter and declared the election results valid. Actually the importance attached to the party in Britain was due to the keen interest taken by the Pakistani Government in its activities. In 1973 one of the national leaders of the party was recruited into the Pakistani Foreign Service and another was appointed as a Liaison Officer for Pakistanis overseas. It appeared, as SCOPO officials felt, that this created an incentive for others to come forward to become leaders with the hope of getting good jobs in Pakistan.

The leaders of the political organizations at the national level and at the local level were educated Pakistanis, in some cases professionals, who were also involved with the welfare organizations. For instance, the President of the Pakistan People's Party, UK, was also the General Secretary of Manchester Pakistan Society, a welfare organization. Similarly, the Chairman of the Rochdale branch of the Pakistan People's Party was also a member of the executive committee of the Pakistan Welfare and Information Centre and the national press secretary of the Pakistan People's Party was the Secretary of the Information Centre in Rochdale. There was considerable duplication of roles among the leadership as those who had political interests became active in the political organizations which related to politics in Pakistan.

Professional Organizations

These are not very common amongst Pakistanis. It was only by chance that the doctor who started the campaign to form a branch of the Pakistan Medical Society in this country happened to live in Rochdale. He was elected as its first General Secretary in 1972 and so it was decided to locate its office in Rochdale. This society has made representations to the Government and the British Medical Association with the help of the local MP, Mr Cyril Smith, about the difficulties Pakistani doctors faced after Pakistan left the Commonwealth. Representations have also been made about the new rules concerning the registration of overseas doctors in this country and the problems this has created for Pakistani doctors.

One of the annual activities of this organization was to arrange a dinner where members from all over the country met and exchanged views, and elections took place. The society had put up two candidates in 1976 to contest the British Medical Association elections. There was an appeal in the *Jang* to support the Pakistani candidates. They were not elected, but the officers of the society claimed that this move helped to make a point about the non-representation of Pakistanis in the BMA and that it also created unity amongst Pakistani doctors. The Overseas Doctors Association (ODA) formed in 1975, of which some individual Pakistani doctors were members, also put up three candidates for the same elections. They were not elected, although each got 4,000-plus votes.

The Pakistan Medical Society was only concerned with the problems and welfare of Pakistani doctors in cases where the BMA, like the Trade Unions, did not recognize or meet the special needs of migrant doctors. Hence, the Society, using other means such as lobbying MPs etc. tried to influence the BMA, the GMC, and the DHSS on different issues facing Pakistani doctors. The feeling of a lack of equality of opportunity in the medical profession amongst the Pakistani (and other migrant) doctors might lead in the future to the formation of their own union on more permanent lines, like the

ODA, to achieve equality in terms of jobs and promotion for its members.

External Hostility and its Impact on Identity, Unity and Incapsulation

I have observed that Pakistanis who did not belong to any of the organizations discussed above, supported them and their leaders when a religious or national issue arose. It was a way of expressing concern over such issues. This type of identification and support on national and local level reinforced national and religious identity and expressed clearly the meaning of Pakistani ethnicity in the community. Ethnic unity was usually demonstrated when there was a conflict with outside groups. This is made manifest in the discussion which follows.

Conflict with other groups such as Indians or Bangladeshis usually arose in relation to the conditions back home. Some felt that they as Pakistanis had a special responsibility in this country to expose India's hostile attitude towards Pakistan since its creation in 1947. The Indo-Pakistani wars of 1965 and 1971 led most Pakistanis both in Pakistan and in Britain to regard Indians as their enemies. In 1971 tensions arose in this country among Pakistanis, Bangladeshis and Indians over the Bangladesh issue. There were marches and counter-marches at both local and national levels in support of government actions back home; collections for defence funds were made and national organizations, such as Pakistan Solidarity Front and Pakistan Action Committee were formed. At the local level special committees were formed to collect funds and to deal with the press and the Pakistan Embassy (then the High Commission) to get news and distribute leaflets and arrange meetings.

In Rochdale Pakistanis formed an Action Committee at the time of the 1971 war to carry out such activities. Members were drawn from all Pakistani ethnic associations. The policy was not to alienate the people from East Pakistan (Bangladeshis) who were few in number, in the hope that Pakistan would remain intact. The Bangladeshis' reaction was not hostile either as they were not sure about the outcome of the independence movement. At a later stage when Bangladesh was declared an independent state, the first thing the Bangladeshis did was to start a new Mosque in one of the houses. This they did, as one of them told me, 'to avoid conflict with West Pakistanis'.

Conflict with the indigenous people could be interpreted as a conflict of interest as Rex and Moore have said. 'They (the Pakistanis) form, in a technical sense, a pariah group, being in the society but not of it. They have clear conflict of interest with the society and have organized themselves to pursue these conflicts and to reach some adjustment compatible with their interests.'[19] This clearly leads to cohesion in the community for mutual aid services and attempts to reinforce values and norms regarded as basic to the group. In turn it leads to the incapsulation of Pakistanis. This type of conflict is usually covert. But there are also situations where it becomes overt such as strikes (see Chapter 6) and local elections (see Chapter 8), when the National Front intimidated Pakistanis. Situations of this sort united Pakistanis, bearing out the thesis put forward by Georg Simmel that external conflict produces internal integration.[20]

Hostility arising from prejudice and discrimination also leads to 'in-group' feeling amongst Pakistanis who then see white people as the hostile 'out-group'. The phenomenon of 'Pakki bashing' and other anti-immigrant movements reinforced the lines of division and the underlying conflict leads on occasions to overt inter-group conflict. Several incidents of racial nature in which Pakistanis were beaten by white people, mainly by youths, were reported during my stay in Rochdale and afterwards.

The activities of Pakistani organizations certainly help Pakistanis to some extent to adapt to the new situation but not wholly. The unity advocated among Pakistanis might make it more difficult for individuals to come to terms with certain aspects of British society. De Witt John in his study of the Indian Workers Association found that the leaders asked their members to participate in British institutions.[21] This willingness to adapt to British ways was absent from the activities of the Pakistani organizations, which emphasized nationalistic, religious and cultural aspects and so had a somewhat negative effect on the degree of participation in indigenous institutions. This situation fits Eisenstadt's hypothesis that if the leaders' attachment to their group is superficial, i.e. is shown in visits, vague friendly relations, etc., without their performing any definite roles in relation to these groups it may have somewhat negative effect on their group's degree of social participation in the wider society.[22] This means that the leaders act as culture-sustaining agents and reinforce the incapsulation of the membership. These organizations were not effective as agents of mutual aid. Mutual support through services revolved around kin/*Biraderi* groups and not around the organizations as did most of the social life of Pakistanis, except for a few functions in the year.

The organizations did however provide symbols of unity and some work towards improving the Pakistani image in British eyes. They also tried to preserve Pakistani culture in the 'difficult circumstances' of migration.

They were concerned to maintain religious observance and the moral welfare of Pakistanis, as they saw it, and to keep their fellows in touch with the home country because of the myth of return. The problem of maintaining Pakistani culture appears to be the responsibility of these organizations along with kinship/*Biraderi* groups (see Chapter 11). Many respondents made this point to me. For instance, one night worker thought that a great responsibility lay on Pakistani organizations and their leaders, who were educated, to provide a lead in protecting 'our values and culture in this progressive society'.

A Pakistani at least until he knows his way around, needs a cultural retreat, where he knows the rules, and knows that other people accept them also. This was provided with the help of kin and friends, and to some extent by the Pakistani organizations.

My observations and the analysis above led me to believe that the leadership of the organizations was in the hands of a few people who were either middle-class professionals or wealthy businessmen. However, the voluntary associations (both welfare and other) were providing a training ground for the new Pakistani urban leadership in the process of social change and adjustment. There was certainly a distinction emerging between the 'old elite', i.e. the host of traditional leaders, and the 'new elite', the educated and professional leaders, because of different backgrounds. It appears, although the traditional kinship/*Biraderi* forces were continually giving way to some extent under the pressure of the Western trend, there were still traditional leaders who carried great weight in Britain. These traditional leaders did not have a recognized status as did the formal leaders in the wider society, but the nature of their traditional hold on the kinship/*Biraderi* made their influence potentially so great that the formal leaders needed their assistance for support when mobilizing the community for various reasons. In this way there seemed to exist a coalition between the traditional leaders and the formal leaders who played a dual role, in the ethnic community and in the wider society.

The forces which united Pakistanis on certain occasions were the issues and feelings of national and religious identification. This reinforced the ties with the homeland. In such situations Pakistani leaders emerged and operated (and this holds for other ethnic minority groups). Support was mobilized at both local and national level. Ethnicity became socially significant. This had a bearing on inter-group relations. In normal circumstances the channels of communication at community level were the formal leaders, and ordinary Pakistanis did not have the opportunity to develop much contact with British people. It seemed unlikely that in the near future the incapsulation of Pakistanis would alter so that these organizations could help to develop relationships cutting across ethnic boundaries.

11. The Incapsulation of Pakistanis: Case Studies

In this chapter I provide individual case studies to illustrate some of the general points which have been raised in this book. These are based mainly on intensive interviews with the respondents but include also observational material about individuals.

In the analysis of the case study data several assumptions were made. First, that the accounts of the individual life histories and in particular the experiences of migration and settlement would provide details which in turn could be analysed to indicate any general points of similarity or contrast. For instance, a Pakistini who migrates to this country comes usually sponsored, not only as an individual but as a member of a village—kin *Biraderi*. His *Biraderi* will ensure that he is met at the airport, accommodated and found work and helped in every possible way. It is important to analyse these stages of settlement to see the pattern which emerges. Also the whole attitude and behaviour to their kin obligations, to the community life, religion, inter-ethnic relations and their own future ambitions and the future of their children, as they see it, will not only demonstrate how the incapsulation of Pakistanis occurs but will also provide illustrations for the points raised in the other chapters.

Employment experience in Britain is relevant to the determination of the life-styles of Pakistanis and, therefore, it was thought useful to select cases from a range of occupations to demonstrate any common elements of experience which could be attributed to the work experience here. Pakistanis who work on night shift have different life-styles from other groups of Pakistanis such as day workers, public transport workers, professionals and the self-employed. Further, the kinship—friendship networks which cut across occupational groupings were also examined for the ways in which they might modify the work experience.

The occupational groupings were discussed above (pp. 103–35) and here I give the individual cases and general details arranged in these groupings. Because of the importance of night-shift work among the Pakistanis living in Rochdale I shall first consider this category.

Night-Shift Workers

I studied four night-shift workers in detail. They were relatively older than those in the other categories. They were all *Muhajirs* and came from villages in Pakistan. They were either illiterate or their educational level was low. Three of them did not speak English. They all worked in textiles in Pakistani groups and changed jobs very infrequently.

On arrival in Rochdale they stayed with relatives and the one who was still without his family here continued to do so. Once settled each sponsored other relatives and aided them by getting work vouchers and making other arrangements on their arrival.

Due to the nature of their work they slept almost all day and whatever spare time was left they spent with their relatives and friends. All activities outside work took place among immediate relatives and the *Biraderi*.

All of the night-shift workers were quite religious and their outlook could be considered a conservative one. They regarded Western education and their non-Muslim surroundings as a threat to their religion and their values and consequently they put a high value on religious education for their children. They were appreciative of the work of the religious and other Pakistani organizations, which they saw as important protectors of religious values.

They all perceived hostility from white people in terms of prejudice and discrimination against coloured people in general and Pakistanis in particular. They were also conscious of immigration policies and considered anti-immigrant organizations as harmful to immigrant interests.

All were investing in Pakistan in terms of buying land and building *Pakka* houses. For the sake of their children's future (who they thought would suffer in this country because of their foreignness, and prejudice and discrimination against them) they regarded their stay in Britain as temporary and hoped to settle in Pakistan eventually. Their kinship obligations towards family and *Biraderi* were another motive for returning to Pakistan. This meant their emotional links with Pakistan were still strong.

To sum up, these Pakistanis were highly incapsulated by a variety of factors, some of which stemming from their background but others connected directly with their work here. The following case study illustrates some of these points.

Mr G. R. was a spinner in a textile mill and worked night shifts. He was born in India (Jullundar) in 1923 and migrated to Pakistan at the time of the 1947 Partition along with his *Biraderi*. He went to school for only four years in India and did not learn any English. His marriage followed the traditional preferential pattern and he was married to his maternal cousin. They had five daughters and one son born in Pakistan. Two of his daughters lived in Pakistan. His married daughter lived in Lyallpur and her husband was her paternal cousin. They had three children. One daughter was unmarried and lived with his parents. His father was a farmer as he himself had been before he ran a grocery shop for three years, which he had to close down as it did not pay.

G. R. came to Britain in November 1961. According to his own account he never thought of coming to Britain; it was just by chance that a person came to their village who had been in Britain for a few years. He was asking for people who wanted to go to Britain to earn good wages. He promised to arrange all the papers and would charge a fee of Rs 4000 (£200). One of G. R.'s cousins asked him if he wanted to start a business in Britain as he had some experience as a grocer. G. R. agreed, and both of them decided to come. He said, 'It was very difficult to convince the family, particularly the women.' After a few days G. R. got a passport and tickets and flew to Britain with his cousin. The agent gave them £5 each and a contact in London in case they needed it. 'It was a difficult parting, everybody in the family was upset.'

G. R. had a distant cousin in Manchester and before leaving Pakistan he wrote to him about his intention to come to Britain. Then he sent a telegram to him, giving the date and flight number. His first experience in Britain was as follows, 'I was expecting my cousin to be at London Airport but he was not there. We did not know how to get out of the airport. We were lucky that in our plane there was an educated Pakistani who had lived in England before. He was helping some people with enquiries and we told him that we wanted to go to Manchester. He took us to the railway station with another Pakistani who was going to Glasgow, and said, "Find a Pakistani when you reach Manchester to show you the way." We were lucky that we had £5 each for the fare. He also warned us to be careful not to get lost. We got a taxi and reached my cousin's place.'

He described his first impression of Britain thus: 'It was great to see so many *Gore Loke* around. The underground was a unique experience particularly the lift they used for the passengers. When the lift was going down I thought what would happen if the wires broke and that would be the end of us. It was frightening, my heart was sinking. Nobody else seemed worried except us.'

When the two men came to G. R.'s cousin's house he was out at work but there were some other Pakistanis in the house who entertained them. G. R. could not sleep properly the first night because of the cold and he was thinking about the journey and about his wife, children and other family members. In the morning his cousin came back from work and was thrilled at their arrival, as he had not received the telegram.

It took G. R. four months to find a job, and according to him, 'It was the most tortuous period of my life.' He used to cry at night and prayed to God for help. In the end he got a job in his cousin's department in the textile mill in Royton. His difficulties in getting a job were, according to him, due to 'unemployment, lack of English and being a Pakistani'. He had changed his job only once. When he brought his family to Britain he changed to the day shift which he did not like. Then he changed back to his old job as a labourer. He worked with five other relatives in the same department, and there were many more Pakistani workers on night shift who were either his *Biraderi* or who were well known to him as he was one of the old hands. He liked working on the night shift as there was a 'homely' atmosphere and he had no language problem as the charge hand was a Pakistani. He did not believe in changing jobs and had been in the present job for the last eight years. He thought it increased one's respect if you worked at one place. He did not envisage getting promotion.

G. R. went to Pakistan in 1966 to fetch his family and he took a lot of gifts for his relations. On his return he brought a lot of presents for the *Biraderi*, friends and fellows from the Pakistani end. He moved to Rochdale in 1966 when he brought his family. He had two brothers, three cousins and five other close relatives living in the town. He claimed that he arranged three work permits for his relatives in 1964 and 1965. He obtained a lot of support from his *Biraderi*. He only went to Pakistani organizations or to the Community Relations Council when nobody in the *Biraderi* was capable of helping.

For instance, when he was trying to bring his unmarried daughter over to Britain from Pakistan he used all these organizations and the local MP to help as she was over 18 years of age. She was refused a visa and then an appeal was lodged against the decision which was also dismissed. During this period G. R. called on all the official sources for help. Once he was told that nothing further could be done he began to look for a Pakistani boy in this country who would marry her, making her eligible to come over. There was a possibility that one of his nephews would agree to this marriage as the girl was educated up to matriculation standard.

G. R. spent his time outside work with his relatives and friends. They visited each other and all the social activities took place among the immediate relations and the *Biraderi*. Usually future plans were discussed and news from Pakistan was exchanged. He perceived a lot of prejudice and discrimination against Pakistanis and thought that to avoid hostility it was better for them to keep to themselves.

When G. R. wanted to buy a house in Rochdale he borrowed £500 from his cousins and paid £700 in cash for the house. He still lived in it and thought that the value of his house was £4,000 in 1974. He supported his family back home and claimed that his family had bought 25 acres of land with his savings. He had also helped to build some rooms in their house in the village. Once his son's education was completed he wanted to go back and settle in Pakistan. He said that there he would be his 'own boss and not a "Paki" labourer in a textile mill'. His wife and daughters did sewing at home for Pakistani manufacturers to add to their savings. They thought if they all could earn good wages then they had a better chance of going back quickly.

G. R. did not have any English friends, although his son had a few, mainly his classmates, whom he usually met outside and not at home; his son sometimes went to his English friends' homes after school. G. R. did not want to mix with English people because he saw them as a 'bad influence'. He often advised his son to come home early and not to waste his time with English friends who could have a bad effect on him. This was one of the reasons for not allowing his son to invite his English friends home. The other reason was that 'it is not a good thing to invite boys in the house when you have grown-up girls.'[1]

G. R. was a very religious person. He used to go to the Mosque regularly every Friday afternoon and during the month of *Ramazan*, and also said his prayers at work whenever possible. His daughters and wife read the Quran almost every day. His son sometimes joined them but usually used his studies as an excuse. G. R. believed that 'the only way to keep ourselves Muslims and Pakistanis is to avoid contact with English people and stick to our religion and our own people. This is needed to protect our values and culture in this progressive society.' He also thought that a great responsibility lay with the Pakistani organizations and their leaders, who were educated, to provide a lead in this direction so that when they went back to Pakistan they were still Pakistanis and not English.

G. R. was very worried about the future of Pakistani children in this country. He felt that if the right sort of action was not taken by the Pakistani community it would lose its religious and national identity. He felt that Pakistani children should get a good education, but not at the expense of their culture.

G. R. thought the children would be discriminated against when they came to look for jobs. 'We have educated Pakistanis working in our mill as labourers. If they were in Pakistan they would get good office jobs. The same thing will happen to our children. If they go back to Pakistan with this education, they could get very good positions.'

G. R. was also suspicious of the immigration legislation. He had become bitter since his daughter was refused entry. He thought that there could come a day in Britain when immigrants and their families would be expelled from this country as others had been from Uganda by President Amin. Therefore, he believed that one should invest in Pakistan and not risk leaving everything in this country, 'should we have to leave in a rush'.

G. R. was considered a very conservative and straightforward person by other Pakistanis. He was respected by his relatives because of his age, and was something of a father figure. Due to his lack of formal education he depended on some of them for certain kinds of help but they still respected him. Particularly, I noticed that his son and nephews would not act in an un-Islamic way in his presence. Nor would they for instance watch 'Top of the Pops' on television while he was there since this would be in the category of a 'bad influence'. His daughters were very shy and hardly went out of the house, although they spent four, three and one year respectively at school. He hoped that their husbands could come here as the girls were British now and he appreciated the Government's decision on this but he was not happy with the delay involved in bringing somebody over. He hoped to take his daughters to Pakistan and arrange their marriages there along with the other daughter who was already there (once he found a boy for her in Britain) and then leave it to them to decide where they would like to live. His personal preference was for all of them to settle back in Pakistan in a few years' time.

Day-Shift Workers

I studied in depth four day-shift workers, all of whom were younger than the night-shift workers. Except for one, all had some formal education. Two were *Muhajirs*, another one's family migrated from India but he was born in Sahiwal and the fourth one was born in Lyallpur. All were sponsored or assisted in migration and on their arrival in Britain by their *Biraderi* or friends. One, for instance, came on a work permit arranged by one of his relatives. One is still unmarried.

They had changed jobs more often than the night-shift workers. Three of them did heavy or dirty work and were more dispersed in the textile mills where they worked. As a consequence of this they were more aware of the problems Pakistanis faced, including discrimination, at work.

They all planned to start their own business, even the one who did not speak English. This was to avoid the hostility at work and to become independent. Some already did market trading over the weekends or helped Pakistani manufacturers in the evenings, to earn extra money and to get experience which would be useful when they started their own businesses.

In terms of dependence and *Biraderi* relations, there seemed no difference between the day-shift and night-shift workers except that the day-shift workers had more time to spend with their families and other relatives. The day workers did not seem very keen on practising their religion although some of them did say their prayers. Their outlook was less conservative but their attitudes towards the religious education of Pakistani children were similar to the night-shift workers. Those who had children, though they were still young, wished them to have a good education. They saw their own future in Pakistan in terms of starting a business and their childrens' future in Pakistan on the basis of the good qualifications they hoped they would acquire in this country. They believed that Pakistani parents had a special duty to look after their children's education and their general interests by not leaving them on their own while working long hours and particularly on the night shift.

All the day-shift workers sent money back to their relations and were investing in Pakistan and hoped to settle there eventually. Like many others they regarded their stay in Britain as a temporary one.

In spite of this attitude they believed that the Pakistani organizations should play a positive role to help the community, unite them, and act as mediators with the wider society. They referred to the Pakistanis' participation in the elections in Rochdale. One of them, a well-educated day-worker, was associated with a Pakistani organization and helped to organize its activities.

In general the day-to-day activities of the day-workers (except at work) were within the community and there were few examples of cross-ethnic inter-personal relationships. Some of these points are illustrated by the case study which follows.

Mr M. K. worked on the day shift as a spinner in a textile mill. He was born in Pakistan in 1942. His father was a school teacher. His family did not migrate from India at the time of Partition, although some of their relatives did. He completed his F. A. ('A' Levels) at the Government College at Lyallpur. He was sponsored to come to Britain by a distant relative and a former student of his father's who arranged his work voucher and ticket.

He came to Britain in 1964 and was received by his sponsor at Manchester Airport and taken to Rochdale. He rested for three days and then got a job as an extra man in the firm where his sponsor was working. He found this job very hard as in Pakistan he had never worked. He explained, 'My father's aim was to send me so that I could do a technical course and also earn some money. I did try but it did not work out.' After a few weeks' work he was trained as a spinner by another Pakistani and was working on the frame after two days of instruction. 'My fellow workers treated me like a son and that was why I adjusted to the night work slowly.' After eight months he changed to another firm to work on the day shift. He did not like night work or sleeping all day as he wanted to see some life.

His next job was also in spinning, but he left after a month because he had to handle dirty materials which was affecting his health. In his next job he worked with some of his friends on the day shift. He was happy and worked there for 5½ years until he went to Pakistan to see his family and to get married.

Before going to Pakistan he went out with other Pakistanis including his workmates to cafés and clubs. Sometimes their English co-workers, at least around Christmas time, accompanied them too. He said he had fun before he got married, although he used to send money to his father regularly. It appeared that his friendship with other Pakistani young people prevented him doing a technical course. For the first one-and-half years he lived with his sponsor, then moved to a lodging-house with his friends. On his return in 1971 his wife did not come with him as she could not get an interview date for an entry certificate in time.

M. K. tried immediately for a job in his old firm but there were no day-shift vacancies. He got a job working on the double day shift elsewhere but after four weeks returned to his old firm on the day shift. He was liked by the management because he was used as an interpreter whenever the need arose. He had some bitter experiences at work with some English workers. He said, 'We are always thought unfit for good and clean jobs and fit only for heavy and dirty jobs. This is based on total misunderstanding and prejudice against Pakistanis.' It was to avoid this situation that M. K. would like to start his own business. While waiting anxiously for his wife he bought a house in the Central Ward area near the house of his relative and sponsor. It was only at the end of 1972 after dozens of letters to the British High Commission in Islamabad by the local Community Relations Council's office, that his wife obtained an interview date and eventually got the entry certificate.

Mr A. S., his relative and sponsor, arranged a big feast for all their Pakistani friends and relatives. Even relatives from other towns were invited to celebrate the arrival of the new bride. It was just like a marriage ceremony. The bride and her husband received many gifts from relatives and friends. They both stayed for two weeks with A. S. so 'that she got used to the life in this new situation'. After that they moved to their own house but she spent a lot of her time with Mrs S. whom she usually called, *Bhabhi*, wife of the elder brother.

On the arrival of his wife, A. S. said, 'The whole life-style has changed.' He had stopped going out with his single friends and had started to exchange visits with other Pakistani families. He added, 'I used to feel so free and now I feel very responsible since I got married.' He had two children and spent his spare time with his family. His wife, who was a nurse in Pakistan, helped other Pakistani women to write and read letters and advised them on various health matters. It appeared that at first she missed her parents very much and used to cry a lot, particularly over *Eid* festivals when family members were supposed to be together. But after three years she felt settled in the community.

Mrs K. wanted to start sewing at home like other Pakistani women but her husband did not like this idea as he thought that Pakistani women with young children should look after them instead of being greedy. He recalled one incident in which a Pakistani woman tied her little child to a chair so that she could do her sewing in peace. The chair fell over and the child injured his head and broke an arm. Later on there was a serious argument between the husband and wife over this issue in which each blamed the other. The wife said that it was her husband who wanted her to do the sewing. The husband argued that he had never suggested that sewing should be done at the expense of the children. This incident was a warning to some families where women were doing sewing but according to the Pakistani manufacturers their business was not affected as a result.

As mentioned above, M. K. would like to start his own business and was exploring the possibilities of getting a stall at the new market in Rochdale for this purpose. He helped a Pakistani manufacturer in the evenings and on Sundays with the view to learning about the business and earning extra money as well.

He did not intend to stay all his life in Britain. He thought that if he started a business he could, after a few years, transfer it to Pakistan. By that time his children would be about the right age to go back to avoid Western influences. Although he was quite Anglicized in his outlook he thought that this was not the right place for children to grow up, particularly for girls. Moreover, his father who still made the decisions, agreed to his daughter-in-law's coming to Britain on condition that when the children were about school age they would go back to Pakistan with their mother. M. K. thought that his father, being a teacher, could look after them better than he could here and also claimed that now he could afford to send them to private schools in Pakistan.

M. K. also perceived a lot of prejudice and discrimination against the second-generation Pakistanis. He explained that this was so 'not due to language difficulties but because they would like equal opportunities in terms of jobs, etc.'. He thought that as a whole there was a lot of hostility against Pakistanis. He mentioned that the anti-immigrant organizations openly intimidated immigrants and no action was being taken by the government.

In general he did not see a bright future for Pakistani children in this country unless parents looked after them properly and spent a lot of their time with them. He thought that a man who worked twelve hours on night shift and then slept all day was being unfair to his wife and children. He explained, 'Some women tell my wife that they feel frightened at night when English youngsters or drunks break bottles in the streets and make noises.' In addition, he thought that the teenage Pakistani children got out of control; when he used to go out with his friends before his marriage he saw dozens of children wandering in the streets.[2]

He often advised some of the parents on taking care of their children and keeping them under control, otherwise they would have caused for regret when their children went out and started acting independently, like the English youngsters.

M. K. thought that the community had a responsibility and should take action to provide facilities, but much depended on the individual parents. He saw the Pakistani organizations' function as one of providing cultural activities and building up the Pakistani image in English eyes, by explaining their cultural background. Here he thought that the role of the local Community Relations Council became important. He appreciated the effort of the local Community Relations Council to arrange a party at the house of a Pakistani, who invited all his Pakistani and English neighbours in for a cup of tea. This helped to create contacts and enabled people to get to know each other. He believed that there should be more activities on these lines.

M. K. did not say prayers as regularly as his wife did, although he did go to *Eid* prayers twice a year. He emphasized, 'I would prefer to be a good Muslim in practice. By this I mean to help others and be good to others, etc.' He believed that children should be taught Arabic (Quran) and Urdu so that they remained Pakistanis. This should facilitate their adjustment when they returned to Pakistan.

Public Transport Workers

I studied four workers in this group. They came to Britain between the ages of 15 and 22 years at arrival and all had some education. None of them was *Muhajir*. Each came with the help of a sponsor or patron. One was still unmarried and another two although married lived as single, because their families were in Pakistan.

One started to work in public transport immediately after his schooling, but the other three first worked in mills for a few years and then joined public transport as a way out of night work which, two of them thought, was affecting their health. They were encouraged by friends and relatives, already in public transport, to do so.

While there were a lot of similarities between the transport workers and the other two groups, mentioned above, on *Biraderi*, *Vartan Bhanji*, etc., they differed on other accounts. One of the most striking was that they came into contact with people much more through their jobs and this had led to inter-personal friendships across ethnic boundaries. These relationships were mostly 'social' and beneficial to adaptation, and were taken as harmless to religious or cultural values. Some referred to Jews as an example who, they considered, were successful in adapting fully to British society without losing their culture and religion to any great extent.

Secondly, as these workers were sufficiently educated, and all could express themselves in English, they were more aware of their rights in British society. Because they were not so incapsulated in their own community, they were, in practice, 'marginal men'.

The two who were married but lived here without their families had both Pakistani and Irish lodgers. One claimed that he did not bring his family to Britain because it would affect his independence. He used to go drinking occasionally but did not drink in the presence of other Pakistanis. Another reason for not bringing his family to this country was that he did not want his daughters to grow up here. (This clearly showed his double standards, one rule for his independence and the other for his family.)

Mr M. S. worked as a driver with SELNEC,[3] public transport. He was born in the Rawalpindi district of Pakistan, in 1932. His father was a soldier in the Indian Army under the British Raj and M. S. studied up to matriculation standard. He could not go to college because of financial difficulties as his father was supporting a large family. His family in Pakistan included his retired father, his mother and his two brothers and their families and his own wife and three children. His marriage to his paternal cousin was arranged by his father when he was 19 years of age and she was only 16.

When M. S. completed his education he applied to join the army but was not accepted. In 1954 when one of his uncles was coming to Britain, his father suggested to him that he should take M. S. with him. The uncle agreed and was even willing to pay the fare. M. S. came with his uncle by sea and they arrived in Southampton. From there they went to Bradford where his uncle had a contact who came from the same area and with whom he had been in the army. (M. S.'s uncle, Mr W. A., was retired from the army in 1951, and was made a 'reserve' like his friend who came to Britain that year.)

Within two weeks of their arrival he and his uncle started work as labourers in a wool factory in Bradford where his uncle's friend was also working. 'There were not so many immigrants in the city in 1954.' M. S. worked with his uncle in the same mill until 1964 when he went back to Pakistan for two years.

M. S. was joined by many relatives between 1954 and 1963. Among those who came with his encouragement and help were two of his brothers, one brother-in-law and at least six cousins. He said, 'It was between 1960 and 1961 that approximately 90 men came from our own village.' He estimated that in 1975 from his village there were 30 families and about 70 men, single or married without their families, living in different areas of Britain.

When M. S. came back from Pakistan in 1966, his close relatives decided to move from Bradford to Rochdale. The reasons were that some of the relatives had jobs there and had bought cheap houses, and also by 1966 there were too many immigrants in Bradford. He explained: 'Up to 1962 there was no hatred against the immigrants in Bradford but after that it started slowly. We decided that before it was too late to go to a place where we could buy houses close to each other, we should go. Before we made the decision my uncle and I came to Rochdale twice to see the jobs and housing situation. It was just unfortunate that as we were still discussing this issue among ourselves, my uncle, W. A., had a heart attack and died. We were all upset as nobody was ready for this sort of accident in this strange situation. We did not know what to do. After making enquiries we managed to send his body to Pakistan by air. Two of his sons who were here went to Pakistan with the body. This incident moved us so much that we did not want to stay in Bradford any more. We came to Rochdale at the end of 1966.'

M. S. bought a big house in the Central Ward area and about seven of them started living there. His other relatives bought houses nearby. They all obtained private mortgages and borrowed money from each other to pay the deposits. M. S., although he owned another two houses, still lived in the house which he bought originally in 1966. His wife and children came to this country in 1969. His family faced no difficulties in getting entry certificates as a friend in Rawalpindi helped them. They stayed until 1971 when he took them back after registering them as British. They lived with his father in a town where they had built a house, for the purpose of the children's education.

M. S. believed that, although one was more comfortable if one's wife was in this country, it created a lot of problems, for instance, looking after children and doing shopping, receiving guests and all sorts of other obligations. He thought that if one lived here as a single person, one could earn more and save more. M. S. added, 'My father did not want my children to grow up in Britain. What he has heard about some families, he does not want to hear about my children. He only allowed my wife and children to come to this country for a visit and to register as British citizens, just to protect their rights of entry to this country.' M. S. had an Irish girl-friend who lived in Nelson. She had her own house and he visited her for weekends. He said, 'I was on duty one day on the bus when I met her in Manchester. I offered her a drink. She left her address with me and I went to see her the same weekend. None of my relatives knew about my affair because she never comes to Rochdale. If somebody came to know, there could be some trouble.' He thought that it was all right to have a friendship but not to get involved as some Pakistanis did.

M. S. worked as a spinner until 1968. He did not like the work as it was affecting his health, particularly the night shift. He changed to day shift for a few months but was not happy. At the end of 1968 one of his relatives who came from Pakistan on a work voucher started working on public transport as a conductor and later as a driver. He was an ex-army man and a trained driver. He encouraged M. S. to join as well. M. S. said, 'One day I decided to join the public transport service. They gave me a language test and I was taken on.' He worked as a conductor for one year and then, because of the introduction of one-man single decker buses, he was trained as a driver. He quite liked it. He explained, 'You meet different types of people. Every day we observe different events.'

M. S. had several English friends. He sometimes went out with them for a drink. He admitted, 'I usually try not to drink in the presence of other Pakistanis who do not drink. If somebody came to know, the news would get home and it would give a bad impression.' He thought it better to avoid such a situation.

M. S. did not seem to be religious. He went for *Eid* prayers twice a year with his relatives and although he believed that if he could say his prayers it was more satisfying for him, he commented, 'Since I came to this country in 1954 I forgot how to recite prayers. My uncle was not very religious either so I did not bother too much.' But he thought that his children should learn all about their religion. They went to the Mosque regularly in Pakistan for religious instruction and prayers. As his father was very religious he obviously made sure his grandchildren followed him.

M. S. admitted frankly that although he liked being free and independent, he would not like his daughters to be very independent. He thought that they should get a good education in single-sex educational institutions. He did not think that his daughters should go out to work. 'If they are educated they will be good mothers. In fact we do not need women to work in our country. Maybe when there is a demand women will start working.'

M. S. being one of the pioneer migrants usually assisted his *Biraderi* and other Pakistanis. He was a representative of the Pakistan Welfare Association. He spoke good English. He attributed this to talking to English people in the early days and later working on the buses. He usually said to his friends, 'If you want to learn a language start meeting people who know the language. You are bound to learn one day.' He felt that the majority of the Pakistanis would never learn the language for two reasons; one, that most of them did not have the basic knowledge of the language; secondly, due to their isolation at work and in residential neighbourhoods, they had little contact with English people.

For himself he said, 'I have three Irishmen living in one of my houses and I sometimes go and speak to them for hours as they are all single men. I get a lot of language practice like this.' He believed that there was no harm in meeting English people socially. Pakistani culture should be firmly protected and much, he believed, would depend on how Pakistani parents brought up their children.

M. S. thought that there was prejudice and discrimination against coloured people in this country. He said that he experienced this in his job. He thought that the ones who were prejudiced were those who did not have contact with immigrants. He said, 'When I talk to some people who work with me I find some of them very ignorant about our customs and culture.' He considered that the majority of English people were good at heart and were not prejudiced. It was a tiny minority which spread anti-immigrant propaganda. 'We are also blamed for not spending and going out for recreation.' In his opinion, different attitudes due to the different family systems and obligations were the real explanation but ignorance on both sides caused misunderstanding.

M. S. recalled how one of his English friends was humiliated by the owner of a pub when he took him (M. S.) for a drink. He said, 'One day I went to a pub with one of my English friends for a drink. Next day my friend was asked by the manager why he brought me. My friend did not like this attitude and told me that he had stopped going to that pub.' M. S. added that he knew another public house where coloured persons were not allowed to go. He thought that if an immigrant did something wrong which was quite normal it was given bad publicity, although if the same thing was done by a white person, it would go unnoticed. He argued that this was how prejudice and discrimination start. But on the other hand, he felt that Pakistanis avoided such situations for various reasons and although this helped to avoid conflict, at the same time it did not provide opportunities for contact with English people, from which understanding could develop.

He believed that the low performance of Pakistani children at school and the disadvantage they would face in this country for some years to come would not provide them an equal opportunity in the field of employment. If the parents assisted and encouraged their children the situation might improve. M. S. would like to stay in this country up to his retirement and then go to Pakistan. He explained, 'I would like to work here but would like to visit Pakistan every two years for a holiday of at least a year. This will give me a chance to see my children regularly and spend some time with them.' However, he did not intend to bring his family to Britain again.

The Professionals

I studied four professionally qualified migrants who came to Britain either to further their education or to work after getting their degrees in Pakistan. On arrival none of them was over 31 years of age. Two of the professionals were *Muhajirs* and the other two were born in Pakistan. Their fathers were in government service and this had given them the chance to live in urban areas in Pakistan. It appears that they obtained information about further education and professional opportunities available in Britain through their friends. They were also helped by relatives and friends during the migration process.

Because of their education, the nature of their jobs and their range of contacts with both the Pakistanis and the English, their awareness of the position of Pakistanis in Britain was greater than that of the other groups. They tended to take up leadership positions and represent Pakistanis to the wider community. All four in this category held positions in the Pakistani organizations. They had formed interpersonal friendships across the ethnic boundaries and exchanged gifts with English people at birthdays, Christmas and *Eids*. At the same time they spent most of their spare time with Pakistanis and participated in the religious and cultural activities of the community. They valued religious education for their children and took part in religious functions. In general, however, their attitude towards formal education was more liberal than that of the majority of Pakistanis in Rochdale.

The professionals were very critical of the immigration legislation and the racial prejudice and discrimination against the ethnic minorities in British society. They felt that the uncertainty created by immigration legislation did not help ordinary Pakistanis to adapt to their new situation. They themselves had faced discrimination in their professions. They also suggested that while individual settlement problems should be left to the Pakistani organizations, bodies such as the Community Relations Council should concentrate on majority—minority relationships, in order to break the prejudice barriers by creating greater understanding.

Their attitude towards settlement varied; two who had daughters planned to go back once their daughters reached puberty, the other two had not yet made up their minds but favoured waiting until their children had completed their education. On the whole, it appeared that the professionals were relatively more settled than some of the other groups. To illustrate some of these points in detail a case study is now discussed.

Dr P. K. was born in Pakistan in 1938. His father died in 1959. He was the eldest son and he had three brothers. Two of his brothers and his mother lived with him in Rochdale. His family in Pakistan included one of his brothers and his uncles and their families. His marriage to one of his uncles' daughters was arranged by his mother.

P. K. completed his MBBS degree in 1963. When his father died in 1959 his uncle started supporting him financially. After completing his medical degree he got a job as a House Physician for six months. Then he was Medical Officer for about a year. In the meantime he applied for a voucher to come to Britain. He got his voucher in 1964 but did not tell his family as he wanted it to be a surprise. When he resigned in January 1965 he told his family and they were very upset on hearing the news, especially his mother.

He explained his reasons for coming to Britain: 'I was undecided about my aim in coming to Britain. There was a salary attraction and to improve my qualifications was an incentive at the back of my mind.' P. K. sent a telegram to a friend (another doctor in London), but not to his maternal uncle in Manchester. He had £10 foreign exchange from the State Bank of Pakistan. When he reached London Airport there was no one to meet him. He took a coach to Victoria and with the help of another Pakistani he found the Pakistan Students Hostel in Knightsbridge, but the warden refused him accommodation because he was not a student. He was given the address of a Pakistani where he stayed as a lodger. Other Pakistanis living there helped him to find his way around London. He said, 'I could not contact my friend on the telephone and wrote to him. He contacted me the same week and I moved in with him and felt at home and confident.'

After three weeks P. K. got his first job in Middlesex. It was a holiday relief job and he worked there for only two weeks as a House Surgeon. His next job was in Macclesfield where he worked for six months as a House Surgeon. Then with the help of a friend, he got a job in Warrington, where again he was supposed to work for six months. In the meantime he applied for full registration with the BMA and was accepted. Then he worked in Sheffield (six months), Ashton-under-Lyne (six months), Rotherham (eight months) and Newcastle-upon-Tyne (one and a half years). In 1970 he was taken into a practice, with the help of a friend, as a General Practitioner in Rochdale. Later on he changed to another partnership where he was still working. He said, 'Now I feel settled, otherwise it was such an unpredictable life that six months in one place and I did not know where the next few months would be spent. It was a terrible life although a good experience of meeting different people.'

For the first few months in Rochdale he stayed with a friend. In 1971 he got a council flat and his wife, mother and youngest brother joined him as his dependants. His other brother had joined him in 1967 when he sponsored him to do an accountancy course, which he completed in 1970. Later, P. K. had a bungalow built in the outer part of the town and moved there with his family at the end of 1973.

His wife, mother and one brother did not face much difficulty in getting passports, but he said that the immigration officers asked them very irrelevant and awkward questions. He added that luckily one of his cousins in government service helped them to answer some of the questions. Once his family arrived here, he admitted, his responsibilities increased and his freedom was restricted. He stopped going out. 'The presence of the family brings comfort but on the other hand it creates some difficulties. For instance, after few months of their arrival my mother fell ill and it created a lot of work and strain for me. But they are settled now.'

Apart from immediate family P. K. did not have any close relations in Rochdale but had uncles and cousins in Manchester, Ashton-under-Lyne and Bolton. They visited each other quite regularly and especially at weekends. They all looked to him as their advisor in any matters related to the family. Before his family came to Britain he supported his joint family, and afterwards he sent money to his younger brother who was a clerk in a government department in Pakistan. P. K. said that he had not invested in Pakistan but was thinking of buying some land in the future. He wished to stay in this country until he retired, 'unless something drastic happens'.

He had many English friends. He claimed, 'Wherever I worked I made some friends, I still visit some of them and exchange gifts at Christmas at least. Similarly in Rochdale there are many friends, in the profession, in the neighbourhood and my patients.' I observed that P. K. received some English friends at his house occasionally. He also exchanged gifts with some of them on *Eids*, at Christmas and on birthdays.

P. K. thought that as a doctor he faced some prejudice but no discrimination. He believed that prejudice was only due to the anti-immigrant organizations who exaggerated issues and instigated people to be prejudiced, and inflamed the situation. He suggested that if immigrant organizations started a positive programme with the help of the Community Relations Council and other concerned local people these misunderstandings could be removed. He explained, 'There is a minority of indigenous people who are prejudiced but the rest are very sympathetic and good people. We should not call the British society a racialist society because the majority of the people hate to be racialist.'

P. K. thought if Pakistanis participated in activities jointly with other groups without losing their identity, this would improve matters. He argued that this could only be achieved if the Pakistani community was united. If they were divided they would not achieve anything and the disunity would be more harmful than anti-immigrant propaganda.

P. K.'s views about the future of Pakistani children in this country were very clear. He said, 'They will face more difficulties. We, the first-generation migrants, accept things and take prejudiced attitudes, etc., for granted. The children born and bred here would not accept this. There should be constant guidance from the community so that they are not isolated and alienated like some West Indian young people.' He also believed that it depended on how the host society brings its children up, hostile or tolerant. He thought the child—parent relationship was very important. He added, 'It is a must and helps to guide the children and keep them under control.'

P. K. suggested that the Pakistani organizations should help parents and their children to cope with this new situation. He thought that this could be achieved if there was unity in the Pakistani community and there was only one organization. He explained, 'There should be only one Pakistani organization and it should deal with religious, and socio-cultural problems. There should be subcommittees to deal with different aspects, with a central body. If this is not achieved these organizations will not be very successful in solving community problems.' He was critical of the activities of the Pakistani political parties in this country.

His prime interest was in the religious education of Pakistani children, adapting to society yet at the same time retaining their Pakistani identity. He felt, 'If mothers have proper control over children it helps a lot. Children should get the proper interpretation of the Quran and not just recitation. This is what we are trying to arrange to provide a full understanding of Islam for our children with the help of the community.'

P. K. was quite religious and went to the Mosque for prayers whenever he could, otherwise he prayed at home. He went to Friday afternoon prayers quite regularly, fasted in the month of *Ramazan* and went to *Eid* prayers. He worked quite hard on community activities. He felt that the way the Community Relations Council was run was not very satisfactory for creating understanding in the community. He suggested, 'I would like to see the whole emphasis shifted from personal problem solving to the relationships of people and to dealing with the situations which created conflict and prejudice.'

He considered that the recent immigration legislation was unnecessary, particularly the 1971 Act and the Pakistan Act 1973. He believed that people should not be forced to change their nationality as it created uncertainties. Those who would like to change nationality could have done so anyway. He said, 'To leave the Commonwealth was the Pakistan Government's decision but those who suffered were the people who were residents of this country. The law should have been that all those already living here would be treated as Commonwealth citizens always. The newcomers will be foreigners. There is some provision on those lines but there was more confusion and people had to go through so many official procedures etc.' He felt that the British government might bring out more legislation which would curtail some rights of those who were not British. He hoped that this would not happen, otherwise it would create more uncertainty for the settlement of immigrants. He thought uncertainty did not help adaptation to the new situation.

It appears that even he, while understanding the consequences of the legislation on his fellow countrymen, had an ambivalent attitude to citizenship rights for immigrants.

The Self-Employed

I studied four self-employed men all of whom, except for one who was in his early forties, came to Britain in their twenties. They all came from Lyallpur and had farming backgrounds. They all had some formal education. Three out of the four informants in this category had lived in urban areas for some time and had also had a business at one time or another or helped a relative in running a business. The kinship—friendship networks were used in the migration process and afterwards.

They all had worked in textiles before starting their own businesses. For instance, the manufacturers passed through these stages: industrial workers, part-time market traders, full-time market traders and then manufacturers. The main reasons given for these moves were to avoid discrimination and to gain independence 'to become one's own boss'. They started their businesses with the help of their relatives and friends, and some ran family businesses. Most of their customers were Pakistanis.

The self-employed were so busy that whatever spare time they had, they spent like the majority of Pakistanis, with relatives and friends. Although through their businesses they had made contacts with white (English) people these relationships were more of a formal than informal nature.

They were aware of hostility against the Pakistanis (and other coloured immigrants) and that was why they intended to start businesses in Pakistan and settle there sometime in the future. The other reason given was the children's future, in particular the girls' 'who should not be exposed to western environment after a certain age' as one of them remarked. That is why they valued and supported the religious education of children in the town.

The long hours which they spent in their businesses meant they did not go to Mosque very often but prayed at home. They supported the Mosque societies financially. They also contributed generously whenever a collection was made at times of a national crisis, for instance, a war or a flood. Other community projects were also supported financially by the self-employed Pakistanis. This gave them the power to influence decisions in the Pakistani organizations and in some cases to become leaders. Their shops were also a source of information and a meeting place for Pakistanis (see above, pp. 48–9).

Like many of my other informants the self-employed were suspicious of immigration policies and believed that inequality of race and colour would continue in employment as well as in other fields. This belief they supported by their own experience in the industry and the knowledge they had about what was happening in the society as a whole.

They believed in a limited participation by minority groups in the wider community and they thought the role of Pakistani organizations an important one to that end. Some of them were personally involved in the social and political institutions of the wider society by representing the Pakistani community. They believed in mobilizing the community on ethnic lines as they had done during the elections.

There appeared to be no cultural integration or even informal interpersonal relationships across ethnic boundaries. Although the position of the self-employed Pakistanis provided an opportunity to create interpersonal relationships with white people such as the suppliers or the few who came as customers, in practice this did not happen that often. The case study which follows illustrates some of these points.

Mr M. T., a ladies' and children's garment manufacturer, was born in 1939 at Jullundur, India. His father was an agriculturist. The family lived in Lyallpur District in Pakistan where they migrated from India at the time of Partition in 1947. M. T. was the second eldest son and had three brothers and one sister. His family in Pakistan consisted of his parents, brothers, uncles and cousins, the joint family totalling 25 members. His family in Rochdale included his wife, one daughter, his sister and her husband and one of his cousins. Some other *Biraderi* members lived in Rochdale as well. His wife's relatives lived in other parts of Britain. In 1969 he married outside his *Biraderi* in Lyallpur city, his father and uncle having arranged the marriage.

M. T. completed his matriculation and went no further with his education as he was not much interested. With the help of his family he opened a grocery shop. A year and a half later a friend of his, a school teacher, whose friend was in Britain, asked him if he was interested in going to Britain. He said, 'Although my family resisted I decided to come to Britain for an experience.' He added, 'As *Muhajirs* we had had experience of migration at the time of Partition, so coming to Britain was not a new venture, but the difference was that I was coming alone without my family to a strange and far country.' His decision was a shock to the family but on his insistence they agreed, he said, 'because with the help of an agent whom I paid Rs 4,500 (£225) I had already got my passport and booked an air ticket, so my family did not have any choice.'

M. T. reached London with his friend in May 1962 and then went on to Huddersfield, where his friend's friend was living. After a week he came to Rochdale to a distant cousin. Recalling the first bad experience he had on his arrival in this country he said, 'When we were travelling from London airport in a taxi to the railway station, we lost our bedding. We informed the taxi driver and he informed the police. This was the first set-back in this new situation. We left for Huddersfield without our bedding and some other things which probably somebody stole when the taxi driver was loading our luggage.' His cousin bought him some essentials such as shaving-kit, etc. and also gave him some money to spend.

After staying a few weeks with his relative in Rochdale who looked after him, he got a job in a textile mill in Heywood where his relative was working, at a wage of £7.00 per week. Commenting on his first experience of industrial work he said, 'It was a very tough job because I had never worked that hard before.' He worked there for a year and then changed to another textile mill in Rochdale where the wage was £11.00 a week on the night shift. He worked there until 1965. 'All this time I was thinking what had been my aim in coming to Britain.' Having had a business background he decided to start market trading. For some time he only worked on Saturdays with his cousin. Then at the end of 1965 he started a full-time business. It was in 1971, through contacts with the wholesalers and a manufacturer, that he started ladies' and children's garment manufacturing in partnership with Mr S. A. This partnership ended in 1972. M. T. kept his stalls to sell some of his materials and employed people to look after the stalls. He had (in April 1974) 16 full-time and 60 part-time people working for him. The wholesalers and market traders from all over the country bought garments from him. M. T. claimed that his weekly turnover in 1975 was £7,000 with a profit of £700–£1,000 per week. He admitted that his business was seasonal, 'sometimes up and sometimes down'.

He did not have a clear-cut time-table and worked late hours. He said, 'My business is twenty-four hours' work particularly when you have Pakistani market traders as your customers, they are free to come to you only either late evenings or on Sundays.' This pattern seemed common with other manufacturers as well.

M. T. lived with his relatives until he bought a house in 1966 where he lived with his cousin. They used part of it as a store for their garments when they started market-trading. This house was demolished in 1968. He bought another house in 1969 when he went to Pakistan to get married. He said, 'There was no resistance from my family in sending my wife to Britain, she joined me later in 1969. She faced some difficulty in getting the entry certificate due to some misunderstanding.'

M. T. considered his life-style had changed when his wife joined him. He said, 'Since my family joined me I feel more settled and responsible. We have created more relationships with other Pakistani families which also helps with manufacturing business.'

M. T. visited his relatives in Rochdale and other parts of Britain but not so regularly. He admitted that usually he spoke to his relatives and friends on the telephone because his time was taken up with his business. They usually came and stayed with him. 'Since my sister came to Rochdale she visits us almost daily and my wife goes to her house as they do not live very far.'

M. T. had been helped by his relatives and friends. Initially when starting his business he borrowed money from relatives but later on he relied on banks. He also used to go to his friends and relatives for general help. For instance, once when he was in hospital his close relatives and some other friends looked after his business for him.

M. T. knew many English people and people of other nationalities through his business but did not call them his friends. He seemed quite active in politics. He openly supported Dr Syed in the local elections of 1973 and campaigned for him. He said, 'We wanted to show that a Pakistani candidate could also win. Pakistanis showed co-operation and he won with the help of the Liberal party.' He thought that Pakistanis should be active in local activities to prove that they were part of the community as a whole, and this would help to create understanding on both sides but they should keep their identity.

M. T. was so occupied with his business that he hardly had any time for prayers. He attended *Eid* prayers and other special religious meetings. He would have liked his children to have a religious education when they were old enough. He contributed to the Mosque and to other appeals quite generously.

M. T. did not think that the future of Pakistani children in this country was good. He said, 'The teenagers are already spoiled. It is too early to say anything about the British-born. The teenagers are losing their contact with the family slowly because their fathers are working mostly on the night shift and cannot look after them properly. Due to this lack of contact the parents are losing respect and control. I think very few Pakistani children will succeed, most will work in the factories as their fathers are doing, although if they were properly looked after they could be successful in this advanced educational system.' M. T. believed it depended on the individual parents, and some help from the Pakistani organizations and leadership was needed as well.

M. T. considered Pakistani organizations quite useful to the community, although he thought that they were more active when there was a crisis or there was some threat to the Pakistani community. He suggested, 'there should be more activities organized by these associations in the community to guide and help the Pakistanis as Jews do for their community.'

M. T. considered that the local Community Relations Council was usually helpful to whoever sought help, particularly with entry certificates, tax queries and other welfare and neighbourhood problems. He said, 'Functions arranged by the local Community Relations Council are usually helpful in getting the English people and immigrants together and also getting to know each other, which could lead to good community relations.' He believed that there should be more everyday contact between ordinary Pakistani and English people to help remove their prejudices.

M. T. thought that some of the British people were prejudiced and discriminated whenever possible against the immigrants. 'There is an overall hate for the (coloured) immigrants.' He gave one example when he himself was beaten up by a gang. 'They shouted, "We will throw you out of the country you Pakis, or kill you".' M. T. also mentioned various examples when he thought he was discriminated against at work. He said. 'That was one of the reasons I started my own business where I am my own boss, and nobody can order me or call me "Oh Paki, do this or do that".'

M. T. thought that the anti-immigrant organizations were doing a lot of damage to community relations. He said, 'They are making the situation flare up and Mr Powell is the head of the group which is using these people for his political motives. Every sensible person knows that if the immigrants left this country there would be the question of who would run their factories, particularly at night, and do the menial jobs.'

M. T. thought that the immigrants in Britain were suffering from every new immigration law. He said, 'It seems that we will have to leave this country ultimately. I keep in mind the example of the British passport holders—Asians who are wandering about in other countries and not getting equal treatment as other British people, although they are British as well.' Relating this to Pakistanis in Britain, he feared that there was a danger particularly after the introduction of the Pakistan Act 1973 that the Pakistanis who did not take British nationality would be pressed to leave Britain. 'There should be protection and security particularly for Pakistani businessmen. Because, if they have to leave this country they should not be treated like the Asians from Uganda, where they had to leave penniless and leaving behind a life-time's earnings. There should be a clear-cut law that if somebody leaves Britain he should be allowed to take all his possessions to the country he wants to go to.' This concern was shared by other Pakistani businessmen particularly when they were changing their nationality to British. A lot of enquiries were made about this point at the Community Relations Council's office.

M. T. sent money to Pakistan but he was also investing here. He claimed that although his brothers and other family members were well off, he helped them whenever necessary. He said, 'I help usually at the time of marriages, as I did at my sister's marriage, or birth ceremonies or if somebody is in trouble and needs financial help.'

M. T. would ultimately like to go back to Pakistan. He had not invested in Pakistan except that his father had bought some land, but he was thinking of going to Pakistan to explore the possibility of starting a business and settling there. (Up until the middle of 1978 he had done nothing about this.)

Incapsulation Continuum

It is clear from the above case material which shows the similarities and differences between different occupational categories that the personal qualities of the migrant and the nature of his work influence his participation in different situations. The life-styles differ. Some Pakistanis in our study were highly incapsulated and had few opportunities to participate in the institutions of the wider community (except in a restricted sense in their work). This increased their dependence on the kinship—friendship groups and reinforced these networks. The night-shift workers were an example of this.

On the other hand, there were those who, because of their education, previous experience of urban life and the nature of their work, had many opportunities (or choices) to participate in the institutions of the wider society and to create relationships across ethnic boundaries. This gave them an opportunity to help other Pakistanis and to become leaders. Therefore, they were the least incapsulated. The professionals were an obvious example.

If we plot all the five occupational categories on a continuum on the basis of the information above to show the degree of incapsulation a picture emerges as shown in Figure 16.

In the analysis of the case material we have seen that their ways of life, and in particular their experiences of migration and settlement, presented different problems for different individuals. But the nature of their occupational experiences played an important role in the determination of the life-styles of Pakistanis. This means that the workers, particularly in textiles, came at one end of the continuum, the professionals and the transport workers on the other and self-employed Pakistanis in the middle.

On the other hand, all groups depended on the kinship—friendship groups for mutual help, support and enduring social relationships. The family was still considered as part of the wider network of the extended family in Pakistan, where most of them would like to return.

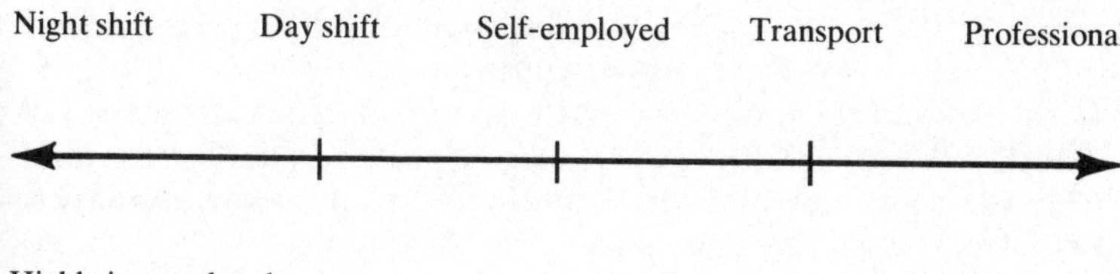

FIGURE 16 *Incapsulation continuum: Pakistani occupational categories*

They had almost similar views on religious matters such as the religious education of their children. They all perceived hostility and racial discrimination against Pakistanis and other coloured people in Britain. Because of this hostility and their kin obligations the majority did not see themselves as 'settlers'. I found a regular pattern of returning home for visits and holidays of varying lengths, from a few weeks up to as much as two years. The remittances and investments made in the country of origin and the kin obligations, it appears, reinforce the 'myth' of return one day in the future. I would suggest that some of these aspects of my informants' behaviour are only grasped if we see them in the British-Pakistani context.

I argue that the settlement of Pakistanis in Rochdale though still home-oriented in psychological and practical ways, was becoming permanent after the arrival of the dependants and other relatives such as their aged parents. The successive immigration legislations and the Pakistan Act 1973 had forced a change in the traditional pattern where,hitherto, migrants kept their families in the villages of their origin. It seemed that some of the accommodative behaviour accepted by migrants as a temporary measure would continue. My informants did not wish to change their values and adapt to the British ways which they regarded as inferior to their own and in some cases as corruptive. It is a situation similar to that described in Mayer's work about Xhosa migrants in East London, which demonstrates the effect of different mental images of city life among the migrant groups. He mentions that 'the question of values is important, for in many situations people might conform outwardly, but still remain inwardly determined to revert to pre-urban patterns when opportunity arises.'[4]

Mayer states that the 'Red's' social network in the city is based on the home society, whereas the 'School' migrants network has no direct connections with his home network. The majority of my informants were very similar to Mayer's 'Red' category of migrants. They saw their status in relation to their home and not to Britain thus hoping to return there one day.

It needs to be understood that the internal value preferences of my informants and the external constraints they faced, discussed above, together prevented the majority of them from coming out of the incapsulation. Furthermore, in the light of the evidence it would be fair to suggest that in the near future at any rate the incapsulation of Pakistanis from the wider society would continue.

12. Conclusions

Both the processes of migration and ethnic relations are difficult and important fields of study. In this work different levels of these processes are analysed by different methods: in case studies at the individual interactional level, for the migrants as a group at the community level, and at the institutional and structural levels focusing on both Britain and Pakistan. The Pakistani community was considered in depth in terms of the activities of the actors in different areas of social life. In this way the processes involved in a series of everyday or special events were highlighted and the resulting incapsulation became apparent.

Process of Migration

No single model explains the migration of Pakistanis to Britain, therefore more than one model was used to illustrate the complexity of this process. Petersen's typology explains the emigrant's motives and the socio-economic causes of migration. The intervening obstacles and difficulties in the process of migration are clarified by the use of Lee's model. The kinship—friendship networks and the clustering of Pakistanis are analysed in terms of chain migration. The role of sponsorship and patronage in the process of mass migration and the way it affected the nature of Pakistani settlement in Rochdale and other parts of Britain helped to illustrate this.

The ways in which the nature of the mass migration is different from that of the early settlers is discussed above (pp. 22–6). For the early migrants the uncertainties and risks were greater than for the later migrants who came to join them. As Petersen says, 'So long as there are people to emigrate, the principal cause of emigration is prior emigration.'[1] The link established with the country of destination, the feedback of knowledge and the sponsorship and patronage of kinsmen help to establish the pattern. 'Migration becomes a style, an established pattern, an example of collective behaviour. Once it is well begun the growth of such a movement is semi-automatic . . . when emigration has been set as a social pattern, it is no longer relevant to enquire concerning the *individual* motivations.'[2] Mass migration resulted in the establishment of institutions, organizations and agents to facilitate the continued migration of other Pakistanis. This is clear from the case study material. Individual case histories also help to explain some of the variables involved in the Pakistani migration. For instance, after the Commonwealth Immigrants Act of 1962, the voucher system reinforced the sponsorship and patronage because the migrants in Britain were in a position to obtain vouchers for their kin and friends in Pakistan. On the other hand, later immigration legislation forced the migrants to bring their dependants to this country. This type of migration has resulted in kinship—friendship networks and a multi-stranded relationship-based ethnic community.

The Southern Italian migration to America between 1889 and 1910 is a case similar to that of the Pakistanis.[3] The introduction of immigration controls in the 1920s initiated a transitional period for the Italian settlement in Chicago, which may well indicate the course of events for the settlement of Pakistanis (and other Asians) in Britain once most dependants have arrived and few new migrants are admitted. Another similarity between Pakistanis and Southern Italian migrants is their loyalties to and continuing relationships with their native villages. Initially their loyalties remained rooted in their native villages rather than transferrring to America. Like the Pakistanis, the early Italian settlers provided an important link for the new arrivals who were helped in the initial stages of settlement, thus facilitating eventual adjustment to the American environment. So the kin/village-based clustered residences of Pakistanis in Rochdale (and other areas) are not a chance phenomenon but the result of social processes distinguished by the obligations of migrants to provide stepping-stones for their relatives and friends.

Ethnic Relations: Change and Adjustment; Continuity and Incapsulation

The migration of kinship and friendship groups has helped to create the *Biraderi*-based Pakistani ethnic community. Residential segregation in some areas demonstrates the role of the kinship—

friendship networks, and a desire to live together near kin and friends. Westernized Pakistanis were geographically far more dispersed than the rest of the Pakistani community.

At work too, sponsorship and patronage had resulted in 'ethnic work groups'. We have seen that *Biraderi* networks contributed to this concentration of Pakistanis in ethnic work groups by helping new migrants to find jobs and at the same time enabling employers to use these channels for the recruitment of more workers.

It is not suggested that this was the only factor which resulted in the formation of ethnic work groups. The management tried to keep the Pakistanis on separate shifts and in separate departments to avoid conflicts with their white workers and to meet the need for a labour supply to do heavy and dirty work. The reliance of the continuous shift system on the willingness of Pakistanis to work on the night shift was demonstrated. While the Pakistanis felt happy working on the night shift and in separate departments in ethnic work groups because of the language differences and as a means of avoiding the prejudice and hostility of the white workers, there was also the added attraction of more money to compensate for their low-paid jobs.

These factors hindered their participation in union activities and in using such facilities as canteens, and their incapsulation was that much greater. Night-shift work also affected their participation in the wider community and strained the relationships between husbands and wives and fathers and children.

Pakistanis were concentrated in certain industrial sectors, in this case largely in textiles. These were the sectors which had either the lowest-paid or the dirtiest jobs, difficult shifts and worst working conditions. Overwhelmingly, the majority of them were manual workers, usually unskilled or semi-skilled. To sum up, I found that generally Pakistanis were employed in occupations rejected by the indigenous population.

They were also at a disadvantage in terms of promotion. The reasons given for this were: their lack of appropriate qualifications and non-industrial background. In addition racial discrimination against them existed. This resulted in Pakistanis, along with other coloured migrants, forming the lowest stratum on the British labour market. This situation clearly demonstrates the external constraints on the migrants. One way to get out of these constraints of unattractive work conditions and to avoid hostility was to become self-employed. This, it was felt, brought independence, prosperity, respect and helped to avoid humiliation.

In Chapters 4 to 10 I showed that the participation of Pakistanis in the wider British community institutions was limited due to the constraints on their options. Certain change-producing factors could not be avoided because of the new urban environment. These included different climate, different jobs, different housing structure and modern amenities, compulsory education for children, and so on. The modified structure of the joint family in Britain rather than the traditional joint family was an example of this: Ballard writing about the Sikh community stated that the wage-based 'economic environment may lead to considerable changes in behaviour, without necessarily affecting the moral and jural norms of the community.'[4] Pakistanis were in a different economic environment and because of that in some situations conformed outwardly but still remained inwardly determined to revert to pre-urban patterns without changing the moral and jural norms of their community. The reason for not participating in the British ways was that the Pakistanis had learnt from childhood that the Western ways were bad, to be despised and regarded as a sign of moral failure. Clearly, resistance to change and non-participation on an individual level in British institutions were characteristic of the majority of Pakistanis interviewed for this work. They reverted back to their 'Pakistani behaviour' as soon as they got the opportunity, because they felt they were here to work, save and wished to return to their villages back home. This whole situation increased Pakistani incapsulation and dependence on the kinship—friendship groups, ethnic institutions and facilities, which were available in the areas of their concentration.

One of the Pakistanis' main concerns which emerged from the case material and other information was the importance attached to the transmission of religion and culture to Pakistani children who were born or brought up in Britain. This was mentioned in almost every context. We saw that the decision to stay in this country was related to how successfully the parents felt they could cope with this very sensitive issue. Western influence on the children was taken as a threat to the authority and control of parents and also to their prestige and the respect considered due to them. The parents thought that it would also take the children away from Islam and Pakistani culture generally. The activities of the religious organizations in particular and the efforts of some individual parents to give their children religious instruction and to teach them Urdu were an attempt to safeguard their culture and identity. The example of success of the Jewish community in protecting their religion and culture was often mentioned by Pakistanis as an example to be emulated. In other words they felt that 'If the Jews can do it why can't we?' Pakistanis seemed to be committed to their religion and were orthodox Muslims. Whether Pakistanis born and brought up in Britain would continue to believe in and practise their religion in the same way is a matter for the future to decide.

The dependence of migrants on kinship groups was facilitated by the presence of *Biraderi* and the functioning of the *Vartan Bhanji* system. This system of *Vartan Bhanji* also fits into Blau's exchange model. Exchange occurs when some goods, services or other benefits are given in the expectation that their equivalent will be returned. The benefits of exchange can be extrinsic or intrinsic; that is, they can consist of things or services which are separate from the process of interaction and from the particular characteristics of those in it, or they can relate directly to interaction as such, and to the nature of those involved.[5] A Pakistani visiting his friends or relatives because he enjoys food is an example of enjoying extrinsic benefits; visiting for the sake of interpersonal contact, or on the occasion of a ceremony such as a marriage within the *Biraderi* to fulfil one's obligations is an example of enjoying intrinsic benefits. There is evidence that *Vartan Bhanji* relationships are hot only found among the relatives in Britain, but are also maintained with kin in Pakistan, because the families in Rochdale are treated as extensions of families in the villages in Pakistan.

The nature of community dependence and help differed from one occupational group to the other. For example, the professionals and other middle-class educated Pakistanis were providing help in day-to-day life while the working-class Pakistanis were mainly at the receiving end. Similarly, dependence on kin for help and companionship differed between the middle-class professionals and the working-class Pakistanis. The professionals depend more on their friends. Geoffrey Gorer has some evidence which supports this finding, that middle-class people are most often separated from their kin, and dependent on their friends and neighbours for help and companionship.[6] Ronald Fletcher also agrees that interest in perpetuating kinship ties and kin and degrees of mutual aid between kin may differ between classes.[7] Although we found an indication of the differences between classes, the picture in terms of mutual help and obligations would probably have been different, had all relatives been living in this country.

We can conclude that in the Pakistani community there were some members, the horizons of whose life were wider than those of others and the number of whose role relationships was therefore potentially greater. This factor, of course, is closely related to various other factors such as the nature of occupation, social class and status, level of education, *Biraderi* strength, age and sex.

Some Pakistanis are highly incapsulated and have few opportunities to participate in the institutions of the wider community. The night-shift workers are such a category. There are those on the other hand whose work is such that they do have many opportunities to participate in the institutions of the wider society and create relationships across the ethnic boundaries. The professionals are such a group. When all the five occupational categories are plotted on the incapsulation continuum, we find that the industrial workers fall on one side of the continuum, i.e. are highly incapsulated, the professionals and transport workers on the other end, less incapsulated, and self-employed Pakistanis fall in the middle. On the other hand, the presentation of network contacts within and between the occupational categories and the way the kinship—friendship networks cut across the occupational boundaries did not only highlight the inter-connections amongst the different groups of actors, but it also underlined how these links were utilized in different areas of activities, which resulted in the incapsulation of the majority of Pakistanis from the rest of the community.

One group in the Pakistani community which has little opportunity to form relationships outside the existing network is the women. Pakistani men in theory are more likely to develop a loose-knit network than are their relatively home-tied women. We see that men's lives are affected more as a result of the change from rural agricultural activities in Pakistan to urban industrial life in Britain but the women, because of the nature of their work, remain enmeshed in a network of kin. Although due to modern amenities, Pakistani women in Britain have more leisure time which they spend in sewing or visiting each other, nevertheless language difficulties and *Purdah* increase their dependence on the kin group and lead to a high degree of incapsulation.

The Pakistanis studied regard Britain as a foreign country, unwelcoming to immigrants. They perceive prejudice and discrimination against coloured immigrants in general and Pakistanis in particular. They also face language barriers which lead to several other difficulties and increase their dependence on one another. So they turn to their own relatives, friends and countrymen for help, assistance and security.

Brown, writing about the South Italians in Bedford, states, 'The world of the first generation is the static world of Southern Italy. Its intensive feeling for the primacy of the family group, its religious respect for the authority of the father, its seclusion and control of unmarried women, its devotion to the Church: all have the force of permanent, unquestioned values. Here is Europe at its most traditional and inflexible.' To this, the world of Bedford is entirely irrevelant, the notion of integration an absurdity.[8] This is clearly pertinent to the situation among Pakistanis in Rochdale.

An important aspect of any situation is the availability of the means to pursue particular goals. The whole complex of ethnic institutions manifests the community's wish not merely to express but also to defend and perpetuate their traditional social norms, values, beliefs and ethnic identity.[9] Pakistanis try to recreate their old community around them in Rochdale but because of the move from their villages in Pakistan to urban areas it cannot be exactly the same. With them, the significance of the colour question and of a different religious system may make for greater differentiation from the British society. Out of necessity, they have formed something different from Pakistan because of situational differences, while the underlying principles remain the same because their aspirations are bound to their homeland where most of them wish to retire. Their relatives in Pakistan expect them to return, and they themselves mention their plans and ambitions (see pp. 185–212). Their obligations to their kin and their economic ties, in the way of remittances and investment and visits, with Pakistan keep alive the wish to return, and so they do not wish to change their norms and values while in Britain. Their ambition and status are related to Pakistan and not to Britain.

On the other hand, the life-styles of those who came from peasant agricultural backgrounds, irrespective of their country of origin, have some fundamental similarities which are different from the industrial urban way of life. Perhaps the most significant aspect of Pakistani migration is the strong inference to be drawn from the life-styles of Pakistanis in Britain, that they have no long-term intention of settling here. For an average Pakistani, migration means that though he has had to come to Britain for economic reasons he is never able to feel that he has come for good. Even if he thought he had come permanently there are kin and friends in Pakistan who cannot follow him because of the migration restrictions. By definition, then, the Pakistani migrant is a person whose network of relations cannot be located in Britain alone. This is why to understand some of the social relationships of my respondents it is necessary to examine the British-Pakistani context.

Consequently, a Pakistani is aware that what he does in Rochdale will be known in Pakistan and he knows how it will be interpreted. If he deviates from the norms of the *Biraderi*, etc., his *Biraderi* in Pakistan, as well as in Britain, will bring pressure on him to conform. This creates a consciousness for the migrant that his activities in Britain are an extension of his home society and that he is operating within the social structure of Pakistani society. Similarly, when he returns to Pakistan for a visit, though he goes dressed like a Westerner, he will behave according to the norms of the *Biraderi* and of Pakistani society. He will be applauded for his economic success by his family and *Biraderi*. This encourages him to remain a part of the traditional society, for it contrasts markedly with the hostility he meets in Britain whenever he tries to participate outside very restricted limits.

The assumption that the changes experienced by migrants invariably lead to a one-way adaptation to the culture of the receiving society has been demonstrated to be too simplistic. We have seen that in the case of the Pakistanis many environmental changes are inevitable while others are accepted only as temporary. The Pakistanis' move from the country of origin to the country of destination is itself instrumental in bringing some social changes but they still derive their meanings and achieve certain statuses through participating in both societies. Similar attempts to recreate the home system in a greatly changed environment have also been found in some ethnic groups in the United States.

The special identity perceived by a social category of people accords with their social interaction with others. I would emphasize that ethnic identity only becomes significant when it is perceived and given a meaning by the people involved. Only then do the participants develop and use those internal mechanisms, such as kinship and friendship networks, and lead others to distinguish them from the rest. Ethnicity has no formal status—there is a vagueness of boundaries and limits and uncertainty about the degree to which any person is associated with any grouping. No member of an ethnic group has to act the way most other members of that group do; nothing but social pressure will hold him to any behaviour. Similarly with persons whom we would consider as 'belonging' to ethnic groups. They may accept that belonging or reject it. Admittedly, there are some groups, marked by race, where belonging is simply imposed by the outside world, as against other less sharply marked groups.[10] Where the members of a social unit share a great many cultural items—religion, language, moral and aesthetic values and other behavioural norms, they are likely to recognize a common allegiance. This in turn implies cohesion.

Pakistanis are such a group differentiated by cultural items as well as by race and national origin.

It is very important to analyse the manipulation of social networks in and by the Pakistani groups for many reasons. Sponsorship and patronage of relatives and friends in the migration process, providing accommodation, helping to get a job, lending money to start a business or to buy a house, mobilizing support at elections by using the *Biraderi* networks, and support and unity within the group at times of conflict with external groups are a few examples of manipulation of social networks in the community. There is a high degree of cohesion within the group which contains these overlapping networks. In small traditional communities and societies, relationships tend to be diffuse, the same individuals who are related to one another by one set of interests being also related by numbers of others.[11] This was found to be the case among Rochdale Pakistanis.

Deviation from norms leads to conflict. Within a Pakistani community this conflict is at different levels; interpersonal, *Biraderi* and regional origin level. There is pressure from the *Biraderi* and the wider group to conform. Where choice is possible in the various spheres of interaction, conflict is inevitable. Thus we have seen that conflict arose from *Zan*, *Zar* and *Zameen*. It is also clear that conflict with outside groups unites Pakistanis. In times of crisis such as the Indo-Pakistan war over Bangladesh in 1971 and the issue of prisoners of war, etc., Pakistanis were united and Pakistani organizations played their part in enlisting effective support for the Pakistan Government. Similarly during elections these organizations, led by the educated members as spokesmen to the outside world, mobilized support for the Liberal Party candidates to counteract the anti-immigrant propaganda first by the British Campaign to Stop Immigration, and later by the National Front. The channels of *Biraderi* were used for this mobilization to achieve unity. External hostility can lead to internal cohesion. Similarly a struggle to end the ethnic discrimination may intensify ethnic cohesion and hence inter-ethnic hostility. Mobilization of ethnic loyalties is not in any sense unique to Pakistanis in Rochdale. Ethnicity, as an undercurrent uniting force has been reported in a number of situations which are separated in time and space; yet the general theme has been the same. The exploitation of ethnic loyalties by politicians on the American political scene is such an example. Robert Dahl has shown how politicians in New Haven manipulated ethnic loyalties for political support and how the Catholic, Jew and the Negro found that ethnic identification coloured his life, his relations with others and his attitudes towards himself and the world.[12]

Looking at the situation as a whole it is clear that the incapsulation of Pakistanis arises because of both the external constraints and the internal cultural norms and values and pressures on them to conform. It must be emphasized that this incapsulation limits inter-ethnic relations across the ethnic boundaries and reinforces the ethnicity. Even those Pakistanis who interact with indigenous people maintain two separate identities. For instance, a professional Pakistani in the company of English people might give the impression that he has been fully assimilated into English culture while in fact that is not the case because he may behave as a strict Pakistani when interacting with other Pakistanis. The same holds true for those Pakistani 'marginal men' (leaders) who represent the community to the wider society and may appear to be 'assimilados'. Indeed it is clear from the information collected in this book that the participation of ordinary Pakistanis on a personal basis in creating interpersonal relationships across the ethnic boundaries is restricted. Lastly, it must be remembered that assimilation is often a misleading proposition for Pakistanis (and other Asians) because of their culture and their skin colour. What appears to have been happening in Britain is a situation of 'pluralism' or 'integration' in which Pakistanis are keeping their structural and cultural identity and are participating in the wider community institutions only where it is inevitable, such as in employment and education.[13] I feel that if the overt hostility continues to grow at the rate it has done in recent years, ethnicity will play an important role in strengthening ethnic boundaries, and reinforcing the myth of return. However, my observations lead me to believe that the Pakistanis have an ambivalent attitude. Many wish to go back but in reality economic circumstances are such that the majority are unlikely ever to return. There is also a possibility that the cultural and familial bonds with Pakistan may weaken with the second generation.

Appendix I Methodology of the Study

The survey and case study data for this work were collected between 1972 and 1975; however, my contact with the Rochdale community was first made in July 1971 when I collected some data for my MA dissertation.[1] After I ceased to live in Rochdale I made frequent visits at weekends up to the time of writing this work. As a result of contacts with the community, I realized that sponsorship and patronage helped in the formation of kinship and friendship networks in Britain. After spending some time in the field and especially working on the local Community Relations Council, I observed that the kinship and friendship networks continued to be major factors in almost all fields of social interaction among Pakistanis. I therefore decided to use a social network analysis not only as a theoretical framework but also as the basic methodological technique.

Social Network as a Method

To collect data using social network as a methodological technique, the researcher needs to be fairly selective in his choice of persons most relevant to the situation to be studied. The nature of the study and the researcher's observation influences the selection of subjects, and the mode of collecting data depends on the occurrence of certain situations, events or actions. Networks are usually seen in operation only partially and connections have to be followed up and recorded.

As a result it is a very slow and sometimes a difficult process. Similarly, it is difficult to follow different parts of different persons' networks in operation at the same time. The researcher may miss some processes and his observation can never be more than partial. To minimize this difficulty and to collect different types of data about the role of kinship—friendship networks in social, political and economic fields and to relate these to the wider community situations, therefore, different techniques were needed. I used a combination of anthropological and sociological methods to get different types of information to fill in the gaps. I was aware, at the beginning, that complete observational techniques would not be possible, keeping in view the scattered nature of the network. I, therefore, decided that observation would be supplemented wherever possible by depth interviews and case studies and by a system of cross-checks with various informants. In one area I also carried out a household survey followed by another survey of the employment patterns of Pakistanis, which included some general questions to set the observations and information collected as a result of the case studies into a broader context. These different procedures were adopted to 'discover their relative strengths and weaknesses so that a rational choice among procedures can be made in the context of a particular study'.[2]

These procedures were adopted, as any piece of research can potentially display what Merton refers to as a serendipity pattern. By this he means that research may unearth findings that are both unanticipated and strategic and that call for the development of a new theory.[3] To cite one example, it has been generally assumed that property values are permanently reduced when non-whites move into an all-white neighbourhood. However, research conducted by Gillette has suggested that this is simply not the case. If anything, the migration of non-whites into a previously segregated neighbourhood serves in the long run to increase property values.[4] This certainly happened in the areas of non-white concentration in Rochdale.

Findings of this kind not only raise questions concerning the validity of 'commonsense' knowledge, but they also create a demand for a new theory. They also require that the same phenomenon is tested by using different techniques in order to modify and improve the theories.

Case Study Method

The case study method was chosen because it enables one to carry out a detailed study of relational aspects which are often difficult to obtain through the use of questionnaires. As C. H. Cooley puts it, 'the case study deepens one's perception and gives us a clearer insight into life. It gets at behaviour directly and not by the indirect and abstract approach.'[5] Outlining the function of case studies, David Morgan mentions that 'case studies may be used to illustrate various aspects of the social structure under examination or the various theoretical perspectives adopted by the investigator.'[6] This is certainly my view of the function of the case study method.

It was clear that the use of intensive methods would allow only a small number of cases to be studied to learn about the patterns of interaction in the community. After prolonged discussions and after study of existing literature, it became clear that Pakistanis were economic immigrants in the sense that the overriding reason for their migration related to work opportunities. Here, five groups reflecting the four main occupations (with the textile group divided into day- and night-shift workers) were chosen.

1. Day-shift workers } mainly textiles
2. Night-shift workers }
3. Public transport workers
4. Professionals
5. Self-employed Pakistanis

Twenty cases in all were studied: four from each group. These cases yielded comparative data within the same category and between categories.

Similarly, having cases from various occupations enhanced the possibility of obtaining data on different social networks within the Pakistani population through which a broader picture could be developed. One reason for not selecting research cases using the kinship—friendship criterion was that there was a possibility that I might get people from one dominant occupational group and miss out the others. My aim was also to analyse how the nature of a Pakistani's occupation structures his life-style and affects his relations with family members, kin, friends, neighbours and the wider community.

The data about the Pakistani community as an ethnic group and the role of ethnicity in the socio-religious, political and economic fields were recorded during the field-work. These activities were recorded in intra-ethnic and inter-ethnic situations. These situations were related to the individuals wherever relevant, thus focusing on two levels simultaneously: individual (cases) and interactional (i.e. social situations and community activities).

Relationship with 'Research Cases' and Reliability of the Data

It is worth recording that the major characteristics of my study were the informal relationships with the informants. This gave a quality of 'free flow' to much of the information obtained relating quite often to intimate affairs, and this helped to draw up a pattern of relationships of the cases within the kinship—friendship networks and in other situations. This also resulted on several occasions in unexpected situations. For instance, I was invited for meals and was asked to solve many problems regarding entry certificates, income tax, passports, UK citizenship and other personal problems. I was asked many questions about the new immigration legislation, particularly the Pakistan Act of 1973 which was going through Parliament at the time of my field-work. This created frequent contact with my informants in the office and in their homes. Sometimes it gave an opportunity to the respondents to relieve their feelings on matters about which they very rarely spoke, such as prejudice and discrimination against Pakistanis.

I was always aware of the problem of invasion of privacy in discussing the intimate affairs of the informants, which presents some delicate moral questions. The problems facing a researcher who is doing a study such as this are likely to be much more acute than those faced by a questionnaire interviewer. Replies required by a questionnaire are usually brief, and more private topics can frequently be blocked off by the person questioned. My job helped me to overcome these difficulties and I tried to handle the situation with tact and judgment.

I was always aware of the distinction between my role as researcher and my official role. The transition from the latter to the former was not easy as the official role was so relevant to the issues discussed. Schwartz writes, 'I was involved yet detached while encountering the research subjects and detached yet involved while engaged in retrospective rumination.'[7] It is very difficult to draw lines about subjectivity and objectivity but during my field-work I tried to avoid personal bias as much as possible.

The question of involvement with the people one studies sometimes may lead to subjective interpretation. I felt this difficulty when I was helping my respondents with their various problems and thought that probably I was influencing the normal course of their life and relationships. But as time passed I realized that only by helping my respondents and winning their confidence was it going to be possible to understand their different situations. A researcher without such an involvement with his subjects would not have insight into some of these situations. It was possible for me to involve and then detach myself from the situation as I was not living with any family. Once I left the field and went home I was able to write my notes.

Good relationships with Pakistanis involved gaining their confidence and respect. I conformed to Muslim traditions and never acted in such a way as to offend the community.

One point relevant to mention is that of *Purdah* practised in some Pakistani families. This created problems for me in the beginning with three families. I was unable for some time to find out what kind of life was lived in the backroom. In two cases however the wives were allowed to come to the front room when I was there. I was able to talk to them though they were still shy and reluctant so I did not press the conversations because this would have embarrassed the women. Papanek points out the kind of problems that a male researcher in a *Purdah* society faces in studying the women's situation.[8] Male researchers in Britain too face these problems in relation to the women who come from *Purdah* society. Hence, Pakistani women were not studied directly, due to *Purdah* limitations on the women.

The research design which underlies the 'ethnographic approach' is not easily applied to the analysis of modern urban communities because of the large populations and diversity of institutions and social interaction involved. I would argue that in order for an ethnographic study to be useful, it must shed light on particular groups formed within the urban situation such as the one covered in this work. If this approach is correct, research on communities will probably become increasingly focused upon specific aspects of community structure and process. Different techniques—described below—were used to collect the data for this work.

Intensive Interviews

In collecting intensive qualitative material, informants were encouraged to talk freely and, within limits, about whatever they wanted to discuss. It was essential not to prevent anyone from raising questions on matters which he felt were relevant, because this helped me to add to the overall picture about the problem under study. The nature of my job as a worker at the Community Relations Council helped me because the informants raised a lot of relevant points and discussed problems they were facing in different situations. Without a set of formal questions I felt free to follow up any answer where I saw interesting leads, without feeling tied to a rigid programme. This was essential in establishing rapport and in creating more informal relationships. My ethnic identity with the informants helped in this situation.

However, this does not mean that the information collected was arbitrary: an interview guide was used. This helped to remind me of the most important questions to be asked before going to see a particular person after checking previous notes. At no time did I take the interview guide with me either for reference or to tick off questions as they were answered by the informants.

By using the intensive technique and unstructured interview combined with personal observation, I was in a position to cover and record anything relevant to the general problem. The structured methods, such as the social survey method are often more limiting, and therefore not exclusively suitable for my purposes.[9]

Participant Observation

One of the main anthropological techniques is participant observation. The advantages and disadvantages of this technique as a data-gathering tool have been well documented.[10] In the classic studies the anthropologist lives among the people being studied, observes or takes part in social activities, and notes all that happens within the community. In this way data gathered are based on direct observation and not simply on informants' accounts. How far the observer actually becomes 'participant' varies a great deal according to the social context and personal qualities of the observer. In a broad sense the social position of the observer determines what he is likely to see.[11] In a modern urban industrial community the situation is quite different as there are a whole range of activities, more individualized dwellings, different work situations, recreational, religious and social activities. So the observation of the researcher is usually restricted to certain activities at any one time in any situation.

The sociologist who decides to study his own society/ community is constantly drawing on his personal background of experience as a basis of knowledge. Participant observation enables the research worker to secure his data within the medium, symbols and experiential words which have meaning to his respondents and to prevent imposing alien meanings upon the actions of the subjects. Anthropologists dealing with cultures other than their own have consciously recognized and utilized the technique as a matter of necessity.[12] Therefore, the role of the participant observer in one's own society/community has the advantage that communication is in the same language and within the same symbolic system. Being a Pakistani I had this advantage and was accepted by the community.

I have mentioned above that during my field-work in the community I took all available opportunities to participate in the local and family/*Biraderi* affairs. I noted events concerning Pakistanis and attended the social functions arranged by them whenever possible. If I was not present at a function I used my informants who had attended to cross-check the information. In addition to the social functions arranged by the Pakistani organizations, I attended family/*Biraderi* affairs in the houses of the informants in particular. This helped me to obtain much valuable material about relatives and friends who were present and provided the opportunity to talk with the wives and children of my respondents. Accordingly, this helped me in elaborating and checking the information gathered through the interviews.

To observe the work situation I managed to get permission to visit and talk to workers in three textile mills in the area. At least one visit, each with the help of the management, was made to three other textile mills who employed Pakistanis. In the three mills I observed Pakistanis working on different shifts. This was not done on a continuous basis throughout the study, but during six months from February to July 1974, I regularly visited all the three mills. I also used informants who worked in these mills and if any interesting matter was reported I made a visit to the work place.

Interview Notes

Naturally nobody can record verbatim everything said by the respondents. I tried to remember a great deal of what was said. In the later writing up of the cases only those words which were recorded verbatim were used as actual quotations. After a sequence of interviews was completed with a person the notes were rewritten on to cards, under different headings as mentioned in the interview guide. Whatever I observed I recorded as well wherever relevant to an informant or to a social situation. Without this organization, the material would have been unmanageable when it came to the analysis stage. As confidentiality was promised to the individuals the case histories were written in coded form.

One point which is relevant to mention here is the reliability of the information. A large amount of data in any field situation is obtained only through the statements of individual informants. It is certainly true that it is customary in a 'primitive' field situation to try to compare the story given with the reality. But every researcher knows that in his notes there are many statements about what people do which are solely based on one source. This problem was solved to some extent in my case through the free access to observe informants in different situations.

Household Survey

The aim of this survey, carried out in 1974, was to find out the basic information necessary for drawing up a sample of working Pakistanis who were to be interviewed. This household survey was conducted in a defined area (see the map, p. 47). Data were collected on: the number of 211 Pakistani households, the number of Pakistanis living in the area, and other characteristics such as age, sex, marital status, employment, place of work, type of work, shift, district of origin in Pakistan, length of stay in this country and year of coming to Britain and then to Rochdale.

The Survey of Employment and Related Aspects

As mentioned above this survey was part of the multi-method technique used for the study as a whole. It was also based on some of the main points which emerged from the case studies and observations along with a survey done in the late 1960s in the Bradford area about the employment and other related factors concerning Indians, West Indians and Pakistanis.[13]

The survey had two main objectives:

1. It helped to present data in a quantitative form and also to test the validity of the qualitative data gathered using mainly anthropological techniques.
2. It offered an opportunity to compare the results of this survey with the Bradford findings after a six-year period. In turn, this helped to present a picture of the local employment situation of Pakistanis and the related factors structuring their lives in the town. Little was known about the local employment situation of Pakistani workers, the main immigrant group in the area, and their own perception of it. The aim, therefore, was to collect data which would enable me to undertake an analysis of the labour market and the employment situation in a racially mixed locality. The data helped to draw a descriptive as well as analytical picture of the situation and factors which structured the life-style of Pakistanis and the meaning they gave to it.

There were 354 'insured'* Pakistanis in the Tweedale Street area.

A quota sample of 103 was drawn. It covered the four groups included in the case studies. A separate interviewing schedule was used for the self-employed Pakistanis.

The interviews with Pakistanis presented some problems. One was the effort to contact the respondents. In one case up to ten visits were made. This was due to their different and sometimes unpredictable working hours. Weekends were a good time for contact, but then additional problems were created by the presence of visiting relatives and friends who made interviewing of the respondent on his own difficult.

Initial contact was created by the household survey and by the time of the employment survey I did not need to use 'sponsors'. I, therefore, avoided being identified with one particular person or faction within the Pakistani community. As a whole, very good co-operation from my respondents was obtained, and the majority welcomed the opportunity to express their views and tell their stories of achievement or failure.

Visit to Pakistan

My visit to Pakistan in March–April 1975 for a few weeks gave me an opportunity to talk to the relatives in Pakistan of some of my respondents, particularly of the 20 research cases. This filled some gaps in the information I had collected. I was able to learn how the relatives felt about their own situation and that of their migrant family members.

Numerical Social Networks: Data Collection[14]

In August 1975 Professor J. C. Mitchell suggested to me that I could test Bernard and Killworth's new technique, which puts ethnographic description and numerical collection about social networks together, with my data.[15] The technique has so far been developed in closed systems such as a ship but nobody has tried using it for an 'open' system. I tested it with my twenty 'cases' as I had already collected the ethnographic data about the social networks. A simple card sort procedure was adopted as follows:

1. I took a deck of file cards, one for each person in the group, and I invented a numbering system. For example, I put the pro-

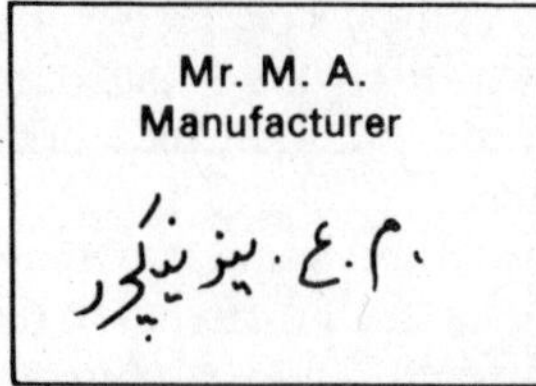

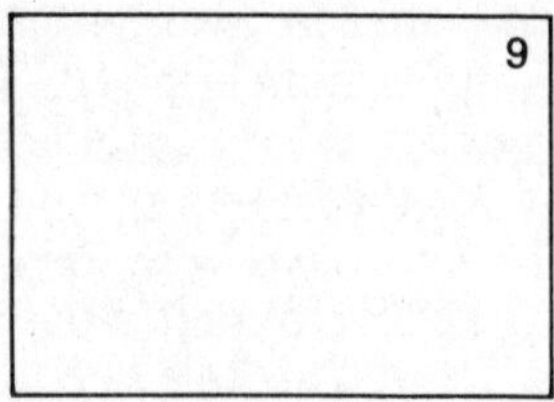

FIGURE 17 *File card*

fessionals first, then the self-employed, then the night workers, then the day workers and the public transport workers last.

2. On one side of the card I put the name, occupation and other related characteristics of the person such as a nickname if relevant, in both English and Urdu as shown in Figure 17. On the other side directly underneath the right-hand corner I put his number so that if the card is turned over left to right it can be read.
3. When I visited my cases I explained the purpose of the exercise and I dealt out the cards (pre-shuffled) same side up in front of a person so that the names were visible. I asked the respondents to sort the cards into four piles: those with whom he has 'close', 'some', 'little' and 'no' interaction. I did not make any attempt to indicate how large, small, even or uneven any of the piles should be. Then I asked the respondents to rank the 'close' pile from top (say, best known, etc.) to bottom (least known) within that category. Then I asked them to do the same with 'some' pile and so on.
4. While a respondent did this I put *his* card on top of his 'close' pile, so that he became his 'closest'. Then I turned the stack over, and fanned the cards out so that all the numbers became visible. Then I wrote the order on a pad, for example:

   Mr. M.A. (9)

'Close'	I: 8, 7, 6, 20 . . .
'Some'	II:10, 11 . . .
'Little'	III:13, 14 . . .
'No'	IV:19 . . .

   This was repeated for all twenty individuals.
5. The second card sorting was quite simple. I asked my respondents to pick up their cards in the order of interaction, beginning with their own card. I allowed them to readjust the order at any time. When a person had chosen fifteen out of twenty I asked him to stop.[16] I did not tell him beforehand that that was the

number of cards he was supposed to pick up. Then I wrote the numbers in the order in which the respondent had arranged them.[17]

At the time of the card-sorting more than half of the people mentioned that they had other close relatives and friends in the town who were not included in the cards.

There were some difficulties to be faced with regard to literacy. Four of the cases could not read any language (although I wrote names and other related information on the cards in Urdu as well). In two cases they were helped by their sons who read the names to them and did the card-sorting. I helped the other two persons following the same procedure as nobody in the house was present who could read either English or Urdu. An effort was made to avoid the influence of the translator during the card-sorting.

From the little experience I have about the technique, I would suggest that card-sorting is difficult for illiterate people, but it works well for educated respondents. If one needs to study networks in a primitive society with a low level of education (or no education at all) then some alternatives have to be developed. This difficulty, I would argue, could be overcome by using photographs in this exercise.

Appendix II
Entry of Dependants—A Social Problem

Thousands of Pakistanis in Britain are kept separated from their wives and children because of long delays in and the complexities of the entry system.* The system is not only slow and cumbersome, but humiliating as well. The average time to get an entry visa in Islamabad where most of the dependants apply, was in 1974 over two years. To get an entry visa, dependants may have to make several long and expensive journeys to the British Embassy. The first step is to get an interview with the Entry Clearance Officer. An interview is not an automatic guarantee of a visa. The dependants who come from far-off villages are mostly illiterate women and unlikely to have ever been interviewed before. They are confronted with a foreign English Entry Clearance Officer who asks innumerable questions (most of them can be said to be irrelevant and personal) during the 90-minute interview. The harshness of the procedure and the strange official situation confuses the dependants and results in inconsistent answers. This means that the dependants are often refused entry visas.

They have a right to appeal. The appeal procedure involves at least another two years before a decision is made despite the United Kingdom Immigrants Advisory Service, a government-financed body, which helps the sponsors in this country to present their cases without charge. It is the time, waiting, journeys, expense and separation from their families which lead the sponsors and their dependants to conclude that the whole system of interviewing, refusal, appeals, etc. is designed to delay the entry of dependants coming to Britain.

The following case which reached the appeal stage and took over four years altogether is typical of the experience of dependants and

*At the end of 1974 there were about 50,000 Pakistani dependants waiting for their turn for an interview.

sponsors. I give in full a statement prepared by the Entry Certificate Officer and submitted to the clerk at the Adjudicator Immigration Appeal Office, London, in order to illustrate the nature of the interviews which dependants undergo.

Entry Certificate Officer's Explanatory Statement

1. The above-named applied on . . . 1970 for an entry certificate to enable them to join Mr R. in Rochdale, Lancashire, as his wife and son. I interviewed them separately with the assistance of an official interpreter, Mr K., who conversed with them in Punjabi; in this way, I asked them if they understood the interpreter and they said they did.
2 The applications were considered under the terms of paragraphs 34 and 38 of Command Paper 4298 'Instructions to Immigration Officers', but were refused because I was not satisfied that they were related as claimed.
3. Documents produced in support of this application, together with application form LM2 and family tree are attached (Annex A to I).

Annex A.	Forms IM2 (Mrs B. had applied first in Lahore and had not kept her appointment because of the Indo/Pak war).
Annex B.	Family Tree of Mrs B.
Annex C.	A declaration of sponsorship signed by Mr M. R. on . . .
Annex D.	Photostat copies of pages 1–7 and 28–31 of the sponsor's passport issued at Karachi on . . .
Annex E.	An affidavit purporting to have signed by Mrs B. on or about . . .
Annex F.	An employer's letter from 'M' Mills Ltd., Rochdale, dated . . .
Annex G.	An employer's letter from 'R' Mills, Rochdale, dated . . .
Annex H.	Medical report submitted by Dr S. M. on . . .
Annex I.	Forms APP 201 and APP 200C.

4. I saw Mrs B. on . . . and took from her the family tree at Annex B. I was surprised when she told me that she was between 60 and 61 years of age, as her date of birth is said to be 1930. On completion of the family tree, therefore, I once more asked Mrs B. to tell me how old she was and she replied that she was sixty

years of age. I noted at the time that she certainly looked that age.

5. In reply to my questions, Mrs B. gave me the following details about her circumstances in Pakistan. She said that she lived in the village of T. R. about 90 miles from Bahawalpur. The house which was owned by her husband was of mud construction with four rooms, it had electric light and water was obtained from a hand pump in the courtyard of the house. She told me that the people who normally resided in the house were:
   1. Herself
   2. Her two sons, M. M. and S. R.
   3. Her daughter — B. B.
   4. Her daughter's husband — M. U.
   5. Her daughter's children — R. and H.
   6. Her brother — A. M.
   7. Her brother's wife — H.

   Mrs B. said that none of her children had ever been to school. The family owned about 10 acres of land which was farmed by her brother, Mr A. M. They owned, in addition to the land, one buffalo and two bullocks, they also kept a white dog. She had last seen her husband about 2½ years previously.
6. M. M. her son, who I interviewed next, gave me a family tree that differed from hers in the following details:
   (a) Hameed was the elder of his sister's two sons, being between seven and eight years of age. Rashid was only 4 years old.
   (b) He did not know the name of G. M.'s wife.
   (c) His paternal uncle Ishaq's son was named Isaan-ul-Haq (this could possibly be the same name as that given by Mrs B.)
   (d) He had two maternal uncles:
      (i) A. M. husband of H.
      One son, Ghulam Qadir, husband of R. B.
      One daughter, Akhtar, 7–8 years old.
      (ii) R. U. husband of D. N. K. (M. M. said that R. U. was dead but his wife was alive and lived in the village of . . . in Wazirabad. She had children but M. M. did not know their sexes or how many there were.)
   (e) M. M. said that he thought that he had two maternal aunts but could not remember their names.
7. I next asked M. M. about the house that he lived in and his

everyday life in the village. He gave me some answers that conflicted with those given by his mother as follows:

(a) M. M. lived in a brick-built house (brick and cement and plastered walls) with seven rooms.

(b) When listing the occupants of the house, he added P. Akhtar, the grand-daughter of A. M. and omitted S. R., his brother, whom he said lived with his sister B. B. three houses down the road.

(c) They did not possess any bullocks.

8. M. M. said that, although he had never been to a proper school, he had been taught at home by one M. Q. and was able to read and write Urdu.
9. I decided at this stage to interview and to ask Mrs B. if she would go to a doctor for an age assessment. She agreed to do this, provided she could be examined by a lady doctor. She was examined by Dr. S. M. whose report is attached at Annex H.
10. Mrs B. returned on . . . with M. M. and they were interviewed separately by me with the assistance of an official interpreter, M. G. K., who spoke to them in Punjabi; they agreed that they understood the interpreter.
11. Once again, I asked Mrs B. to tell me how old she was and she replied that she was forty-two years old, she added that her parents had told her age and that she had been upset at the last interview and had been unable to give me her correct age. I pointed out that the doctor estimated her age as about 49–50 years. She made no comment.
12. In an effort to clear the discrepancies on the family tree, I asked Mrs B. the following questions. Her answers follow each question:
    1. How many brothers have you? One only, A. M.
    2. Are you quite sure that you have no other brothers dead or alive? Yes, certain.
    3. Have you ever had a brother called R. A.? No, never.
    4. Is A. M. married? Yes, his wife's name is H. B. and they have one son called Ghulam Qadir, husband of R. Bibi and a grandaughter named Parveen.
    5. How many sisters have you, living or dead? Two, both are dead, A. and F. Was A. married? No.
       How old was A. when she died? I was not born when she died. Was F. married? No, she also died before I was born.
    6. How many brothers has your husband? Three. (The only change she made in listing the three brothers was that F.

M. has had two wives, first wife dead, with two sons T. and I., there were no other children. The second wife was S. who had no children.)

7. What was the name of M. M.'s private tutor? M. A. K.

13. I next asked Mrs B. whether she had ever lived in Karachi. She replied that they (the family) had lived in Karachi, at the time of partition of India and Pakistan. She did not know exactly when she left Karachi. I asked her whether it was before or after the birth of her daughter, Bibi, to which she replied that it was about two months before B. Bibi's birth. She was quite definite that B. Bibi had been born in T. R.
14. I asked Mrs B. where her son S. R. lived and she said that he lived with her daughter B. Bibi. When I asked where Parveen lived, she said that Parveen did not normally live with them but lived with her (Parveen's) paternal aunts. I then asked Mrs B. to tell me the names of Parveen's paternal aunts and she replied that Parveen had no paternal aunts. I asked her if she was telling me that she was not A. M.'s sister. She made no reply. Mrs B. said that the occupants of the house were herself, her son, M. M., A. M. and H. only
15. I asked Mrs B. whether she could write and she replied that she could not but added that she was able to sign her name. I went on to ask her if she had signed any papers for her husband, such as an affidavit. Mrs B. replied that she had signed nothing before her husband returned from the United Kingdom. I asked whether she could recall signing any papers before her husband went to the United Kingdom for the first time or shortly after he had left for the United Kingdom. She said that she was sure that she had not.
16. M. M. was next seen by me for the second time. He had changed his version of the family tree to more or less coincide with that given by R. B. on her second visit.
    1. He had no other maternal uncles barring A. M.
    2. He had never heard of R. U.
    3. No maternal aunts. He was absolutely sure of this fact.
    4. He still insisted that Parveen lived with them. I asked him if she lived there all the time and he said that she did.
    5. He told me that R. son of G. M., was single. I asked him what had happened to his wife S., whom he had told me about last time. He replied that he had never mentioned S., R. was single and worked in a sugar mill in Potwari.
17. M. M. told me that he had lived in Karachi till . . . when his father went to the United Kingdom. I asked him when he left

Karachi and he replied that he did not know. I asked him how he knew that he had lived in Karachi, he answered that he knew because he was old enough in . . . to know which city he lived in. I asked him once more whether he could tell me when he had left Karachi—reminding him at the same time that he was able to tell me exactly when his father had left Karachi for the United Kingdom. He replied that he did not know when they had moved from Karachi.

18. I recalled Mrs B. to the office and questioned both her and M. M. together about the affidavit. Together they told me that the affidavit had been signed by Mrs B. at the time of application for their Pakistani passports. Both mother and son agreed that no papers had been signed by Mrs B. before or after the time of application for passports.
19. I next asked them to explain to me why they had both changed their stories, with particular reference to the following points:
    1. Mrs B.'s age.
    2. Who was older — H. or R.
    3. Size and nature of construction of their house.
    4. Occupants of house.
    5. The name of M. M.'s tutor at home.
    6. Where had the two bullocks that Mrs B. had said they owned gone?
    7. Why had R. M. been given two dead wives and lost a daughter at the second interview?
    8. R. Bibi had said that S. was still the wife of R. on the second interview, but M. M. had denied this.
    9. How was it that R. B. was able to recall that her brother had a son and grand-daughter on her second visit when she was sure that she had no children at the first interview.
    10. What had happened to Rahmatullah, his wife and children?
    11. Maternal aunts R. B.'s sisters. R. B. had said one then two, M. M. had said two and then definitely none.
    12. Had they ever lived in Karachi? If so, when had they left?
    13. How could I accept at face value an affidavit purporting to have been signed in 1963, when both mother and son insist that it was not signed until they applied for passports? Passports were issued on . . . at Lahore.

    Both applicants became very excited when confronted in this manner but although they argued hotly between themselves they were unable to offer any explanations for the discrepancies.

20. I next asked them both if they could explain one or two details in the few documents they had presented in support of their application which did not ring true to me.
    1. The passport of M. R. showed that he had left Pakistan on . . . (we do not know his date of arrival in the United Kingdom). But an employer's letter emanating from 'M' Mills Ltd., of Rochdale, Lancashire, and dated . . . states that a Mr M. R. had been employed by them since . . . at least three months before he left Pakistan.
    2. Why had the date of marriage and the date of birth of Mrs B. been altered on the affidavit?

    They both said that there must surely be some simple mistake in the first instance but offered no explanation for the alterations to the affidavit.
21. I explained to Mrs B. and M. M. my reasons for refusal and that they had the right to appeal against my decision. An appeal was lodged on . . . nothing in the grounds of appeal prompts me to alter my decision.
22. Mrs B. and M. M., who showed no signs of strain or nervousness at any time during the interviews, were asked at their conclusion whether they had had any difficulty in understanding what the interpreter had said and they replied that they had not.

Mr M. R. and his relatives were very upset and concerned about the decision and, in particular, the questions the Entry Certificate Officer asked. They think, 'It is a deliberate Government policy to discourage people from coming to Britain.'

It took over two more years after Mr M. R. had submitted the appeal before he got the hearing date at the end of 1974. It was adjourned because the Adjudicator was not satisfied with the papers and Mr M. R. was asked to produce more papers. His relatives from Rochdale went as witnesses but 'It was not sufficient evidence.' Mr M. R. approached the Pakistani organizations, the Community Relations Council, the local MP and the UKIAS several times in this connection. He was still waiting desperately for a date for the hearing in early 1975. This was roughly five years after his wife and son originally applied at Islamabad for entry certificates to Britain. He was given another date and his appeal was successful.

During my field-work, I came into contact with many Pakistanis who were more or less in the same situation. They told me how their children's education suffered once they applied for the entry visa to come to Britain; they lost interest in school hoping that they would start their education in Britain. Both in Britain and in Pakistan cases of stress result from the uncertainty. One educated respondent described the process, 'The waiting of letters, news, dates of interviews, decisions of the Entry Certificate Officers, demands for more papers, agents' misleading advice to the simple villagers in Islamabad, etc. upset the life at both the Pakistani and British ends.' He added, 'This is not justice, but rather discrimination. It starts, not only in Britain, but from the day one applies to come to this country.' These processes raise many questions. They are constantly discussed within the Pakistani community, and the officials appear to remain unaware of the real feelings of Pakistanis towards the treatment they receive. It is obvious that this treatment has serious implications for the views they develop about Britain.

Glossary

Apaji	Elder sister
Apna	Own, 'own family' father, mother, brother, sister, etc. relatives
Arian	Man of vegetable grower caste
Azan	Muslim call for prayer
Barat	Wedding procession
Barati	Members of wedding procession
Bhabhi	Wife of the eldest brother
Bhanji	Sweet pastry (a kind of sweetmeat)
Biraderi	Patrilineage, brotherhood, fraternity
Chacha	Paternal uncle
Chapati	Native bread; a flat, round cake made of unleavened dough
Chowdhry	Village chief, headman, honorary role for a *Zamindar*; sometimes used as a sub-caste
Dadke	Paternal home
Dupata	Headcloth for women
Eid-ul-fite	Muslim religious festival at the end of *Ramazan*
Eid-ul-azha	Muslim religious festival after the *Haj* when sheep and other animals are sacrificed
Gala	Ceremony officially opening wedding celebrations
Ghar	House, household
Ghi	A liquid butter, clarified by boiling, made from cow's and buffalo's milk
Gore Loke	White people
Haj	Pilgrimage to Mecca
Imam	Priest of a Mosque
Izzet	Prestige, status, honour
Jat	Landowner class
Jowra	Set of clothes for men and women

Kabila	*Biraderi*, patrilineage
Kamiz	Tunic worn by a man or woman
Kammi	Village craftsman
Katchi	Weak and temporary
Khara	Ritual bath taken by bride or bridegroom as part of wedding ceremony
Laag	Money received by *Kammis* of the house at wedding ceremony at the house they work for
Lambardar	Revenue head of a village, *Chowdhry*
Maiyan	Ceremony of tying bracelet of coloured thread around wrist of bride or bridegroom
Mamu	Mother's brother
Masi	Maternal aunt
Meylis	Wedding guests
Mhendi	Henna, ceremony of putting henna on bride or bridegroom
Mithyai	Sweets
Muklawa	Second visit of bride or bridegroom to family of parents-in-law
Nai	A barber
Nanke	Mother's parents' home
Neondra	Money given to parents of bridegroom by male *meylis*
Nikah	Religious ceremony of marriage registration
Opera	Non-kin, stranger
Pak	Purified, clean, holy
Pakka	Solid brick- and cement-made
Pakki	Firm and permanent
Phuphi	Father's sister
Purdah	Curtain, veil
Quom	Sub-caste
Ramazan	Month of fasting, ninth month of Muslim calendar
Rishtadar	Kin group
Rupee	Pakistani currency. One rupee equal to approximately 5p
Selami	Money given to welcome bride or bridegroom
Sepoy	Soldier
Shariat	Islamic Law
Shelwar	Baggy pants worn by men, women and children
Tahsil	District sub-division
Vag Pharari	Holding of reins, money given by bridegroom to sisters and female cousins
Vartan Bhanji	System of reciprocal gift exchange

Vartan	Dealing (noun)
Vartna	To deal (verb)
Zakat	Religious assessment of property to give away, about 2½% every year
Zamin	Land
Zamindar	Landowner
Zan	Women
Zar	Money, gold or property
Zat	Caste or identity

Bibliography

Ahmad, K. S. *A Geography of Pakistan*, Lahore, Oxford University Press, 1964.

Alavi, H. 'The Politics of Dependence: A village in West Punjab', *South Asian Review*, Vol 4, No. 2, Jan , 1971.

—— 'Kinship in West Punjab Villages', *Contributions to Indian Sociology*, New Series, Vol VI, December, 1972.

Allen, S. *New Minorities Old Conflicts, Asian and West Indian Migrants in Britain*, New York, Random House, 1971.

—— 'Black Workers in Great Britain' in Hans Van Houte and Willy Melgert (eds.). *Foreigners in Our Community*, Amsterdam, Keesing Publishers, 1972.

—— 'Immigrants or Workers' in S. Zubaida (ed.). *Race and Racialism*, London, Tavistock Publications, 1970.

—— and Barker, D. (eds.). *Dependence and Exploitation in Work and Marriage*, London, Longmans, 1976.

—— Bornat, J. and Bentley, S. *Work, Race and Immigration*, University of Bradford, 1977.

Allport, G. W. *The Nature of Prejudice*, New York, Doubleday and Co., 1954.

Anwar, M. 'Perceptions, Adjustments and Aspirations of Pakistani Immigrants in Rochdale'. An unpublished dissertation for part fulfilment for M.A. (Econ.), University of Manchester, 1971.

—— 'A Sociological Study of Pakistanis in a Northern Town in England' Ph.D. thesis, University of Bradford, 1977.

—— 'Pakistani Participation in the 1972 Rochdale By-Election' *New Community*, Vol II, No. 4, Autumn, 1973.

—— 'Pakistani Participation in the 1973 Rochdale Local Elections', *New Community*, Vol III, Nos 1–2, Winter–Spring, 1974.

—— 'Pakistanis and Indians in the 1971 Census: Some Ambiguities', *New Community*, Vol III, No. 4. Autumn, 1974.

—— *Muslim Burials*, London, Community Relations Commission, 1975.

—— 'Asian Participation in the 1974 Autumn Election', *New Community*, Vol IV, No. 3, Autumn, 1975.

—— *Between Two Cultures*, London, Commission for Racial Equality, 2nd ed., 1978.

—— 'Young Muslims in a Multi-cultural Society: Their Educational Needs and Policy Implications—The British Case' Paper for the First World Conference on Muslim Education, Mecca, Saudi Arabia, March/April, 1977.

—— and Kohler, D. *Ethnic Minority Participation in the October 1974 General Election*, London, Community Relations Commission, 1975.

Aurora, G. S. *The New Frontiersmen, A Sociological Study of Indian Immigrants in the United Kingdom*, Bombay, Popular Parakasham, 1967.

Baijier, G. *Rural Migrants in Urban Settings*, The Hague, Martinus Nijhoff, 1963.

Ballard, R. 'Family Organisation Among the Sikhs in Britain', *New Community*, Vol II, 1, 1972–73.

Barnes, J. A. 'Class and Committees in a Norwegian Island Parish', *Human Relations*, VII, 1954.

—— 'Network and Political Process' in J. C. Mitchell (ed.). *Social Networks in Urban Situations*, Manchester University Press, 1969.

Barth, F. (ed.). *Ethnic Groups and Boundaries: The Social Organisations of Cultural Difference*, Boston, Little Brown and Co., 1969.

Becker, H. and Geer, B. 'Participation and Interviewing: A Rejoinder', *Human Organisation*, **17**, No. 2, 1958.

Bell, C. and Newby, N. *Community Studies*, London, George Allen and Unwin, 1971.

Bentley, S. 'The Structure of Leadership Among Indians, Pakistanis and West Indians in Britain'. Unpublished M.Sc. thesis, University of Bradford, 1970.

Bernard, H. R. and Killworth, P. D. 'On the Social Structure of an Ocean-Going Research Vessel and Other Important Things', *Social Science Research*, **2**, 1973.

Bernard, W. D. 'The Integration of Immigrants in the United States'. *International Migration Review*, **1**, Spring, 1976.

Blau, P. M. *Exchange and Power in Social Life*, London, John Wiley and Sons, 1964.

Blunt, E. A. H. *The Caste System of Northern India*, London, Oxford University Press, 1931.

Bott, E. *Family and Social Networks*, London, Tavistock Publications, 1957.

Breton, R. 'Institutional Completeness of Ethnic Communities and the Personal Relations of Immigrants', *American Journal of Sociology*, **70**, September, 1964.

Brenton, R. and Pinnard, M. 'Group Formation among Immigrants: Criteria and Processes', *Canadian Journal of Economic and Political Science*, 26, August 1960.

Brown, J. *The Un-Melting Pot*, London, Macmillan, 1970.

Burney, E. *Housing on Trial*, London, Oxford University Press for IRR, 1967.

Butler, D. and Stokes, D. *Political Change in Britain*, London, Macmillan, 1969.

—— and Kavanagh, D. *The British General Election of February 1974*, London, Macmillan, 1974.

Castles, S. and Kosack, G. *Immigrant Workers and Class Structures in Western Europe*, London, Oxford University Press for IRR, 1973.

Charsley, S. R. 'The Formation of Ethnic Groups' in Abner Cohen (ed.). *Urban Ethnicity*, London, Tavistock Publications, 1974.

Cohen, A. (ed.). *Urban Ethnicity*, London Tavistock Publications, 1974.

—— and Middleton, J. (eds.). *From Tribe to Nation in Africa*, Scranton, Pennsylvania, Chandler Publishing, 1970.

Cooley, C. H. 'Primary Groups' in A. P. Hare *et al* (eds.). *Small Groups*, Knopf, 1955 also in Pauline V. Young *Scientific Social Surveys and Research* (2nd edition), New York, Prentice Hall Inc., 1951.

Coser, L. A. *The Functions of Social Conflict*, New York, Free Press of Glencoe, 1956.

Crewe, I. *British Political Sociology Year Book: The Politics of Race*, London, Croom Helm Ltd, 1975.

Crissman, L. W. 'The Segmentary Structure of Overseas Chinese', *Man*, **2**, 1967.

Dahl, R. *Who Governs?* London and New Haven, Yale University Press, 1961.

Daniel, W. W. *Racial Discrimination in England*, Harmondsworth, Penguin, 1968.

Davies, K. *The Population of India and Pakistan*, Princeton, Princeton University Press, 1957.

Deakin, N. *Colour, Citizenship and British Society*, London, Panther, 1970.

—— (ed.). *Colour and the British Electorate, 1964*, London, Frederick A. Praeger, 1965.

—— and Bourne, J. 'Powel, the Minorities and the 1970 Election', *Political Quarterly*, Vol 41, No 4, 1970.

Dean, J. P. *et al.* 'Observation and Interviewing' in John R. Doby (ed.), *An Introduction to Social Research* (2nd edition) New York, Appleton–Century–Crofts, 1967.

Department of Employment, *Monthly Gazette*, years 1973–1975.

Department of Employment Wages Inspectorate, *Note on Homeworkers in the Clothing Industry*, H.M.S.O. 1973.

Desai, R. *Indian Immigrants in Britain*, London, Oxford University Press for IRR, 1963.

Dhaya, B. 'The Nature of Pakistani Ethnicity in Industrial Cities in Britain', in A. Cohen (ed.). *Urban Ethnicity,* London, Tavistock Publications, 1974.

Downie, J. H. *Some Social and Industrial Implications of Shift Work*, Industrial Welfare Society, 1963.

Duncan, O. D. and Lieberson, S. 'Ethnic Segregation and Assimilation', *American Journal of Sociology*, **64**, January, 1959.

Eisenstadt, S. N. *The Absorption of Immigrants*, London, Routledge and Kegan Paul, 1954.

—— 'Analysis of Patterns of Immigration and Absorption of Immigrants', *Population Studies*, **7**, November, 1953.

Eglar, Z. *A Punjabi Village in Pakistan*, Columbia University Press, 1960.

Engels, F. *The Conditions of the Working Class in England in 1844*, London, George Allen and Unwin, 1952.

Firth, R. 'Family and Kinship in Industrial Society', *The Sociological Review*, Monograph No. 8, Keele, 1964.

Fletcher, R. *Britain in the Sixties, The Family and Marriage*, Harmondsworth, Penguin, 1962.

Foot, P. *Immigration and Race in British Politics*, Harmondsworth, Penguin, 1965.

—— 'The Strike at Courtaulds, Preston 24 May–12 June 1965', *IRR Newsletter*, July 1965.

Form, W. H. and Nosow, S. *Community in Disaster*, New York, Harper and Row, 1958.

Fox, R. *Kinship and Marriage*, Pelican Books, 1967.

General Registrar Office. *Census 1951, 1961, 1966 and 1971*, New Commonwealth Immigrant Tables, London, H.M.S.O.

Gillettee, T. L. 'A Study of the Effects of Negro Invasion on Real Estate Values', *The American Journal of Economics and Sociology*, **16**, January, 1957.

Glazer, N. *Affirmative Discrimination*, New York, Basic Books, 1975.

Gluckman, M. 'The Bonds in the Colour Bar' in *Custom and Conflict in Africa*, Oxford, Basil Blackwell, 1955.

Goode, W. J. *The Family*, Englewood Cliffs, N.J., Prentice-Hall, 1964.

Gordon, M. *Assimilation in American Life*, New York, Oxford University Press, 1964.

—— 'Assimilation in America: Theory and Reality', in M. Kurokawa (ed.), *Minority Responses*, New York, Random House, 1970.

Gorer, G. *Exploring English Character*, London, The Cresset Press, 1955.

Greenfield, S. M. 'Industrialisation and the Family in Sociological Theory', *American Journal of Sociology*, Vol 67, 1961.

Halsey, A. H. 'Race Relations: The Lines to Think On', *New Society*, 19 March, 1970.

Hepple, B. *Race, Jobs and Law in Britain*, London, Allen Lane, 1968.

Heywood, T. T. 'New Annals of Rochdale', *Rochdale Times*, 1931.

Hill, M. J. and Issacharoff, R. M. *Community Action and Race Relations*, London, Oxford University Press, 1971.

Hiro, D. *Black British White British*, London, Eyre and Spottiswoode, 1971.

Hoffnidu Nowotny, H. J. 'Global Social Aspects of Relationships Between Trade Unions and Migrant Workers', *Migration Today*, No. 11, Autumn 1968.

Homeworkers Study Group. 'Homeworkers in North London' in Sheila Allen and D. Barker (eds.), *Dependence and Exploitation in Work and Marriage*, London, Longmans, 1976.

Horrock, J. E. Editor's Foreward in Muzafar Sharif, *Group Conflict and Co-operation: Their Social Psychology*, London, Routledge and Kegan Paul, 1967.

Hubbell, C. H. 'An Input–Output Approach to Clique Identification', *Sociometry*, XXVIII, 1965.

Industrial Society. *Survey of Shift Working Practices*, 1970.

Isaac, J. *British Postwar Migration*, Cambridge, Cambridge University Press, 1954.

Jackson, J. A. *The Irish in Britain*, London, Routledge and Kegan Paul, 1963.

Jahoda, M. *et al. Research Methods in the Social Sciences*, New York, Dryden Press 1951.

Jeffery, P. 'Pakistani Families in Bristol', *New Community*, Vol. II, Autumn 1972.

John, D. W. *Indian Workers Association in Britain*, London, Oxford University Press for IRR, 1969.

Johnston, R. 'A New Approach to the Meaning of Assimilation', *Human Relations*, **16**, August 1963.

Jones, K. and Smith, A. D. *The Economic Impact of Commonwealth Immigration*, Cambridge, Cambridge University Press, 1970.

Jones, F. L. 'Ethnic Concentration and Assimilation: An Australian Case Study', *Social Forces*, **45**, March 1967.

Key, W. H. 'Rural–Urban Differences and the Family', *Sociological Quarterly*, Vol. 2, 1964.

Khan, V. S. 'Pakistani Villagers in a British City', unpublished Ph.D. thesis, University of Bradford, 1974.

Kluckholn, F. R. 'The Participant Observer Technique in Small Communities', *American Journal of Sociology*, XLVI November, 1940.

Kohler, D. *Ethnic Minorities in Britain: Statistical Data*, London, Community Relations Commission, 1975.

Korson, J. H. 'Student Attitudes Towards Mate Selection in a Muslim Society: Pakistan', *Journal of Marriage and the Family*, XXXI, No. 1, February 1968.

Lee, E. S. 'A Theory of Migration' in Jackson (ed.), *Migration*, Cambridge University Press, 1969.

Leicher, H. J. and Mitchell W. E. *Kinship and Case Work*, New York, Russell Sage Foundation, 1967.

Le Lohe, M. J. 'Participation in Elections by Asians in Bradford', in Ivor Crewe (ed.), *The Politics of Race*, Croom Helm, 1975.

—— and Goldman, A. 'Race in Local Politics', *Race: the Rochdale Central Ward Election of 1968*, Vol X, No. 4, 1969.

Lewis, O. *Life in a Mexican Village: Tepoztlan Restudied*, Springfield, University of Illinois Press, 1951.

Liberal Party. *Immigration and Race Relations*, London, Liberal Publication Department, 1974.

Lieberson, S. 'The Impact of Residential Segregation on Ethnic Assimilation', *Social Forces*, **40**, October 1961.

Linton, R. 'The Natural History of the Family', in R. N. Anshen (ed.). *The Family: Its Functions and Density,* New York, Harper and Row, 1959.

Lomas, G. B. *Census 1971, the Coloured Population of Great Britain*, The Runnymede Trust, 1973.

Lord, A. 'Asians in Wardleworth', 1975, unpublished.

Lyon, M. 'Race and Ethnicity in Pluralistic Societies. A Comparison of Minorities in the U.K. and U.S.A'. *New Community*, Vol 1, No. 4, Summer 1972.

MacDonald, J. and MacDonald, L. D. 'Chain Migration, Ethnic Neighbourhood Formation and Social Network,' *Social Research*, **29**, 4, 1962.

Marsh, P. *Anatomy of a Strike*, London, IRR Special Series, 1967.

Maududi, S. A. A. *Purdah and the Status of Women in Islam*, Lahore, Islamic Publications Ltd, 1972.

Maw, L. *Immigrants and Employment in the Clothing Industry: The Rochdale Case,* The Runnymede Trust, 1974.

Mayer, P. *Townmen and Tribesmen*, Cape Town, Oxford University Press, 1974 (first published 1961).

McCall, G. J. and Simmons, J. L. *Issues in Participant Observation*, Reading, Addison-Wesley Publishing Co., 1969.

Merton, R. K. *Social Theory and Social Structure*, New York, Free Press, 1957.

Ministry of Housing and Local Government, *The Deeplish Study*, H.M.S.O., 1966.

Mitchell, J. C. (ed.). *Social Networks in Urban Situations*, Manchester University Press, 1969.

—— 'Social Networks', *Annual Review of Anthropology*, Vol. 3, 1974.

Morgan, D. H. J. 'Theoretical and conceptional problems in the study of social relations at work: An analysis of the differing definitions of women's role in a northern factory' unpublished Ph.D. thesis. University of Manchester, 1969.

Morris, H. S. *The Indians in Uganda*, Weidenfeld and Nicolson, 1968.

Mott, P. *Shift Work: The Social, Psychological and Physical Consequences*, Ann Arbor, The University of Michigan Press, 1965.

National Board for Prices and Incomes, *Hours of Work, Overtime and Shift Work*, Report No. 161, N.B.P.I.

—— *Pay and Conditions in the Clothing Manufacturing Industries*, Report No. 110, HMSO, 1969.

Nelli, H.S. *The Italians of Chicago 1880–1930*, New York, Oxford University Press, 1970.

Nimkoff, M. F. *Comparative Family Systems*, Boston, Houghton Mifflin, 1965.

O'Flannery, E. 'Social and Cultural Assimilation', *American Sociological Review*, **22**, Spring 1957.

Orenstein, H. 'The Recent History of Extended Family in India', *Social Problems*, Vol 8, 1961.

Pahl, R. E. *Pattern of Urban Life*, Longman, 1970.

Papanek, H. 'The Woman Fieldworker in a Purdah Society' *Human Organisation*, Vol 23, No. 2, 1964.

—— 'Purdah in Pakistan: Seclusion and Modern Occupations for Women', *Journal of Marriage and the Family*, August 1971.

Park, R. E. and Burgess, E. W. *Introduction to Sociology*, Chicago University Press, 1921.

Parsons, T. 'The Social Structure of the Family, in R. H. Anshen (ed.). *The Family: Its Functions and Density*, Harper and Row, 1959.

—— and Bales, R. F. *Family, Socialization and Interaction Process*, Glencoe, Free Press, 1955.

Patterson, O. 'Content and Choice in Allegiance: A Theoretical Framework and Caribbean Case Study', in N. Glazer and G. Moynihan (eds.), *Ethnicity*, Cambridge (Mass.), Harvard University Press, 1975.

Patterson, S. *Immigrants in Industry*, London, Oxford University Press for IRR, 1968.

—— *Dark Stranger*, Harmondsworth, Penguin, 1965.

Peach, G. C. K. *West Indian Migration to Britain*: London, Oxford University Press for IRR, 1968.

Petersen, W. 'A General Typology of Migration', *American Sociological Review*, Vol. 23, 1958.

Price, C. A. *Southern Europeans in Australia*, Melbourne, Oxford University Press, 1963.

—— 'A Study of Assimilation' in J. A. Jackson (ed.), *Migration*, Cambridge, Cambridge University Press, 1969.

Radin, B. 'Coloured Workers and British Trade Unions', *Race*, Vol. III, No. 2, October 1966.

Rex, J. and Moore, R. *Race, Community and Conflict, A Study of Sparkbrook*, London, Oxford University Press for IRR, 1967.

Richmond, A. H. *Ethnic Residential Segregation in Metropolitan Toronto*, Toronto, Institute of Behavioural Research, 1972.

Rose, A. (ed.) *Human Behaviour and Social Process: An Interactional Approach*, Boston, Houghton Mifflin and Co, 1962.

Rose, R. (ed.). *Electoral Behaviour: A Comparative Handbook*, New York, Free Press, 1974.

Rose, E. J. B. and associates *Colour and Citizenship, a Report on British Race Relations*, London, Oxford University Press for IRR, 1969.

Rosenthall, E. 'Acculturation without Assimilation: The Jewish Community of Chicago, Illinois' in Munako Kurokawa (ed.). *Minority Responses*, New York, Random House, 1970.

Rossi, P. H. *Why Families Move*, New York, Free Press, 1955.

Schneider, D. M. 'Some Muddles in the Models', *The Relevance of Models for Social Anthropology*, A.S.A. Monograph I. London, 1965.

Schwalzweller, H. K. and Segger, J. F. 'Kinship Involvement: A Factor in the Adjustment of Rural Migrants' *Journal of Marriage and the Family*, No. 29, November 1967.

Schwartz M. S. 'The Mental Hospital and the Research Person in the Disturbed Ward', in A. J. Vidich, J. Bensman and M. R. Stein (eds.). *Reflections on Community Studies*, London, Harper and Row, 1971.

Shah, S. *Immigrants and Employment in the Clothing Industry, The Rag Trade in London's East End,* The Runnymede Trust, 1975.

Sharif, M. *Group Conflict and Co-operation*, London, Routledge and Kegan Paul, 1967.

Sharp, H. and Axelrod, M. 'Mutual Aid Among Relatives in an Urban Population', in R. Freedman *et al.* (eds.), *Principles of Sociology*, Holt, Rinehart and Winston, 1956.

Simmel, G. *Conflict*, (trans. by Kurt Wolff), Free Press of Glencoe, 1955.

Simmons, O. G. and McPhee, W. N. 'Time Trend and Analysis of the Urban Experiences of Rural Migrants to the City', Paper presented to the conference on adaptation to change, San Juan, Puerto Rico, June 1968.

Smith, D. *The Facts of Racial Disadvantage*, London, PEP, 1976.

Spencer, R. 'The Minorities and the General Elections 1970, Lambeth,' *Race Today*, July 1970.

Studlar, D. T. 'British Public Opinion, Colour Issues, and Enoch Powell: A Longitudinal Analysis' *British Journal of Political Science*, Vol 4, No. 3, 1974.

Sussman, M. B. 'The Help Pattern in the Middle-Class Family', *American Sociological Review*, Vol. 18, 1953.

—— 'Family Community: Selective Factors which Affect Relationships between Families at Generational Levels', *Marriage and Family Living*, Vol. 16, 1954.

Textile Council, *Cotton and Allied Textiles—A report on present performances and future prospects*, Manchester, 1969.

Thomas, W. I. and Znaniecki, F. *The Polish Peasant in Europe and America*, Chicago, Chicago University Press, 1965 (first published 1918–20).

Thompson, E. P. *The Making of the English Working Class*, Harmondsworth, Penguin, 1968.

Townsend, P. 'Family and Kinship in Industrial Society: A Comment', *Sociological Review*, Monograph No. 8, Keele, 1964.

Union of Muslim Organizations, *Islamic Education and Single Sex Schools*, London, U.M.O., 1975.

—— *Guidelines and Syllabus on Islamic Education*, London, U.M.O., 1976.

Van Velsen, J. *The Politics of Kinship*, Manchester University Press for Rhodes–Livingstone Institute, 1964.

Vidich, A. J. 'Participant Observation and the Collection and Interpretation of Data', *American Journal of Sociology*, **60**, 1955.

Wakil, P. A. 'Explorations into the Kin-networks of the Punjabi Society: A Preliminary Statement', *Journal of Marriage and Family*, November 1970.

Whyte, W. F. *Street Corner Society*, Chicago, University of Chicago Press, 1943.

—— 'Observational Fieldwork Methods' in M. Jahoda *et al. Research Methods in the Social Sciences*, New York, Dryden Press, 1951.

Williams, R. M. Jnr, *Strangers Next Door: Ethnic Relations in American Communities*, Englewood Cliffs, N. J., Prentice-Hall, 1964.

Wilson, B. R. 'The Migration Sects', *British Journal of Sociology*, 18, September 1967.

Wirth, L. *The Ghetto,* Phoenix Books, Chicago, Chicago University Press, 1956.

—— 'Urbanism as a way of life', *American Journal of Sociology*, Vol. 44, 1938.

—— 'The Problem of Minority Group' in Ralph Linton (ed.), *The Science of Man in the World Crisis*, New York, Columbia University Press, 1945.

Young, K. *Sociology, A Study of Society and Culture*, New York, American Book Co. 1949.

Zubaida, S. (ed.) *Race and Racialism*, London, Tavistock Publications, 1970.

Zubrazycki, J. *Polish Immigrants in Britain*, The Hague, 1956.

Notes and References

Introduction

1. Taking Western Europe together (Britain, Switzerland, France, West Germany, Belgium, Holland, Austria and Scandinavia) there are nearly eleven million immigrants living in these countries. They make up over five per cent of the total population.
2. New Commonwealth will be used here to refer to all the countries of the Commonwealth, except Australia, Canada and New Zealand and including Pakistan, even though she is no longer a member of the Commonwealth.
3. See also the White Paper on *Racial Discrimination*, HMSO, 1975, and *Race Relations Act 1976*, HMSO, 1977.
4. E. P. Thomas, *The Making of the English Working Class*, Harmondsworth, Penguin, 1968, pp. 469–85.
5. J. A. Jackson, *The Irish in Britain*, London, Routledge and Kegan Paul, 1963, p. 11.
6. F. Engels, *The Condition of the Working Class in England in 1844*, London, George Allen and Unwin, 1952, pp. 9–94.
7. J. A. Jackson, op. cit., p. 14.
8. See J. Isaac, *British Postwar Migration*, Cambridge, Cambridge University Press, 1954.
9. ibid., p. 182.
10. P. Foot, *Immigration and Race in British Politics*, London, Penguin, 1965, p. 119.
11. For details see E. J. B. Rose *et al*, *Colour and Citizenship*, London, Oxford University Press for the Institute of Race Relations, 1969, pp. 65–90.
12. Nicholas Deakin, *Colour, Citizenship and British Society*, London, Panther, 1970, p. 52.
13. See the White Paper, *Racial Discrimination*, op. cit.
14. See F. Barth (ed.), *Ethnic Groups and Boundaries: The Social Organisation of Cultural Difference*, Boston, Little, Brown and Co., 1969. He uses the term 'insulated' in more or less the same sense.

15. This book is a revised and abridged version of a Ph.D. thesis. See M. Anwar, 'A Sociological Study of Pakistanis in a Northern Town in England', Ph.D. thesis, University of Bradford, 1977.

Chapter 1

Theoretical Issues

1. W. I. Thomas and F. Znaniecki, *The Polish Peasant in Europe and America*, Chicago, 1965 (First published 1918–20).
2. Louis Wirth, *The Ghetto*, Phoenix Books, University of Chicago Press, 1956, and R. E. Park and E. W. Burgess, *Introduction to Sociology*, Chicago, 1921, deal with the theoretical aspects.
3. Referring to the American situation three ideologies of assimilation have been operative at different times; these are 'Anglo-conformity', 'the melting pot' and 'cultural assimilation'. See M. Gordon, 'Assimilation in America, Theory and Reality' in M. Kurokawa (ed.), *Minority Responses*, New York, Random House, 1970, pp. 87–94.
4. R. Johnston, 'A New Approach to the Meaning of Assimilation', *Human Relations*, **16** (August 1963), pp. 295–8.
5. ibid., Gordon argues that there are two major categories of assimilation, the structural and the cultural. Cultural assimilation refers to the adoption of the values and behaviour of the host society while structural assimilation entails the development of primary group relationships with members of the host society. See M. Gordon, *Assimilation in American Life*, New York, Oxford University Press, 1964.
6. E. O'Flannery, 'Social and Cultural Assimilation', *American Sociological Review*, **22**, Spring 1957, pp. 195–206.
7. R. E. Park and E. W. Burgess, op. cit.
8. K. Young, *Sociology, A Study of Society and Culture*, New York, American Book Co., 1949, p. 615.
9. S. N. Eisenstadt, 'Analysis of Patterns of Immigration and Absorption of Immigrants', *Population Studies*, **7**, November 1953, pp. 167–80.
10. O. D. Duncan and S. Lieberson, 'Ethnic Segregation and Assimilation', *American Journal of Sociology*, **64**, January 1959, pp. 364–74.
11. ibid.
12. W. D. Bernard, 'The Integration of Immigrants in the United States', *International Migration Review*, **1**, Spring 1967, p. 23.
13. R. E. Park and E. W. Burgess, op. cit., Jerzy Zubrazycki, *Polish Immigrants in Britain*, The Hague, 1956, p. 75; Sheila Patterson, *Dark Strangers*, Harmondsworth, Penguin Books Ltd., 1965, pp. 19–26.
14. C. Price, 'A Study of Assimilation', in J. A. Jackson (ed.) *Migration*, Cambridge, Cambridge University Press, 1969, pp. 215–6.

15. John Rex and R. Moore, *Race, Community and Conflict: A Study of Sparkbrook*, London, Oxford University Press. 1967, p. 14.
16. A. H. Halsey, 'Race Relations: The Lines to Think On', *New Society*, 19th March, 1970, p. 473.
17. In Britain the much used definition of integration is as follows: 'It is not a flattening process of assimilation but of equal opportunity accompanied by cultural diversity, in an atmosphere of mutual tolerance.'
18. See for instance, S. Lieberson, 'The Impact of Residential Segregation on Ethnic Assimilation', *Social Forces*, **40**, October 1961, pp. 52–7; F. L. Jones, 'Ethnic Concentration and Assimilation: An Australian Case Study', *Social Forces*, **45**, March 1967, pp. 412–23; A. H. Richmond, *Ethnic Residential Segregation in Metropolitan Toronto*, Toronto, Institute of Behavioural Research, 1972, p. 3.
19. F. L. Jones, op. cit., p. 413.
20. A. H. Richmond, op. cit., p.4.
21. See Erich Rosenthall, 'Acculturation without Assimilation? The Jewish Community of Chicago, Illinois', Minako Kurokawa (ed.), op. cit., pp. 145–51.
22. See F. Barth (ed.), op. cit., p. 13.
23. ibid.
24. L. W. Crissman, 'The Segmentary Structure of Overseas Chinese', *Man*, **2**, 1967, p. 188.
25. R. Breton, 'Institutional Completeness of Ethnic Communities and the Personal Relations of Immigrants', *American Journal of Sociology*, **70**, September 1964, pp. 193–205.
26. R. Breton and M. Pinard, 'Group Formation Among Immigrants: Criteria and Processes', *Canadian Journal of Economic and Political Science*, **26**, August 1960, pp. 465–77.
27. Orlando Patterson, 'Content and Choice in Allegiance: A Theoretical Framework and Caribbean Case Study', in N. Glazer and D. Moynihan (eds.), *Ethnicity: Theory and Experience*, Cambridge, Mass., Harvard University Press, 1975, pp. 306–7.
28. F. Barth (ed.), op. cit., p. 13.
29. The existence of a 'minority group' in a society implies the existence of a corresponding dominant group with higher social status and greater privileges. In Western societies minority groups can be objectively distinguished by one or more of four characteristics. These are race, nationality, language and religion. See Louis Wirth, 'The Problem of Minority Group', in Ralph Linton (ed.), *The Science of Man in the World Crisis*, New York, Columbia University Press, 1945.
30. As a result of the Pakistan Act 1973 most of them have British nationality but they are also Pakistanis in the technical sense as well, due to the dual nationality provisions.
31. See Michael Lyon, 'Race and Ethnicity in Pluralistic Societies: A Comparison of Minorities in the UK and USA', *New Community*, Vol. I, No. 4, Summer 1972, pp. 256–62.

32. John MacDonald and Leatrice D. MacDonald, 'Chain Migration, Ethnic Neighbourhood Formation and Social Networks', *Social Research*, **29**, 4 (1962), pp. 443–8. Also see B. R. Wilson, The Migration Sects', *British Journal of Sociology*, **18**, 1967, pp. 303–17.
33. J. Van Velsen, *The Politics of Kinship*, Manchester University Press, 1964.
34. ibid; p. XXVI.
35. Barnes was the first one to use this approach—see J. A. Barnes, 'Class and Committees in a Norwegian Island Parish', *Human Relations*, VII, 1954, pp. 39–58.
36. J. C. Mitchell, 'Social Networks', *Annual Review of Anthropology*, Vol. 3, 1974, pp. 279–99.
37. Philip Mayer, *Townsmen and Tribesmen*, Cape Town, Oxford University Press, 2nd ed., 1974 (first published 1961).
38. The terms 'loose-knit' and 'close-knit' are used following E. Bott, *Family and Social Networks*, London, Tavistock Publications, 1957. The difference between single-stranded and multiplex relationships is that the former entails only one content and the latter may have several strands.
39. Mitchell, op. cit., p. 283.
40. ibid; p. 295, also see J. C. Mitchell (ed.), *Social Networks in Urban Situations*, Manchester University Press, 1969.
41. Lewis A. Coser, *The Functions of Social Conflict*, New York, Free Press of Glencoe, 1956, p. 7.
42. Georg Simmel, *Conflict* (Kurt Wolff's translation), Free Press of Glencoe, 1955.

Chapter 2

Migration of Pakistanis

1. A. Cohen and J. Middleton (eds.), *From Tribe to Nation in Africa*, Scranton, Pennsylvania, Chandler Publishing, 1970.
2. Everett S. Lee, 'A Theory of Migration', in J. A. Jackson (ed.), *Migration*, Cambridge University Press, 1969, p. 285.
3. See Sheila Patterson, op. cit., pp. 64–6.
4. W. Petersen, 'A General Typology of Migration', *American Sociological Review*, Vol. 23, 1958, pp. 256–66.
5. Sheila Allen, *New Minorities, Old Conflicts, Asian and West Indian Immigrants in Britain*, New York, Random House, 1971, pp. 29–33.
6. John MacDonald and Leatrice D. MacDonald, op. cit.
7. ibid.
8. ibid.
9. Louis Wirth, op. cit.
10. C. A. Price, *Southern Europeans in Australia*, Melbourne, Oxford University Press, 1963.

11. C. A. Price, op. cit., p. 113, quoted in S. R. Charsley, 'The Formation of Ethnic Groups' in Abner Cohen (ed.), *Urban Ethnicity*, London, Tavistock Publications, 1974, p.357.
12. For the Italian communities in the United States, see H. S. Nelli, *The Italians of Chicago 1880–1930*, New York, Oxford University Press, 1970, and Thomas and Znaniecki, op. cit., the study of Polish peasants migrating to America, which also provides the subjective accounts of migrants themselves which portray the elements of chain migration. See in particular Vol. III, p. 376.
13. This freedom was first restricted in 1962 and virtually withheld since 1973 by the Immigration Act 1971 and after Pakistan left the Commonwealth in 1973.
14. Kingsley Davies, *The Population of India and Pakistan*, Princeton, Princeton University Press, 1951, p. 181.
15. Dilip Hiro, *Black British, White British*, London, Eyre and Spottiswoode, 1971, pp. 121–2.
16. B. Dahya, 'The Nature of Pakistani Ethnicity in Industrial Cities in Britain', A. Cohen (ed.), op. cit., p. 84.
17. G. S. Aurora, *The New Frontiersmen: A Sociological Study of Indian Immigrants in the United Kingdom*, Bombay, Popular Prakashan, 1967, p. 27.
18. The later immigration restrictions have forced decisions on migrants who might never have come to stay in Britain but who did not want to lose the opportunity in case of further restrictions in the future. The difficulties of entry and re-entry for returning migrants have forced many to bring over their families and to take British citizenship particularly after Pakistan left the Commonwealth in 1973.
19. Dr K. S. Ahmad, *A Geography of Pakistan*, Lahore, Oxford University Press, 1964, p. 154.
20. Sheila Allen, op. cit., p. 32.
21. See Verity Saifullah Khan, 'Pakistani Villagers in a British City', Ph.D. thesis, University of Bradford, 1974. She also stresses this point.
22. There were only 11,117 Pakistanis in England and Wales in 1951, and it is estimated that 6,130 of these were 'White' Pakistanis (British born in India during colonial rule). The figure was still under 20,000 in 1960. In 1961 and 1966 the number of Pakistanis rose to 30,737 and 73,120 respectively. In 1971 the total number of people born in Pakistan was 139,455. This shows that most of the Pakistanis migrated in the 1960s.
23. Everett S. Lee, op. cit., p. 291.
24. G. C. K. Peach, '*West Indian Migration to Britain*', London, OUP for IRR, 1968. It appears that this does not apply to the period just before the Immigration Act 1962, because many respondents told me that they had been unemployed for some periods.
25. In some cases this led to exploitation of fellow Pakistanis by those who turned hospitality into profitable business by charging higher rents.

Chapter 3

Context of the Study

1. T. T. Heywood, *New Annals of Rochdale, Rochdale Times*, 1931, pp. 44 and 108.
2. 'A Pageant for Rochdale'. A document used at one of the Centenary processions, 1973, p. 11.
3. ibid.
4. ibid.
5. It is called 'Rochdale Equitable'. The Toad Lane shop is now a museum which attracts visitors from all over the world interested in the co-operative movement.
6. F. Engels op. cit.
7. Rochdale Local Authority information.
8. A. Lord, 'Asians in Wardleworth', 1973, unpublished.
9. Ministry of Housing and Local Government, *The Deeplish Study*, HMSO, 1966, p. 1.
10. Census 1971, County of Birth tables, HMSO, table 14, p. 177.
11. Department of Employment. An 'insured person' is one who holds an insurance card.
12. Rochdale received 34 families of Ugandan Asians at the end of 1972 when Ugandan Asians were expelled by President Amin. For approximately the same period of time (end of 1972):

	North West	*Great Britain*
Total unemployed migrant workers	2,176	23,768
of whom adults	1,992	22,107
per cent unemployed	1·7	2·1

    See: *Department of Employment Gazette*—Feb. 1973

13. Census 1971—Quoted in David Kohler, *Ethnic Minorities in Britain, Statistical Data*, London, Community Relations Commission, 1975.
14. See Muhammad Anwar, 'Pakistanis and Indians in the 1971 Census: Some Ambiguities', *New Community*, Vol. III, 4, Autumn 1974, pp. 394–6.
15. Estimate of the local Community Relations Council and the local Indian Association.
16. For example, according to the 1966 Census out of 73,130 people whose birthplace was recorded as Pakistan, 5,400 were estimated to be white.
17. Later on dual nationality provisions allowed them to have Pakistani nationality as well.
18. This was demonstrated in a survey done by the Opinion Research Centre on behalf of the Community Relations Commission during the October 1974 General Election; see Muhammad Anwar and David

Kohler, *Ethnic Minority Participation in the October 1974 General Election*, Community Relations Commission, October 1975.
19. *Census 1971,* Ward Data, supplied by the Planning Department of the Local Authority.
20. The information for the Wardleworth area was mainly collected by Mr A. Lord, working with the Public Health Department, Rochdale. I am grateful to him. Also see his paper 'Asians in Wardleworth' (see above n. 8).
21. Survey area is not the complete ward but part of the Central Ward; see map on p. 47.
22. English is taught in Pakistan at the age of 11 or after 5 years' schooling. In some schools (very few in number) there are no English classes up to the 9th year of schooling. In this case students spend two extra years learning English to reach the same level as the other students. This means two additional years for their education as compared to the students who have the facilities to learn English at the age of 11.
23. Chapter 6 deals with employment in greater detail.
24. R. Breton, op. cit.
25. In 1971 when I came to Rochdale there were only two manufacturers on a small scale.
26. There was only one collection booth in 1971.
27. Elizabeth Burney, *Housing on Trial*, London, Oxford University Press for IRR, 1967, p.208.
28. In 1977 the name of the CRC was changed to Rochdale and District Council for Racial Equality but throughout this work its name at the time of the field-work has been used to avoid any confusion.

Chapter 4

Kinship Networks: The Family Structure and Functions

1. See Raymond Firth, 'Family and Kinship in Industrial Society', *The Sociological Review*, Monograph No. 8, Keele 1964, pp. 65–81.
2. J. C. Mitchell (ed.), op. cit.
3. William J. Goode, *The Family*, Englewood Cliffs, N. J., Prentice-Hall, 1964, p. 108. Talcott Parsons in Talcott Parsons and Robert F. Bales, *Family Socialization and Interaction Process.* Glencoe Free Press, 1955, p. 9; M. F. Nimkoff, *Comparative Family Systems*, Boston, Houghton Mifflin, 1965, p. 343.
4. See R. Linton, *The Natural History of the Family*, in R. N. Anshen (ed.). *The Family: Its Functions and Density*, New York, Harper and Row, 1959, L. Wirth, 'Urbanism as a Way of Life', *American Journal of Sociology*, Vol. 44, 1938, pp. 1–24; T. Parsons, 'The Social Structure of the Family', in R. N. Ashen (ed.), op. cit.
5. 'Family and Kinship in Industrial Society; A comment', by Peter Townsend, *Sociological Review*, Monograph No. 8, Keele 1964, p. 89.

6. S. M. Greenfield, 'Industrialisation and the Family in Sociological Theory', *American Journal of Sociology*, Vol. 67, 1961, pp. 312–22.
7. H. Orenstein, 'The Recent History of the Extended Family in India', *Social Problems*, Vol. 8, 1961, pp. 241–50.
8. See Michael Anderson (ed.), *Sociology of the Family*, Penguin Modern Sociology Readings, Part 2, 1971, pp. 97–8.
9. P. H. Rossi, *Why Families Move*, New York, Free Press, 1955.
10. Raymond Firth, op. cit.
11. See A. G. Mayer, *Caste and Kinship in Central India*, London, Routledge and Kegan Paul, 1960, p. 177.
12. See also Z. Eglar, *A Punjabi Village in Pakistan*, Columbia University Press, 1960, p. 26.
13. ibid.
14. In a nationwide study of Asians, which the author supervised on behalf of the Community Relations Commission, it was found that out of 1,427 households, 67 per cent were living as nuclear families and 33 per cent as extended families. Of the households interviewed, 549 were Muslim (mostly Pakistani); 71 per cent of these were living as nuclear families and 29 per cent as extended families. For details see Muhammad Anwar, *Between Two Cultures*, London, Commission for Racial Equality, 1978 (2nd edition).
15. See also Patricia Jeffrev, 'Pakistani Families in Bristol', *New Community*, Vol. 5, Autumn 1972, pp. 364–9.
16. See Muhammad Anwar, op. cit. (1978).

Chapter 5

Biraderi and *Vartan Bhanji:* Institutions of Kinship Networks

1. The term *Kabila* (an Arabic word) for 'Big family' is also used with the same meaning but *Biraderi* is the more common usage.
2. Zekiye Eglar, op. cit., p. 76.
3. E. A. H. Blunt, *The Caste System of Northern India.* London, Oxford University Press, 1931, Ch. 1.
4. J. H. Korson, 'Student Attitudes towards Mate Selection in Muslim Society: Pakistan', *Journal of Marriage and The Family*, Vol. XXXL, Feb. 1968, No. 1 pp. 153–65.
5. P. A. Wakil, 'Explorations into the Kin-networks of the Punjabi Society: A Preliminary Statement', *Journal of Marriage and The Family*, November 1970, pp. 700–7.
6. H. Alavi, 'Kinship in West Punjabi Villages', *Contributions to Indian Sociology*, New Series, December 1972, Vol. VI, p. 3.
7. A. G. Mayer, op. cit.
8. H. Alavi, op. cit. p. 3.
9. I have heard my informants use the term *Biraderi* in the 'kin', 'village', 'region' and even 'Pakistan' sense. It depends in which referent it is being used. A Pakistani talking to an English or Indian person would

say 'my Pakistani Biraderi' (to replace the word 'community'). If he (a Punjabi) is talking to a Sindhi or Pathan he will say 'my Punjabi *Biraderi*'; if he is talking to another Jat he might delimit it to his endogamous *Biraderi*. As we can see, it very much depends on the level of contact and on the context in which the term is being used.

10. See David M. Schneider, 'Some Muddles in the Models', *The Relevance of Models for Social Anthropology*, A.S.A. Monographs, 1, London 1965, pp. 25–8; Robin Fox, *Kinship and Marriage*, Pelican Books, 1967, *passim*.
11. W. H. Key 'Rural—Urban Differences and The Family'. *Sociological Quarterly*, Vol. 2, 1961, pp. 49–56.
12. These kinds of services are widespread, see M. B. Sussman, 'The Help Pattern in the Middle-Class Family', *American Sociological Review*, Vol. 18, 1953, pp. 22–8; H. Sharp and Axelrod, 'Mutual Aid among Relatives in an Urban Population', in R. Freedman *et al.* (eds.), *Principles of Sociology*, Holt, Rinehart and Winston, 1956. Also, M. B. Sussman, 'Family Continuity: Selective Factors which Affect Relationship between Families at Generational Levels', *Marriage and Family Living*, Vol. 16, 1954, pp. 112–20.
13. Z. Eglar, op. cit., p. 105.
14. ibid.
15. ibid.
16. H. Alavi, op. cit., (1972), p. 11.
17. V. S. Khan, op. cit., p. 51.
18. See H. Alavi op. cit. (1972) and Z. Eglar, op. cit.
19. H. Alavi, op. cit., (1972), p. 12.
20. ibid., p. 13.
21. This practice sometimes creates problems as well, see pp. 93–4.
22. Those in Pakistan who had *Pakki Vartan* should have been present in person but due to the migration situation it was not possible; however, they symbolized their presence by attending celebrations in Pakistan.
23. See W. H. Form and S. Nosow, *Community in Disaster*, New York. Harper and Row, 1958, pp. 54 and 82. According to Form and Nosow, as many as 75% of the people struck by major natural disasters may be rescued in the first few hours by neighbours living nearby.
24. For a review of the history of the Italian migration to United States see John S. MacDonald and Leatrice D. MacDonald, op. cit. pp. 433–48.
25. J. C. Mitchell, 'Social Networks', *Annual Review of Anthropology*, Vol. 3, 1974, p. 295.
26. Max Weber, *The Theory of Social and Economic Organisation* (trans. A. A. Henderson and Talcott Parsons), William Hodge, 1947, pp. 104–7.
27. The basic method which was used was developed by Bernard and Killworth as generally applicable to the study of networks in closed social systems. (See H. R. Bernard and P. D. Killworth, 'On the

Structure of an Ocean–Going Research Vessel and Other Important Things', *Social Science Research*, **2**, 1973, pp. 145–84.) The object of the exercise was to test this method for non-structural situations like the one I have studied. Hubbell's procedure and Beam and Broundage procedures were also modified by Mitchell.

28. J. C. Mitchell (ed.) op. cit., p. 20. He also mentions that this approach converges with that of the symbolic interactionalists. See for example, Arnold Rose, *Human Behaviour and Social Process; An Interactional Approach*. Boston, Houghton Mifflin and Co., 1962.
29. Technically a clique is a 100 per cent dense segment of network—a cluster is less than 100 per cent dense.
30. C. H. Hubbell, An Input—Output Approach to Clique Identification', *Sociometry*, XXVIII, 1969, pp. 377–99.
31. 1, 2—doctors, 3—school teacher, 5, 6, 7—self-employed. 10 is 7's brother, and so has roughly the same social networks. Also, 5 comes from the same area in Pakistan as 1, 6, 7 and 10. No. 8 is an exception, although he is self-employed.
32. The clusters, nature, density and direction of the social network would be different if we were dealing only with one *Biraderi*. One assumes that it would be more closely knit and dense compared to this analysis.
33. Bernard and Killworth, op. cit.
34. E. Bott, op. cit., pp. 101–2.
35. J. C. Mitchell (ed.), op. cit., p. 15. The procedure adopted to measure reachability is Mitchell's procedure.
36. Matrix raw data coded '3' for 'close', '2' for 'some', and '1' for 'little' and '0' for 'no' interaction (see pp. 232–3).
37. E. Bott, op. cit., p. 60.
38. J. A. Barnes, 'Networks and Political Process' in J. C. Mitchell (ed.), op. cit. pp. 58–66.
39. Barnes proposed a measure of density, 200 a/n (n–l) where 'a' refers to the actual number of links and 'n' to the total of persons involved including Ego. For details see J. A. Barnes, ibid.
40. The return fare to Pakistan by air was £200-plus. The cost multiplies when one has to buy gifts for relatives in Pakistan on each visit or if the wife and children are travelling as well.
41. H. J. Leichter and W. E. Mitchell, *Kinship and Casework*, New York, Russell Sage Foundation, 1967.
42. Muzafar Sharif, *Group Conflict and Co-operation: Their Social Psychology*, London, Routledge and Kegan Paul, 1967, p. VII.

Chapter 6

Economic Activity and the Role of Social Networks: Workers

1. See Sheila Allen, J. Bornat and S. Bentley, *Work, Race and Immigration*, University of Bradford, 1977.

2. Some of these points are raised in: H. K. Schwalzweller and J. F. Seggar, 'Kinship Involvement: A Factor in the Adjustment of Rural Migrants', *Journal of Marriage and the Family*, November 1967, No. 29, pp. 662–71; B. Beijer, *Rural Migrants in Urban Settings*, The Hague, Martinus Nijhoff, 1963; O. G. Simmons and W. N. McPhee, 'Time trend and analyses of the urban experiences of rural migrants to the city.' Paper presented to the Conference on Adaptation to Change, San Juan, Puerto Rico, June 1968, sponsored by the Foundations Fund for Research in Psychiatry.
3. See Stephen Castle and Godula Kosack, *Immigrant Workers and Class Structure in Western Europe*, London, OUP for IRR, 1973, p. 57.
4. For males only the economic activity rate was 91·2 per cent which is very high when compared with the other ethnic minority groups and the indigenous population.
5. K. Jones and A. D. Smith, *The Economic Impact of Commonwealth Immigration*, Cambridge, Cambridge University Press, 1970, pp. 66–7.
6. The recent PEP survey, David Smith, *The Facts of Racial Disadvantage*, 1976, p. 85, shows that a higher proportion of minority men than of white men works shifts which attract premium rates of pay.
7. Textile Council, *Cotton and Allied Textiles—A report on Present Performance and Future Prospects*, Manchester, 1969, p. 177.
8. PEP (1976), op. cit., pp. 77–9, found that although shiftwork was more common among four minority groups (W. Indians, Indians, Pakistanis and African Asians) than among whites, (31 per cent minority groups and 15 per cent white), there were important variations between the four groups. Pakistanis were particularly likely to work night shifts of some kind, including alternate two-shift and three-shift systems as well; in fact, 27 per cent of Pakistani men were working some kind of night shift, compared with only 9 per cent of white men, a difference of the order of 3 to 1. Analysis by region showed additional important variations. As many as 45 per cent of minority men in the North West were working shifts; this of course, corresponds with the concentration of Pakistanis in the textile industry.
9. ibid; pp. 74–5.
10. As a consequence of the British Government's decision the Indian Medical Council decided that British medical degrees will not be recognized in India from 1977. *Garvi Gujrat* (weekly), 23 November, 1975.
11. See PEP, *The Extent of Racial Disadvantage*, Broadsheet No. 547.
12. Some employers told me that they generally expect a job history to follow a fairly set pattern.
13. Taking those with qualifications to degree standard, PEP (1976), op. cit., found that 79 per cent of white men were in professional or managerial positions compared with only 31 per cent of minority

men. Furthermore, 21 per cent of minority men with degree standard qualifications were doing manual jobs, whereas none of the white men with equivalent qualifications were doing manual jobs of any kind.

14. See W. W. Daniel, *Racial Discrimination in England*, Harmondsworth, Penguin 1968, and PEP (1976), op. cit.
15. Sheila Allen *et al*, op. cit., p. 52.
16. *The Guardian*, 'Migrants' Aid to the Town's Trade', 12th May, 1971.
17. Sheila Allen *et al.*, op. cit., p. 5.
18. Paul Foot, 'The Strike at Courtaulds, Preston, 24th May–12th June 1965', *IRR Newsletter*, July 1965; P. Marsh, *Anatomy of a Strike*, London, IRR, special series, 1967. More recently see the Grunwick dispute.
19. There were 142 Pakistanis in all (except 3 trainees) working on night shift and double day shift out of 587 workers (not including the office staff of 84—all locals).
20. Because the Census figures do not tell us the actual nature of the jobs. For example, in professional and scientific services, it includes both highly skilled doctors and women who wash hospital floors. Therefore, it is necessary to obtain information which reveals the actual nature of the job. This is only possible in local-level studies.
21. Sheila Allen *et al.*, op. cit., p. 151, also found low wages in textiles as compared with other industries in Bradford area. This notion is also confirmed if we look at the monthly statistics about earnings and hours in different industries in the *Department of Employment Gazette*, for the years 1974–5.
22. Sheila Allen *et al.*, op. cit., pp 187–8.
23. S. Patterson, *Immigrants in Industry*, London, Oxford University Press, 1968, p. 240.
24. Castles and Kosack, op. cit., p. 128.
25. ibid., pp. 138–9.
26. B. Hepple, *Race, Jobs and the Law in Britain*, London, Allen Lane, 1968, p. 50, quoted in Castles and Kosack, op. cit., p. 139.
27. See B. Hepple, op. cit.; Sheila Allen in S. D. Zubaida (ed.), *Race and Racialism*, London, Tavistock Publications, 1970. Sheila Allen, op. cit. (1971); Beryl Radin, 'Coloured Workers and British Trade Unions', *Race*, Vol. VII, No. 2, October 1966; and the PEP report quoted in W. W. Daniel, op. cit., p. 132.
28. *Daily Telegraph*, 27th January, 1970.
29. *Guardian*, 29th April, 1970.
30. See also Sheila Allen *et al.*, op. cit., p. 242.
31. This remark is made in the concluding chapter in Sheila Allen *et al.*, op. cit.
32. H. J. Hoffnidu Nowotny, 'Global Social Aspects of Relationships Between Trade Unions and Migrant Workers', *Migration Today*, No. 11, Autumn 1968.
33. Sheila Allen *et al.*, op. cit., p. 220.

34. Pakistanis usually know who is looking for night-shift work. Managements normally allow this sort of exchange as they need workers and are not concerned about who they are.
35. P. Mott, *Shift Work: The Social, Psychological and Physical Consequences*, Ann Arbor, The University of Michigan Press, 1965, p. 232.
36. The effects on health which have been demonstrated in a number of studies, include loss of appetite and difficulties in sleeping and digestion, experienced by shift workers. These disorders occur because shift working when it involves night work, disturbs the circadian (24-hour) rhythms in sleeping activity, body temperature, eating and elimination. In effect, the individual is forced to work against his natural 'internal clock'. Similarly, sleeping is made more difficult due to poor housing conditions which give inadequate insulation from noise in the daytime. See NBPI, *House of Work, Overtime and Shift Working*, Report No. 161; Industrial Society *Survey of Shift Working Practices*, 1970; J. H. Downie, *Some Social and Industrial Implications of Shift Work*, Industrial Welfare Society, 1963.

Chapter 7

Economic Activity and the Role of Social Networks : Self-Employed Pakistanis

1. Hairdressers usually belong to a *Kammi* group whose status is usually lower in Pakistani society, and therefore no person from another class is likely to start such a business. Those who belong to *Nai* families in the *Kammi* group usually learn hairdressing skills from their fathers as apprentices, and therefore can easily start the business once they have gained the confidence.
2. Sheila Allen, *et al*., op. cit., p. 256. The categories of sources of finance are not mutually exclusive, as respondents may have had more than one source of finance available to them.
3. Rashmi Desai, *Indian Immigrants in Britain*, London, OUP for IRR, 1963, Chapter on 'The Internal Economy: Grocer and Hawking'.
4. The majority of the factory workers in Greater London rag trade are Cypriots, Greek and Turkish. They work side-by-side, cutting, machining and pressing ready-to-wear fashion in thousands of small businesses in Finsbury Park, Stoke Newington and Camden Town areas. They also use homeworkers for sewing the garments. Most of these businesses are owned by Jews.
5. Jewish manufacturers also used homeworkers as cheap labour but their workers were relatively better paid than the Asian homeworkers who had newly arrived and were less aware of the payments rate in the industry (personal communication from a manufacturer).

6. See Leila Maw, *Immigrants and Employment in the Clothing Industry: The Rochdale Case*, The Runnymede Trust, 1974.
7. It was noticed that some manufacturers had started using homeworkers from other areas such as Bury, Huddersfield and Burnley.
8. These points and others are to be found in Department of Employment, Wages Inspectorate, *Note on Homeworkers in the Clothing Industry*, HMSO, January 1973; National Board for Prices and Incomes, *Pay and Condition in the Clothing Manufacturing Industries*, NBPI, Report No. 110, HMSO, April 1969; The Homeworkers Study Group, 'Homeworkers in North London' in Sheila Allen and D. Barker (Eds), *Dependence and Exploitation in Work and Marriage*, London, Longmans, 1976; Samir Shah, *Immigrants and Employment in the Clothing Industry, The Rag Trade in London's East End*, The Runnymede Trust, September 1975.
9. It was in 1973 that one Pakistani started buying 'seconds tights' and encouraging women to sort out the good ones and do the packing. It was shown that women earned more money doing this than sewing.
10. As a result of some complaints the Rochdale Council took action: as the *Rochdale Observer* reported, 'Action to prevent a number of houses in Boundary Street, Rochdale, being used as small industrial premises producing clothes, is being taken.' (21st February 1976).
11. The Homeworkers Study Group, op. cit.
12. The Homeworkers Study Group, op. cit., found that husbands in the North London area usually helped their wives with housework.
13. *Sunday Times*, December 1973, article about 'Bangladeshi Community in the East End' touches on this subject.

Chapter 8

Ethnic Group Mobilization and Political Participation

1. Parts of this chapter are published in M. Anwar, 'Pakistani Participation in the 1972 Rochdale By-Election', *New Community*, Vol. II, No. 4, Autumn 1973, pp. 418–23; 'Pakistani Participation in the 1973 Rochdale Local Elections', *New Community*, Vol. III, Nos. 1–2, Winter–Spring, 1974, pp. 67–72; 'Asian Participation in the 1974 Autumn Election', *New Community*, Vol. IV, No. 3, Autumn, 1975; and Muhammad Anwar and David Kohler, op. cit.
2. See Nicholas Deakin (ed.), *Colour and the British Electorate 1964*, London, Federick A. Praeger, 1965; Richard Spencer, 'The Minorities and the General Election 1970, Lambeth', *Race Today*, July 1970; and Ivor Crewe (ed.), *British Political Sociology Year Book*, Vol. 2, *The Politics of Race*, London, Croom Helm Ltd, 1975.

3. D. Butler and D. Stokes, *Political Change in Britain*, London, Macmillan, 1969, pp. 349–54.
4. R. Rose (ed.), *Electoral Behaviour: A Comparative Handbook*, New York, The Free Press, 1974, p. 253.
5. Butler and Stokes, op. cit.
6. Danley T. Studlar, 'British Public Opinion, Colour Issues, and Enoch Powell: A Longitudinal Analysis', *British Journal of Political Science*, Vol. 4, No. 3, 1974, p. 378.
7. N. Deakin and J. Bourne, 'Powell, The Minorities and the 1970 Election', *Political Quarterly*, Vol. 41, No. 4, 1970, p. 407.
8. M. J. Le Lohe, 'Participation in Elections by Asians in Bradford', in Ivor Crewe (ed.), op.cit, pp. 84–122; and M. Anwar (1973), (1974), (1975) op. cit.
9. M. J. Le Lohe and A. Goldman, 'Race in Local Politics: the Rochdale Central Ward election of 1968', *Race*, Vol. X, No. 4, 1969.
10. This was noted by the press; for instance, there was a long article in the *Guardian* (24th October 1972) headed 'Loyalty of Asian Voters Crucial for Labour'.
11. Lewis E. Coser, op. cit, p. 7.
12. Georg Simmel, *Conflict*, op. cit.; and Robert C. Angell, 'The Sociology of Human Conflict' in Elton B. McNeil (ed.), *The Nature of Human Conflict*, London, Prentice-Hall Inc., 1965, Chapter 5.
13. *Rochdale Observer*, 25th October, 1972.
14. *Guardian*, 23rd October, 1972.
15. ibid.
16. *Rochdale Observer*, 25th October, 1972.
17. *The Guardian*, 28th October, 1972.
18. *Rochdale Observer*, 18th November, 1972.
19. From a leaflet published by the Rochdale Anti-Racialist Committee for the public meeting on 8th May, 1973.
20. Gordon W. Allport, *The Nature of Prejudice*, New York, Doubleday & Co., 1954, p. 254.
21. *Rochdale Observer*, 14th April, 1973.
22. ibid.
23. Figures calculated from the Electoral Register by identifying Pakistani names.
24 In Pakistan each elector is approached by the candidates on an informal basis.
25. J. E. Horrock, Editor's Foreward to Muzafar Sharif, op. cit, p. viii.
26. Max Gluckman, 'The Bonds in the Colour Bar in *Custom and Conflict in Africa*, Oxford, Basil Blackwell, 1955, pp. 137–65.
27. D. Butler and D. Kavanagh, *The British General Election of February 1974*, London, Macmillan, 1974, pp. 24, 60, 139–42 and 335.
28. After the disappointing results of the 1973 local council elections the local BCSI group joined the National Front.
29. *Rochdale Observer*, 2nd March, 1974.

30. Where the number of immigrant voters (approximately) was larger than the majority in the February election.
31. The *Daily Jang*, 3rd September, 1974.
32. *Morning Star*, 27th September, 1974.
33. *Daily Telegraph*, 2nd October, 1974.
34. The *Daily Jang*, 4th October, 1974.
35. Dr M. J. Le Lohe, op. cit., pp. 99–100.
36. 'Non-Asian' includes all voters who are not Asian, such as whites and Afro-Caribbeans.
37. Conservative Party Manifesto, *The Times*, 11th September, 1974.
38. Labour Party Manifesto, *The Times*, 17th September, 1974.
39. A Liberal Party Report, *Immigration and Race Relations*, London, Libral Publication Department, 1974.
40. BBC Television, *Nai Zindagi Naya Jeevan*, Sunday 29th September, 1974, 9 a.m.
41. Calculated from the Electoral Register 1973.
42. A survey of 97 Pakistanis which I did in conjunction with Dr Le Lohe after the election shows this.
43. *Arian Biraderi* in particular met twice to discuss whom they should support and why. The decision was in favour of the Liberal candidate.
44. *Rochdale Observer*, 19th October, 1974.
45. ibid.
46. M. J. Le Lohe, op. cit.
47. M. J. Le Lohe and A, Goldman, op. cit.
48. Muhammad Anwar and David Kohler, op. cit.
49. Lewis E. Coser, op. cit., p. 87.

Chapter 9

Religion as a Binding Force

1. Recently at least three Pakistani workers were reported to have been sacked because they wanted to say their prayers at work.
2. H. S. Morris, '*The Indians in Uganda*', Weidenfeld and Nicolson, 1968, p. 64.
3. A new Mosque, *Jamia* Mosque (the big central Mosque) is to be built and another was started in William Street in 1976.
4. The Union has published two policy documents as part of their programme in this direction; see *Islamic Education and Single Sex Schools*, London, U.M.O., 1975, and *Guidlines and Syllabus on Islamic Education*, London, U.M.O., 1976. There are other organizations which also play their role for the religious education of Muslim children. These include the UK Islamic Mission, the Islamic Foundation, Leicester and the Islamic Cultural Centre, London.

5. The second *Eid* comes two months and ten days after the first one.
6. Rochdale Muslim Society; Golden Mosque Society and U.K.Islamic Mission (*Neeli* Mosque Society).
7. The society was formed in 1972 and has a Chairman, a Secretary and a Treasurer, all doctors, as its officials.
8. H. Papenek, 'Purdah in Pakistan: Seclusion and Modern Occupations for Women', *Journal of Marriage and The Family*, August 1971, gives a detailed account of the attitude towards women going out to work in Pakistan.
9. See S. A. A. Maududi, *Purdah and the Status of Women in Islam*, Lahore, Islamic Publications Ltd., 1972.
10. There are co-educational schools in Pakistan but usually even Westernized parents send their children to those schools only up to a certain age.
11. The trouble over single-sex schools in Bradford in early 1970s and the support given to Muslims there by the majority of Muslims in Britain is an example. Even the Pakistani Government intervened and decided to help Pakistanis to set up two single-sex schools for girls, one in Bradford and the other in Birmingham, to overcome the difficulties created for Pakistanis by the introduction of the comprehensive school system in Britain. There are also some moves by the Arab States to help British Muslims to set up such schools. A National Education Council was set up in 1978 (the idea was approved in 1974) to look after the educational needs of Muslim children in Britain.
12. J. A. Jackson, op. cit., p. 303.
13. There are over 300 Mosques and many centres for religious education in the country, and there is a concerted effort to practise Islam and transmit its teachings to the next generation. National and local Muslim organizations try to stress the values of Islam in Britain, and to emphasize the importance of its continuation.
14. See M. Anwar, 'Muslim Burials: A Policy Paper', London, Community Relations Commission, 1975.

Chapter 10

The Structure of Leadership and Ethnic Organizations

1. See Stuart Bentley, 'The Structure of Leadership Among Indians, Pakistanis and West Indians in Britain', unpublished M.Sc. thesis, University of Bradford, 1970.
2. S. N. Eisenstadt, *The Absorption of Immigrants*, London, Routledge and Kegan Paul, 1954, p. 195.
3. ibid., p. 193.

4. Stuart Bentley, op. cit., p. 59, presents it in a scheme of new, modified and unchanged authority relationships taking intra-ethnic, minority –minority and minority–majority on the vertical axis.
5. Formal leader is defined here as a person believed to be a representative of a Pakistani organisation whether elected, nominated or self-appointed.
6. M. J. Hill and R. M. Issacharoff, *Community Action and Race Relations*, London, O.U.P 1971, p. 146.
7. Religious leaders are discussed in Chapter 9.
8. R. E. Pahl, *Patterns of Urban Life*, Longman, 1970, p. 135.
9. These are:
    1. Pakistan Welfare Organization
    2. Pakistan Welfare and Information Centre
    3. Pakistan Social Circle
    4. Pakistan People's Party, U.K. Rochdale Branch
    5. Tehrik-i-Istaklal, U.K. Rochdale Branch
    6. Pakistan Muslim League
    7. Kashmir Liberation League U.K.
    8. Pakistan Medical Society U.K.
    9. Rochdale Muslim Society
    10. Rochdale Mosque Society
    11. U.K. Islamic Mission (Mosque Society), Rochdale Branch
10. Because the CRO at that time was asked by the Race Relations Board for recommendations from Rochdale.
11. *Meena Bazaar* originated during the period of Mogul rule in India, it was designed as a fair at which people from all over the Empire should display their wares, skills and achievements. There was however, one basic difference between this and the conventional 'fair': the people allowed in the *Bazaar* were women only, and it was organized by the noble ladies of the Royal Household. Over the years the objective has been to raise money for charity. This *Bazaar* was organized by Rochdale Pakistanis in the traditional spirit to raise funds, but was attended by both men and women.
12. The Ronald Gorton Centre is an old people's home. After this the Pakistan Welfare Association organized a *Spring Fair*, to raise money for the same fund. The Rochdale Muslim Society also arranged a charity dinner to raise funds to provide a cardiac care ambulance for the Birch Hill hospital. All three functions were attended by English people as well. In the main the English had been specially invited.
13. See Robin M. Williams Jnr, *Strangers Next Door: Ethnic Relations in American Communities*, Englewood Cliffs, N. J. Prentice Hall, 1964, p. 201.
14. The Standing Conference of Pakistani Organizations, a national body, also made several representations to the Home Office about this issue until it was resolved.
15. I observed that after the office was opened Pakistanis sought more help from the association officers, on regular basis, than they did

before. Particularly over the weekend the office usually seemed full of clients who needed help for different reasons.

16. The Vice-Presidents included one teacher and one doctor. In 1974 the General Secretary was elected President and another businessman (Mirpuri) took his place. The Vice-Presidents remained the same.
17. See M. Le Lohe, op. cit., pp. 105-6.
18. In May 1976 SCOPO wrote to the Prime Minister of Pakistan and to all the leaders of the political parties in Pakistan asking them to close their branches in Britain for the sake of the unity amongst Pakistanis in this country. This was not done.
19. Rex and Moore, op. cit., pp. 171–2.
20. Lewis E Coser, op. cit., p. 87.
21. De Witt John, *Indian Workers Association in Britain*, London, Oxford University Press for IRR, 1969.
22. S. N. Eisenstadt, op. cit., (1954) p. 193.

Chapter 11

The Incapsulation of Pakistanis: Case Studies

1. In another case a Mr M. S.'s English neighbour took some interest in his children's education. His neighbour's children sometimes came to their house and they also exchanged gifts at Christmas. So the children were a source of contact between the two families (this family did not have any teenage daughters).
2. I observed that the lack of parental control, because of father' absence from the home while working on the night shift, was creating problems in some families.
3. South East Lancashire, North East Cheshire.
4. P. Mayer, op. cit., p. 6.

Chapter 12

Conclusions

1. W. Petersen, op. cit., p. 263.
2. ibid.
3. H. S. Nelli, op. cit., p. 3.
4. R. Ballard, 'Family Organization among the Sikhs in Britain', *New Community*, Vol. 2, No. 1, 1972–3, p. 13.
5. Peter M. Blau, *Exchange and Power in Social Life*, London, John Wiley and Sons, 1964, pp. 1–32.

6. Geoffrey Gorer, *Exploring English Character*, London, The Cresset Press, 1955, p. 46.
7. Ronald Fletcher, *Britain in the Sixties, The Family and Marriage*, Penguin Books, 1962, pp. 69–76.
8. J. Brown, *The Un-Melting Pot*, Macmillan, 1970, p. 90.
9. For instance, the Mosque plays an important role in the transmission of Islamic religion, culture, values and identity to the second generation. By so doing, it is maintaining clear ethnic boundaries.
10. Nathan Glazer, *Affirmative Discrimination*, New York, Basic Books Publishers, 1975, p. 29.
11. The term 'diffuse' is used here in the Parsonian sense: diffuse ties are those in which many interests are compounded in the same relationships; on the other hand 'specific' ties are those in which one or a few interests are contained in the same relationships.
12. Robert Dahl, *Who Governs*?, London and New Haven, Yale University Press, 1961, pp. 32–3.
13. Using Gordon's seven assimilation variables and three hypotheses in which he shows processes by which they related to each other, the Pakistanis in Rochdale were substantially not assimilated. There was no evidence of much cultural or behavioural assimilation, structural assimilation, marital assimilation, identificational assimilation, attitude receptional assimilation, behaviour receptional assimilation and civic assimilation. See M. Gordon, op. cit, (1964), pp. 71–81.

Appendix 1

Methodology of the Study

1. Muhammad Anwar, 'Perceptions, Adjustments and Aspirations of Pakistani Immigrants in Rochdale', an unpublished dissertation for part fulfilment for M.A.(Econ.), University of Manchester, 1971.
2. Howard S. Becker and Blanche Geer, 'Participation and Interviewing: A Rejoinder', *Human Organization*, **17**, No. 2, 1958, pp. 39–40 and Editor's comment.
3. Robert K. Merton, *Social Theory and Social Structure*, New York, The Free Press, 1957, pp. 103–8.
4. Thomas L. Gillette, 'A Study of the Effects of Negro Invasion on Real Estate Values', *The American Journal of Economics and Sociology*, **16**, January 1957, pp. 151–62.
5. C. H. Cooley, quoted in Pauline V. Young, *Scientific Social Surveys and Research*, 2nd ed., New York, Prentice Hall Inc., 1951, p. 265.
6. D. H. J. Morgan, 'Theoretical and conceptual problems in the study of social relations at work: An analysis of the differing definitions of

women's role in a northern factory', unpublished Ph.D. thesis, University of Manchester, 1969, p. 113.

7. M. S. Schwartz, 'The Mental Hospital and the Research Person in the Disturbed Ward' in A. J. Vidich, J. Bensman and M. R. Stein (eds), *Reflections on Community Studies*, London, Harper and Row, 1971, p. 106.
8. H. Papanek, 'The Woman Fieldworker in a Purdah Society', *Human Organization*, Vol. 23, No. 2, 1964, p. 60.
9. See George J. McCall and J. L. Simmons, *Issues in Participant Observation*, Reading, Addison-Wesley Publishing Co., 1969 in particular Chapter Eight, 'Comparison of Methods', pp. 289–341. John P. Dean *et al.*, 'Observation and Interviewing' in John T. Doby (ed.), *An Introduction to Social Research*, 2nd ed., New York, Appleton-Century-Crofts, 1967, pp. 274–304.
10. See in particular William F. Whyte, *Street Corner Society*, Chicago, University of Chicago Press, 1943, Preface, pp. v–x, and also his 'Observational Fieldwork Methods' in Marie Jahoda, Merton Deutsch and Stuart W. Cook (eds), *Research Methods in the Social Sciences*, New York, Dryden Press, 1951, Vol. II, pp. 383–514; Marie Johoda *et al.*, 'Data Collection: Observational Methods', ibid., Vol. 1, Chapter v; and Florence R. Kluckholn, 'The Participant Observer Technique in Small Communities', *American Journal of Sociology*, XLVI, November 1940, pp. 331–3.
11. Oscar Lewis has dealt with this point in his *Life in a Mexican Village: Tepoztlan Restudied*, Springfield, University of Illinois Press, 1951.
12. Arthur J. Vidich, 'Participant Observation and the Collection and Interpretation of Data', *American Journal of Sociology*, **60**, 1955, pp. 354–60.
13. Sheila Allen, J. Bornat and S. Bently, op. cit.
14. For details see H. Russell Bernard and P. D. Killworth, op. cit., pp. 145–84.
15. I am grateful to Professor J. C. Mitchell for all the encouragement and help he gave me to use and test this new technique and other network techniques with my data.
16. I decided to have the 'certain number' fifteen because the 'certain number' twenty for a group of twenty as suggested by Bernard and Killworth did not work in practice.
17. The analysis using Bernard and Killworth *Catij* technique and other procedures is given in Appendix 1, pp. 231–3. I have also tried to relate it to the 'cases' wherever possible.

Index